Using the *Sams Teach Yourself in 24 Hours* Series

Welcome to the *Sams Teach Yourself in 24 Hours* series. You're probably thinking to yourself, "What? They want me to stay up all night and learn this stuff?" Well, no, not exactly. This series introduces a new concept in teaching you about exciting new products: 24 one-hour lessons, designed to keep your interest and keep you learning. By breaking the learning process into smaller units, you will not be overwhelmed by the complexity of some of the new technologies being introduced in today's market. Each hourly lesson has a number of special items, some old, some new, to help you along.

10 Minutes

In the first 10 minutes of the hour, you will be given a complete list of all of the topics and skills you will have a solid knowledge of by the time you finish the hour. You will be able to know exactly what the hour will bring, with no hidden surprises.

20 Minutes

By the time you have delved into the lesson for 20 minutes, you will know what many of the newest features of the software application are. In the constantly evolving computer arena, knowing everything a program can do will aid you enormously, if not right now, then definitely in the near future.

30 Minutes

Before 30 minutes have passed, you should have learned at least one useful task, oftentimes more. Many of these tasks will take advantage of the newest features of the application. These tasks take the hands-on approach, and tell you exactly which menus and commands you need to step through to accomplish the goal. This approach is found through each lesson in the *24 Hours* series.

40 Minutes

As you will see after 40 minutes, many of the tools you have come to expect from the *Sams Teach Yourself* series are still here. Notes and Tips offer you quick asides into the special tricks of the trade to make your work faster and more productive. Warnings give you the knowledge to avoid those nasty time-consuming errors.

50 Minutes

Along the way, you may run across terms that you haven't seen before. Never before has technology thrown so many new words and acronyms into the language, and the New Terms elements you will find in this series will carefully explain each and every one of them.

60 Minutes

At the end of the hour, you may still have questions that need to be answered. You know the kind— questions on skills or tasks that may come up every day for you, but weren't directly addressed during the hour. That's where the Q&A section can help. By asking and answering the most frequently asked questions about the topics discussed in the hour, Q&A will possibly not only get your specific question answered, it will definitely provide a succinct review of all that you have learned in the hour.

The Photoshop 5 Toolbar

- Keyboard shortcut in parentheses
- Shift+shortcut=Cycle through multiple tools

Rectangular Marquee
Elliptical Marquee
Single Row Marquee
Single Column Marquee
Crop (C)

Marquee tools (M)

Lasso
Polygonal Lasso
Magnetic Lasso

Lasso tools (L)

Rubber Stamp
Pattern Stamp

Stamp tools (S)

Blur
Sharpen
Smudge

Focus tools (R)

Pen
Magnetic Pen
Freeform Pen
Add Anchor Point (+)
Delete Anchor Point (–)
Direct Selection (A)
Convert Point

Pen tools (P)

Cut Here

Adobe Online

Move (V)

Magic Wand (W)

Airbrush (J)

Paintbrush (B)

History Brush (Y)

Eraser (E)

Measure (U)

Paint Bucket (K)

Pencil
Line

Drawing tools (N)

Dodge
Burn
Sponge

Tone tools (O)

Type
Type Mask
Vertical Type
Vertical Type Mask

Type tools (T)

Linear Gradient
Radial Gradient
Angle Gradient
Reflected Gradient
Diamond Gradient

Gradient tools (G)

Eyedropper
Color Sampler

Eyedropper tools (I)

Hand (H)

Foreground Color

Default Foreground and
Background Colors (D)

Edit in Standard Mode (Q)

Standard Screen Mode (F)

Zoom (Z)

Switch Foreground and
Background Colors (X)

Background Color

Edit in Quick
Mask Mode (Q)

Full Screen Mode (F)

Full Screen Mode with Menu Bar (F)

Photoshop 5 Keyboard Shortcut Quick Reference

Top-level menus have keyboard mnemonics (accessed by pressing Alt+) for Windows users. Windows users should use the Control key instead of Command except where indicated.

FILE MENU

New	Cmd+N
Open	Cmd+O
Open As (Windows only)	Alt+Cmd+O
Close	Cmd+W
Save	Cmd+S
Save As	Shift+Cmd+S
Save a Copy	Option+Cmd+S
Page Setup	Shift+Cmd+P
Print	Cmd+P
Preferences->General	Cmd+K

EDIT MENU

Undo	Cmd+Z
Cut	Cmd+X
Copy	Cmd+C
Copy Merged	Shift+Cmd+C
Paste	Cmd+V
Past Into	Shift+Cmd+V
Free Transform	Cmd+T
Transform->Again	Shift+Cmd+T

IMAGE MENU

Adjust->Levels	Cmd+L
Adjust->Auto Levels	Shift+Cmd+L
Adjust->Curves	Cmd+M
Adjust->Color Balance	Cmd+B
Adjust->Hue/Saturation	Cmd+U
Adjust->Desaturate	Shift+Cmd+U
Adjust->Invert	Cmd+I

LAYER MENU

New->Layer	Shift+Cmd+N
New->Layer Via Copy	Cmd+J
New->Layer Via Cut	Shift+Cmd+J
Group with Previous	Cmd+G
Ungroup	Shift+Cmd+G
Arrange->Bring to Front	Shift+Cmd+]
Arrange->Bring Forward	Cmd+]
Arrange->Send Backward	Cmd+[
Arrange->Send to Back	Shift+Cmd+[
Merge Down	Cmd+E
Merge Visible	Shift+Cmd+E

SELECT MENU

All	Cmd+A
Deselect	Cmd+D
Reselect	Shift+Cmd+D
Inverse	Shift+Cmd+I
Feather	Alt+Ctrl+D (Windows)
	Shift+Cmd+D (Macintosh)

FILTER MENU

Last Filter	Cmd+F
Fade	Shift+Cmd+F

VIEW MENU

Preview->CMYK	Cmd+Y
Gamut Warning	Shift+Cmd+Y
Zoom In	Cmd++
Zoom Out	Cmd+-
Fit on Screen	Cmd+0 (zero)
Actual Pixels	Shift+Ctrl+0 (zero) (Windows)
	Alt+Cmd+0 (zero) (Macintosh)
Hide Edges	Cmd+H
Hide Path	Shift+Cmd+H
Show Rulers	Cmd+R
Hide Guides	Cmd+;
Snap To Guides	Shift+Cmd+;
Lock Guides	Alt+Cmd+;
Show Grid	Cmd+"
Snap To Grid	Shift+Cmd+"

HELP MENU (Windows only)

Contents	F1

OTHER SHORTCUTS

Move view up/down 1 screen	Page Up/Down (W)
	Opt+PageUp/Down (M)
Nudge view up/down	Shift+Page Up/Down (W)
	Opt+Shift+PageUp/Down (M)
Move view left/right 1 screen	Ctrl+Page Up/Down (W)
	Cmd+PageUp/Down (M)
Nudge view left/right	Shift+Ctrl+Page Up/Down (W)
	Cmd+Shift+PageUp/Down (M)
Previous History Entry	Ctrl+Shift+Z
Next History Entry	Ctrl+Alt+Z
Scroll through blending modes	Shift++ and Shift+-

Carla Rose

SAMS
Teach Yourself
Adobe® Photoshop® 5
in 24 Hours

SAMS

A Division of Macmillan Computer Publishing
201 West 103rd St., Indianapolis, Indiana, 46290 USA

Sams Teach Yourself Adobe® Photoshop® 5 in 24 Hours

Copyright © 1998 by Sams Publishing

International Standard Book Number: 0-672-31301-4

Library of Congress Catalog Card Number: 98-84022

Printed in the United States of America

First Printing: May, 1998

00 99 98   4 3

Interpretation of the printing code: the rightmost double-digit number is the year of the book's printing; the rightmost single digit, the number of the book's printing. For example, a printing code of 98-1 shows that the first printing of the book occurred in 1998.

Trademarks

PUBLISHER
Jordan Gold

EXECUTIVE EDITOR
Beth Millett

MANAGING EDITOR
Brice Gosnell

ACQUISITIONS EDITOR
David Mayhew

DEVELOPMENT EDITOR
Bob Correll

PROJECT EDITOR
Katie Purdum

COPY EDITOR
Michael Brumitt

INDEXER
Rebecca Salerno

TECHNICAL EDITOR
Raymond Pirouz

PRODUCTION
Carol L. Bowers
Mona Brown
Ayanna Lacey
Gene Redding

COVER DESIGNER
Aren Howell

BOOK DESIGNER
Gary Adair

Overview

Contents

Dedication

This book's for Carroll Spinney; artist, clown, and bird.

Acknowledgments

No project this big could ever get started, much less completed, without help from a lot of wonderful people. I'd like to thank the folks at Macmillan, especially Beth Millett, David Mayhew, Bob Correll, Michael Brumitt, and Katie Purdum. Thanks to Christie Cameron and the Adobe folks for providing beta software, and for coming up with a wonderful product. Thanks to my friends in the ABC's for their moral support as I worked 20-hour days to meet the deadlines. Special thanks to Carole Harrison for lending me her relatives to restore, and to Geoff Steadman.

Finally, hugs and eternal gratitude to the kids and cats for staying out from underfoot. And the biggest hug and deepest gratitude of all to my wonderful husband, Jay, who always does what needs to be done.

About the Author

CARLA ROSE started her photography career at the age of 8 with a Brownie Hawkeye. A graduate of the School of the Museum of Fine Arts in Boston, she has been a TV news photographer and film editor, as well as advertising copywriter and graphic artist, before discovering the Macintosh. She has written all or part of more than twenty computer books, including *Maclopedia, Sams Teach Yourself Digital Photography in 14 Days, Sams Teach Yourself Photoshop in 14 Days, The Whole Mac, Managing the Windows NT Server, PageMaker 6.5 Complete, Sams Teach Yourself Photoshop 4 in 24 Hours, Mac Online, It's a Mad, Mad, Mad, Mad Mac, Turbocharge Your Mac,* and *Everything You Ever Wanted to Know About the Mac.* She lives near Boston, Massachusetts, with her husband, audio guru Jay Rose, sons Joshua and Daniel (both presently in college), and a fluctuating number of cats. She welcomes e-mail addressed to momcat@pinkcat.com.

Introduction

Photoshop 5 is the very newest version of a program that's set the standard for image manipulation since 1987. The new version has lots of new features, including new "magnetic" tools and a system for undoing changes you've made, even if you have already saved the page. It's also brought you improved color-management capabilities, support for 16-bit channels, and improved type handling. If you've used an earlier version, you'll be amazed at how much more powerful this one is. If this is your first experience with Photoshop, you'll be blown away. It's that good! The big surprise for first-time users is that it's really not as difficult as it looks. If you have used any other Adobe software, the Photoshop interface will be immediately familiar to you. If this is your first step into digital graphics, you'll find the going easier if you work on the chapters of this book one at a time and don't skip the activities or exercises.

There's honestly no way to become an overnight expert, be it in Photoshop or anything else, but this book will get you up and running in 24 hours or less. It's divided into two dozen one-hour "lessons," rather than chapters. Each one should take you about an hour to complete. Some lessons may need more time, others less. You could probably sit down and blast through all 24 in half a day, if necessary. Should you? Only if you must....

The best way is to take an hour or two between the lesson hours to try out what you've learned, and to simply poke around and see what's on the menus and what happens when you click here and there.

Here's one for you to start with: Open the About Photoshop window and wait for a minute. You'll see it start to scroll through the list of all the people who worked on the program. Watch carefully for the very last name on the list.

Please note that this book was produced using beta software, and it's possible that some screenshots may not exactly match what you see in the final version. Every effort has been made to make the book as accurate as possible.

Ready? Let's get to work.

Hour 1

The Basics

Photoshop is the ultimate graphics program. Although it's mainly used for photo-retouching and image manipulation, you can also use it to create original art, either from scratch or based on a photograph. It's fun to use and not as complicated as you might think.

Finding Your Way Around

When you first open Photoshop, you'll see its toolbox on the left side of the screen, menu headings at the top of the screen, and four windows on the right. (You'll also see your desktop, or whatever else is open at the time.)

You won't see a work area, because Photoshop, unlike most graphics programs, doesn't automatically open a new page for you. This makes sense, because most of your work in Photoshop will be done on pictures that you have brought in from some other source. Maybe you'll be using digital images from your digital camera or scanner. Possibly you'll work on files you've downloaded from the Internet or on photos from a CD-ROM. In Hour 2, "Opening and Saving," you will learn all about opening these pictures. Right now, let's open a blank page so you can try out some of Photoshop's tools.

Starting a New Page

File→New is the first item on the first Photoshop menu. When you select it, you open the New dialog box, shown in Figure 1.1. You may enter a title for your new file at the top of the dialog box, such as My New Page, or leave it untitled for now. The following sections will give you a brief overview to get you started on setting up a new file.

FIGURE 1.1.

Use the New dialog box to start a blank page.

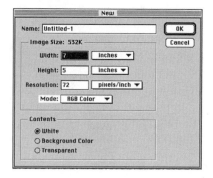

Image Size

In the Image Size dialog, you specify the size of your image—width and height—in pixels, inches, centimeters, points, picas, or columns. These measurements are available in drop-down menus that you can access by clicking the small arrow next to the unit of measurement. For now, choose inches. Make your page big enough to work on comfortably. The page in the figure is 7 inches by 5 inches, which is a convenient size to display on a typical screen.

Resolution

Resolution refers to the number of dots of ink per inch (if you're printing) or pixels per inch (if you're looking at the computer screen). It's important because the resolution of the image determines the quality. Higher resolution gives you a better quality image but uses more memory. Most images that you see in print are close to a resolution of 300 dpi—or dots per inch.

Your computer's monitor, on the other hand, has a dpi of 72, which is substantially lower. Therefore, you always set the resolution depending on what your output will be. For now, keep the resolution at 72 dpi (Mac) or 96 dpi (PC), because we're just looking at the screen. For the same reason, set the Mode to RGB Color, as shown in the figure. RGB color is the kind of color that monitors display. (You'll learn all about color modes in Hour 5, "Color Models and Modes.")

Click the button to set the page contents to white. This gives you a white "canvas" to paint on.

> If you intend to publish your images on the Web, then anything over 72 dpi is a waste of pixels. Computers can't display pictures at higher resolutions. If, on the other hand, you are printing to a high quality laser printer, set the resolution to 200 dpi. You really would only use 300 dpi if you were looking to create professional color prints.

After you click OK in the New dialog box, you see a new window. This is the active window and the canvas is the large white square within it. Figure 1.2 shows the canvas. You can have more than one window open within Photoshop at a time, but only one can be the active window. The active window is always in the foreground. This is where you create and edit images.

FIGURE 1.2.

This is your "canvas."

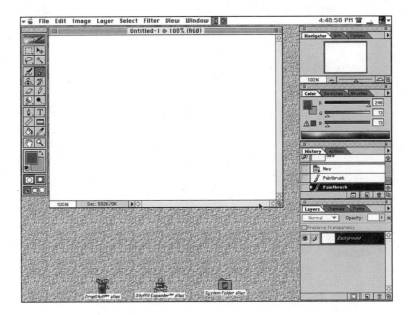

Set your mouse cursor at the lower-right corner of the window, and then click and drag. The window expands, but notice that the canvas size stays the same. After you have created a new file, you can only change the size of the canvas by selecting Image→Canvas Size. This command allows you to specify a new height and width for the canvas, as in Figure 1.3. The Anchor section lets you specify the base area from which the canvas expands or shrinks. (Changing the image size, obviously, changes the size of the canvas, too. The difference is that changing the canvas size gives you more room around your existing image.)

FIGURE 1.3.

Click a white square to locate your current canvas in the corresponding part of the new canvas.

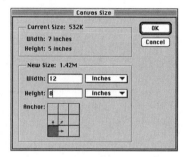

The Toolbox

The toolbox, like an artist's worktable or paint box, holds all the tools you'll use to draw, paint, erase, and otherwise work on your picture. There are four kinds of tools in the box:

- Selection tools
- Painting tools
- Specialized tools for working with type, gradients, and so on
- Viewing tools

Let's take a quick look at these tools. (We'll talk about them in detail later on.) Figure 1.4 shows the toolbox with the tools labeled.

Notice that some of the tool icons have a tiny black triangle in the lower-right corner. This means that there are more tools of the same general kind available on a pop-out menu. Point to any tool that has a triangle, click, and hold down the mouse button to see what other tools are available.

Selection Tools

At the top of the toolbox is a group of tools called Selection tools. They are used to select all or part of a picture. There are three: the Marquee, the Lasso, and the Magic Wand. A selected area is indicated onscreen by a blinking selection border, called a

FIGURE 1.4.

In the Photoshop tool-box, the tools are grouped by type.

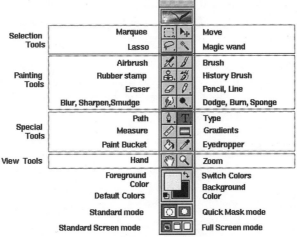

Marquee after the movie theater marquee lights that flash on and off. The Marquee and Lasso tools work by clicking and dragging the tool over the part of the image that you want to select. Figure 1.5 shows the pop-out menu for the Marquee Selection tools.

FIGURE 1.5.

The Marquee Selection tools.

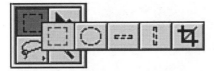

The fourth tool in this set is the Move tool. After you have made a selection, use the Move tool to move the selected area to another place on the page.

Painting Tools

Within the set of Painting tools, there is an Airbrush, Paintbrush, Pencil, and Rubber Stamp. These all apply "paint" to the screen in one way or another, just like the real tools they imitate. The Airbrush and Paintbrush can change width and angle. The Pencil draws or erases a single pixel line. The Line tool, which pops up when you click the Pencil, draws straight lines at 45 and 90 degree angles, just as if you had an artist's or architect's T-square and triangle. There's also an Eraser that, as you might expect, takes away part of the picture.

NEW TO VERSION 5 New to Photoshop 5 is the History brush, a tool that, combined with the History window, gives you the ability to selectively undo and redo as many of your changes or individual brushstrokes as you want.

Finally, there are tools that move, blur, and change the intensity of the image. These are the Smudge, Blur/Sharpen, and Dodge/Burn/Sponge tools. The latter two are found on pop-out menus. These tools will be covered in detail in Hour 7, "Paintbrushes and Art Tools," Hour 8, "Digital Painting," and Hour 9, "Moving Paint."

Viewing Tools

There are two Viewing tools: the Hand tool and the Zoom tool. The Zoom tool is shaped like an old-fashioned magnifying glass, and the Hand tool, not surprisingly, like a hand. The Zoom tool lets you "zoom in" by clicking the tool on the canvas to see a magnified view of your picture or "zoom out" again by pressing (Option) [Alt] as you click the image. When you zoom in, the picture is usually too big to see all at once. The Hand moves it within the window and is helpful after you use the Zoom tool to enlarge the picture. Use the Hand, as shown in Figure 1.6, to slide the part of the picture you want to see or work on into a convenient spot. You can also click and drag the Zoom tool to enlarge a specific part of the image.

FIGURE 1.6.

The Hand tool moves an image within its window.

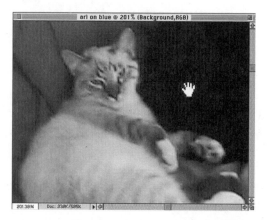

Special Tools

These tools aren't as easy to classify as the Painting tools or the Selection tools. They do different, useful things. The letter T represents the Type tool, which puts type on your picture. The Pen tool draws paths, which are a means of drawing a curved line or shape. Paths can be used as a Selection tool or as a Drawing tool. (See what I mean about being hard to classify?) In Hour 13, "Paths," you'll learn how to work with paths.

NEW TO VERSION 5 The Measure tool, also new to Photoshop 5, can be used to measure dimensions and angles in the picture. Click and drag a line to measure a distance between two points, and see it displayed in the Info window. To measure an angle, first create a measured line. Then place your cursor on one of its two end-points. Hold down the (Option) [Alt] key while clicking and dragging from the endpoint of the first line in the direction of the angle. Figure 1.7 shows an angle measurement.

FIGURE 1.7.

The angle is measured between the two lines.

The Gradient tool lets you create backgrounds that shade from one color to another, or even all the way through the rainbow. The Paint Bucket (which really belongs up with the Painting tools) pours paint into any area you select. The Eyedropper tool picks up a sample of any color you click it on, making it the "active" color, so you can paint with it.

Tool Shortcuts

NEW TO VERSION 5 Every one of these tools can be selected by clicking its icon in the toolbox, but Photoshop gives you another, even easier way to access the tools. Instead of clicking the tools you want to use, you can type a single letter shortcut to select each tool. To toggle through the available tools where there are pop-out menus, type Shift plus the shortcut letter until you reach the tool you want. Table 1.1 lists the tools with their shortcuts. Dog-ear this page so you can refer to the table until you have memorized the shortcuts.

TABLE 1.1. TOOLS AND THEIR SHORTCUTS.

Tool	Shortcut	Tool	Shortcut
Marquee	M	Move	V
Lasso	L	Magic Wand	W
Airbrush	J	Brush	B

continues

NEW TO VERSION 5 TABLE **1.1.** CONTINUED

Tool	Shortcut	Tool	Shortcut
Rubber Stamp	S	History Brush	Y
Eraser	E	Pencil	N
Blur	R	Dodge	O
Pen	P	Type	T
Measurement	U	Gradient	G
Paint Bucket	K	Eyedropper	I
Hand	H	Zoom	Z
Crop	C	Switch background/ foreground colors	X

Caution! If you're used to using an earlier version of Photoshop, be aware that some of the shortcuts have changed.

What's on the Menus?

The menus across the top of the screen contain the commands that allow you to open and manipulate files. They are accessed by simply clicking and holding the mouse button and dragging down to the desired command. Whenever you see an arrow or an ellipsis off to the right of a menu command, it indicates that there is either a submenu, in the case of the arrow, or a dialog box, in the case of the ellipsis.

File and Edit Menus

The first two menus are File and Edit. Photoshop's File and Edit menus hold no surprises for anyone who has used any other Macintosh or Windows program. The File menu lets you work with files: opening, closing, saving, exporting, and printing them and, of course, quitting the program. The Edit menu includes all the editing commands you're familiar with from other applications: Cut, Copy, Paste, Clear, and the most important one—Undo.

The six menus that are unique to Photoshop are

- Image
- Layer
- Select

- Filter
- View
- Window

The Image Menu

The Image menu, which is shown in Figure 1.8, has several submenus. The first of these, Mode, is shown in the figure. As you can see, it allows you to select a color mode to work in. Most of the time, you will be working in RGB mode, because that's what your monitor displays. Color modes are discussed in detail in Hour 5.

FIGURE 1.8.

The Image→Mode menus.

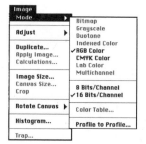

The Image menu also has the tools to adjust the colors and the lightness and brightness of your picture. You will learn how to use the tools on the Image→Adjust menu in Hour 6, "Adjusting Color."

When you want to make a picture bigger or smaller, or turn all or part of it sideways, you'll use the Image→Size and Image→Rotate Canvas menu. In Hour 4, "Transformations," you'll learn how and when to use these tools.

The Layer Menu

Arguably the most powerful feature of Photoshop is the capability to work on different layers. This enables you to combine images, create collages, and make corrections without fear of damaging the original picture. Think of it as working on sheets of transparent plastic. Each layer is totally separate from the others. You can paint on a layer, change its opacity, or do whatever you want with it without disturbing the background or other parts of the picture on other layers.

The Layer menu opens dialog boxes to create new layers. It also has commands to merge and work with them. Figure 1.9 shows what's on the Layer menu. Hour 6 and Hour 11, "Layers," will teach you about working with layers.

FIGURE 1.9.

The Layer menu.

The Select Menu

You have Selection tools, so why do you need a Selection menu? In Hour 3, "Selection Modes," you'll learn all the tricks for selecting and working with selected parts of a picture. The Select menu works with the tools to let you modify areas you have selected. You can enlarge or shrink the selected area by as many pixels as you want, or feather its edges so the selection appears to fade into a background you paste it on.

The Filter Menu

Filters are the tools that make Photoshop fun. The Filter menu lists a dozen different categories of filters: Some blur or sharpen the picture, some distort it, and some turn it into imitation paintings, colored pencil drawings, or neon light sculpture. There's so much for you to do with filters that we'll spend Hours 14, "Filters That Improve Your Picture," 15, "Filters to Make Your Pictures Artistic," and 16, "Filters to Distort and Other Funky Effects," applying them to your pictures.

Photoshop filters are called plug-ins, and many work with other graphics programs as well. If you install any third-party filters or plug-ins, like Alien Skin's Eye Candy series or MetaTools KPT, they'll appear at the bottom of the Filter menu.

The View Menu

Like the Zoom tool, the View menu has commands that let you zoom in and out on the picture. As you can see in Figure 1.10, it also has the Ruler, Grid, and Guides commands that enable you to measure and place objects precisely within the work area.

Figure 1.10.

The View menu.

The ruler can be set to measure in pixels, inches, centimeters, points, or picas. Choose the measurement you're most familiar with. The setting is done in a Preferences dialog box: File→Preferences→Units&Rulers.

Guide lines are lines that you place over your picture to position type or some other element that you're going to add to the picture. To place guide lines, follow these steps:

1. Select View→Show Rulers. This makes the rulers visible at the edges of the canvas.

2. Select View→Show Guides or use the keyboard shortcut (command+;) [Ctrl+;].

3. To place a horizontal guide line, put the mouse pointer on the ruler at the top of the screen and drag downward. You'll see a line scrolling down the canvas as you drag. The left ruler shows you the position of the line.

4. To place a vertical guide line, put the mouse pointer on the ruler at the left of the screen and drag across. You'll see a line scrolling across the canvas as you drag. The top ruler shows you the position of the line. See Figure 1.11 for an example.

Figure 1.11.

Guides let you place type right where you want it.

Once you have placed a guide line, you can't move it unless you use the Move tool. (You can place a guideline regardless of what tool is selected.) You can hide it by choosing View→Hide Guides or using the keyboard shortcut in step 2 to toggle back and forth. To get rid of the guide lines, choose View→Clear Guides.

The Show Grid command, which is also found on the View menu, places an entire grid of guidelines over your image, rather like a layer of transparent graph paper. The Snap to... commands make it easier to position an element, such as a block of type. In effect, they make the guideline or gridline "magnetic," so that when you place the element near it, the line pulls the element right up against it.

The Windows Menu

Most of Photoshop's commands can be accessed in several different ways. The windows at the right of the Photoshop screen give you information about your picture, options for many of the tools in the toolbox, a choice of brush sizes and shapes, colors, and access to Layers, Paths, and Channels. The Windows menu shows and hides these windows. If there are some, like Actions, that you're not ready to use, close them to keep your screen uncluttered.

Setting Preferences

As you become more familiar with Photoshop, you may want to change the ways it handles certain tasks. You may want to use the System Color Picker instead of the Photoshop version. You might decide to measure in inches for one project and centimeters for another. You might need to change the color of the guide lines because they're too close to the background in your photo. All these changes and many more are made in the File→Preferences dialog boxes. The General Preferences dialog box is shown in Figure 1.12.

FIGURE 1.12.

Set preferences here.

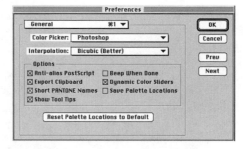

Use the Next button to scroll through the Preferences dialog boxes. You may encounter some preferences that you don't understand. For now, leave the default settings. As you learn more about the program, you can come back and change preferences as necessary.

Summary

You are starting to learn your way around the Photoshop screen, and you learned how to open a new page. You've looked at the toolbox and Photoshop's menus, and learned about grids and rulers. Finally, you learned about setting preferences.

Q&A

Q What are foreground and background colors?

A The foreground color is the uppermost of the two colored squares in the toolbox. It's the color the brush applies. The background color is the lower square. It's the color you see when you erase the canvas.

Q How do I change the size of a picture?

A Use the Image→Image size dialog box. Enter new numbers in the Print size windows. (If you change one number, the other(s) change in proportion.)

Quiz

Questions

1. What's the picture at the top of the tool bar for?

   (a) It's the Adobe Photoshop logo.

   (b) It's your connection to Adobe Online.

   (c) It looks pretty.

2. Why are there trash cans at the bottom of the History and Layers windows?

   (a) Oscar the Grouch was here.

   (b) To delete a layer, or an unwanted action.

   (c) To erase the page if you change your mind.

Answers

1. (b) If you click it, *and* if you have an Internet browser and modem, you'll open a browser window linked to Adobe Online, a place for ideas, tips, and late-breaking Photoshop news.

2. (b) Clicking the trash can for the Layers window deletes a selected layer. Similarly, clicking the trash can for the History window deletes an action. You'll learn more about this later on.

Activities

1. Open a new page and try out some of these tools. Click the Paintbrush and draw some squiggles and lines. Click the Eraser and erase part of them. Try dragging the Smudge tool across one of the lines. Select a piece of line with one of the Selection tools and move it to another part of the page. Explore. You're not going to break anything.

2. If you have an Internet connection, click the Adobe logo at the top of the toolbar. Visit Adobe Online and see what's there.

HOUR **2**

Opening and Saving

Before you can do anything exciting with Photoshop 5, you need to learn how to open and view files. Photoshop can open a wide variety of file formats, so you can work on pictures from many different sources. If you have a scanner or a digital camera, you can bring in pictures that you've taken. You can also use photos from CD-ROM collections or images that you have downloaded from some online or Internet source. This chapter will also cover methods of saving your work because if you don't save, all the changes you make will be lost.

Working with Files

Photoshop can open and save images in many different file *formats*. Formats are ways of saving the information in a file, so it can be used by other applications, printed, or placed on a Web page for use on the Internet.

In the Windows world, file formats are defined by three-letter extensions to filenames, such as .doc for a word processing document or .bmp for a bitmapped graphic.

Mac users are lucky because they don't need to deal with file format extensions. Macintosh files have a *resource fork* and a *data fork*. The data fork contains the file's data, and the resource fork contains the file's information—whether it is a graphic file, a word processing document, or even a sound. Don't let this worry you, Windows users. Filenames are kind of a nuisance, but they aren't that difficult.

The most common file format in Photoshop is .psd, which is the native Photoshop file format (Photoshop document). The drawback to .psd is that, because it is native to Photoshop, other applications may have trouble opening this format. To move files between applications, to print, or to publish on the World Wide Web, you must save your files in a compatible format.

Here are some common formats with brief definitions of their uses. Note that Photoshop can handle many other graphics formats as well.

- **Bitmap (.bmp)**   This is a standard file format for Windows.
- **GIF (.gif)**   GIF stands for Graphics Interchange Format. It is one of the three formats you can use for Web publishing. Because it is a compressed format, it takes less time to send by modem.
- **JPEG (.jpg)**   JPEG stands for Joint Photographic Experts Group. JPEG is another popular format for Web publishing.
- **PDF (.pdf)**   Adobe's Acrobat Page Description Format, a system for creating documents that can be read cross-platform.
- **PNG (.png)**   Stands for Portable Network Graphic, or PNG's Not GIF, depending on whom you ask. It's the newest and arguably best format for Web graphics, combining good compression like GIFs with the JPEG unlimited color palette. However, older browsers don't support it. (We'll discuss these formats and their use in Web publishing in the final hour.)
- **TIFF (.tif)**   TIFF stands for Tagged-Image File Format. These files can be saved for use on either Macs or Windows machines. This is also often the preferred format for desktop publishing applications, such as PageMaker and QuarkXpress.
- **EPS (.eps)**   Encapsulated PostScript is another format often used for desktop publishing. It uses the PostScript page description language and can be used by both Macs and PCs.
- **PICT (.pct)**   This is mainly a Macintosh format. It, too, is widely used in desktop publishing.
- **Raw (.raw)**   This format saves image information in the most flexible format for transferring files between applications and computer platforms.

NEW TO
VERSION 5 These file formats, and some less common ones like Amiga IFF and Scitex CT, are available in the Save dialog boxes—File→Save, File→Save As, and File→Save a Copy. Just look for the drop-down menu. Figure 2.1 shows the Save dialog box with the formats available. A new feature in Photoshop 5 is the ability to choose whether to append a file extension within the Save As dialog box. (This appears as a Preference option under File→Preferences→Saving Files.) Just click the check boxes to add an extension and to keep it in lowercase (as required by DOS users).

2

FIGURE 2.1.

Photoshop 5 can save your work in any of these formats.

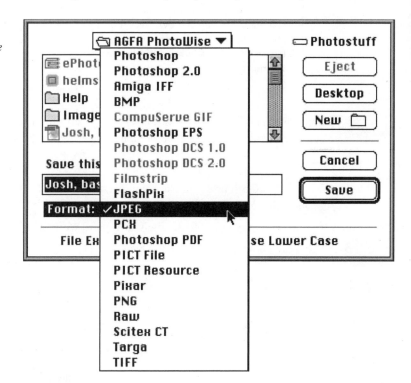

Opening and Importing Files

Opening a file in Photoshop is as easy as opening it in any other application. You can open as many images as you want or as many as your RAM can hold. If a file is of the proper type (a file format that Photoshop recognizes), all you have to do is double-click it with your mouse to not only open it, but to open Photoshop as well. If Photoshop is already open, you can either double-click a file or use the File→Open command. You can also drag and drop a compatible file on the Photoshop 5 icon to open it.

A technical note for Windows users: Double-clicking on an image file will open Photoshop only if the extension (BMP, for instance) is associated with Photoshop. Sometimes installing new applications will change the extension mapping to other programs. GIFs and JPGs are notoriously remapped to Microsoft Internet Explorer, whereas BMP usually is grabbed by Paint. If double-clicking doesn't work for you, check your extensions. Mac people: You don't have to worry about this.

When you open the dialog box, Photoshop displays all the files in formats it can open. Figure 2.2 shows the Photoshop Open dialog box. As you can see, Photoshop displays *thumbnails* of any image that has one, and it can even create a thumbnail for any usable image that doesn't have one. To make a thumbnail, click the Create button.

 Thumbnail, or thumbnail sketch, is an artist's term for a small version of a picture, so called because they are often no bigger than a thumbnail.

To open a file:

1. Choose File→Open or use the key command (Command-O) [Control-O] to open the Open dialog box.

2. Use the dialog box to locate the file you want to work on.

3. Select it and double-click, or click Open.

FIGURE 2.2.

Any file that's shown can be opened in Photoshop.

Importing a File

The Import command (File→ Import) lets you open files that have been saved in formats that use plug-in import modules. Typically, these include files saved with the TWAIN interface, Scitex files, antialiased PICT files and PICT resources (Macintosh), and files imported directly from any digital camera that has a Photoshop plug-in import filter.

Importing from Digital Cameras

The Agfa e307 is one of several digital cameras that can import pictures directly into Photoshop. The plug-in filter comes with the camera. Drop it into the plug-ins folder. (Remember that you need to quit the application before you install plug-ins. If you install while Photoshop is running, it can't see the new plug-in until you quit and restart it.) To import a picture, you simply plug the camera cable into the computer's modem (Mac) or Com1 (Windows) port and choose File→Import→Agfa e307. Figure 2.3 shows the Agfa import window. Pictures in the camera are displayed as if they were slides on a sorting table.

FIGURE 2.3.

Other cameras use a similar system.

Importing Files with the Twain Interface

The TWAIN Acquire and TWAIN Select commands found under the File→Import submenu don't actually import images. Instead, they enable you to open the appropriate scanner software to be used from within Photoshop and to use it to import the scanned images. Photoshop supports TWAIN, TWAIN32, and TWAIN_32 standards for scanning. Consult the scanner manual for more information.

Importing PICT Resources and Antialiased PICTs

These commands open dialog boxes just like the regular Open box, but they enable Mac users to open specialized kinds of PICT files. Antialiased PICTs are simply PICTs that have been processed to avoid sharp contrasts between dark and light pixels. PICT resources are images saved within the document's resource fork, often used as icons for the document, or as splash screens for a program. When you attempt to open a PICT resource for editing, you first open the document and then Photoshop scans its resource fork for PICT resources. Any it finds are displayed in a window like the one in Figure 2.4. Open the resource and edit it from this dialog box.

FIGURE 2.4.

*You won't find these in
the Windows version of
Photoshop.*

Saving Your Work

There's one very important thing to know about saving your work: Do it often!
Computers are prone to unexpected shutdowns and errors. Saving takes only a couple of
seconds and it can make the difference between having to do your work all over again or
just reopening it if the computer shuts down.

The first time you save a picture, you'll see the Save As dialog box, just as in Figure 2.5.
Give the file a name and select an appropriate format to save it in, from the pull-down
menu. After this, choose File→Save or just type (Command-S) [Control-S] to save the
file.

FIGURE 2.5.

*Saving a file in
Photoshop.*

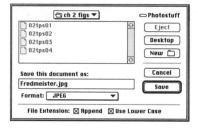

For Macintosh users only: If you have to work cross-platform, that is, on
both Mac and PC, you should always choose to include file extensions with
your files. This option is found in the Save As dialog box. Check both
Append and Use Lower Case to be sure your file is Windows/DOS-
compatible.

In addition to the familiar Save and Save As commands, Photoshop has a third command, Save a Copy. This command, like Save As, lets you save the file with a new name
and in a new location. The difference is that after you use Save As, you're working in the
new file.

If you use Save a Copy, you save a copy of the file as it is at that moment, but you'll still be working on the original file, not the copy. Save a Copy is especially useful for making a backup copy before you try a drastic change or for saving the file in a different format. Suppose you create a logo for your business and want to use it in print and on the Web. You'd save it as a TIFF or EPS file to print from and you'd save a copy as a JPEG or PNG file for your Web page. The word "copy" is automatically added to the filename. The Save a Copy box also gives you the option of flattening the image, if applicable, and excluding Alpha channels and nonimage data. If you don't know what that means, don't worry. You'll learn later on.

2

Reducing File Size

As you start to work with different Photoshop files, you'll notice that your hard drive is starting to fill up. Photoshop files can get very large, very quickly. You can make your files smaller in several ways:

- Reduce the resolution.
- Reduce the number of colors in the image palette.
- Use a format that compresses the file.
- Use compression after the file is saved.

Reducing the resolution is not a good idea if you're going to print the image. If the picture is only going to be viewed on your computer screen or on the Web, reduce the resolution to 72dpi (Mac) or whatever resolution (72–120dpi) your PC monitor uses. You can change the resolution in the Image→Image size dialog box.

Reducing the number of colors means reducing the bit depth. This can make your colors look blotchy onscreen and in print. If you are working in grayscale (no color in the picture), reduce the bit depth to 8 bits. This gives you 256 shades of gray, which is more than a printer can print. You can make this change from the Image→Mode submenu.

Using a compressed format means choosing a file format, such as TIFF with LZW compression, which automatically shrinks the file down as small as possible when it saves. It does this by a means called "lossless" compression, so there's no image degradation or blotchy color. LZW compression (named for its inventors, Lempel, Ziv, and Welch) is also used by GIF, PDF, and Postscript formats.

There are also formats, such as JPEG, which use "lossy" compression. This means, as you might guess from the name, that some of the data that makes up the image is lost in the compression process. Instead of 20 shades of blue in the sky in a TIFF file, the same image in a JPEG file might have only five shades of blue. And yes, you *can* see the difference. Unfortunately, compression is necessary when you are putting images on the

Web, in a multimedia presentation, or in another situation where upload time or storage space is limited. JPEG saves files in the least possible amount of disk space.

When you have files that you want to save for future reference, you can save them in the normal way as .psd's (Photoshop documents) or in whatever format you prefer to work in, and then compress the files with a utility like StuffIt (Mac) or PkZip (PC). Both of these file compression utilities use lossless compression algorithms and shrink your image files by anywhere from 20 to 50 percent.

Figure 2.6 is a typical digital photograph, which I saved in a number of different file types. The following chart shows the more common file types and the sizes of the files that this picture required. The version shown is a high-quality JPEG.

FIGURE 2.6.

If storage space isn't a problem, don't compress the picture.

TABLE 2.1. FILE FORMAT/FILE SIZE COMPARISON.

Format	File Size
.bmp	891K
.eps	1.3MB
.fpx	119K
.jpg (high quality)	344K
.jpg (low quality)	60K
.pdf	257K

Format	File Size
.pct	572K
.png (interlaced)	837K
.png (not interlaced)	495K
.psd	891K
.tif	797K

2

Choosing a Format

With so many possible formats, how can you decide which one to use? It's really not so difficult. As long as you are working on a picture, keep saving it as a Photoshop document (.psd). This makes sense, especially when you learn to work in layers, because Photoshop's native format can save the layers, whereas other formats require that you merge the layers into one. After you have flattened the layers, you can't split them apart again. So, bottom line, as long as you think you'll want to go back to a picture and work on it more, save a copy as a .psd.

When you finish working on the picture and are ready to place it into another document for printing, save a copy as an .eps file if it's going to a PostScript-compatible printer or as a .tif. If you're going to place your picture onto a Web page, choose .gif if the picture is line art (a drawing, with limited color). Choose .jpeg or .png if the picture is a photograph or continuous tone art (lots of colors). If you want to import the picture into some other graphics program for additional work, choose PICT if you are working on a Macintosh or .bmp if you use Windows. These two are the most generally compatible graphic formats.

Undoing and Redoing

NEW TO
VERSION 5

The single biggest change in Photoshop 5 is that Adobe has finally responded to years of pleading from users and given us a means to undo more than just the very last thing we did to a picture. The new palette in your Photoshop desktop is the History palette, so called because it keeps a listing of every tool you used and every change you made, up to a predetermined number you can set in the History Options menu. You can also take "snapshots" of the work in progress and use these as saved stages to revert to. Figure 2.7 shows the History palette for a picture with a lot of changes made to it.

FIGURE 2.7.

*The History palette
and its pop-out menu.*

You can click any previous step to revert to it if you don't like what you've done. It's
more useful in some ways than multiple undos because the History palette lets you undo
and redo selectively. More importantly, it lets you save your work as you do it and still
go back and undo. In previous editions of Photoshop, and in most other programs, after
you save your work, Undo isn't available. We'll discuss the uses of the History palette
and the History brush (which lets you undo as much or as little of a change as you want)
in greater detail in Hour 7, "Paintbrushes and Art Tools."

Summary

Photoshop can work with many different kinds of graphics files from many sources.
Those that it doesn't open directly, either by double-clicking or by using the File→Open
dialog box, can be imported through plug-in filters. If you have a digital camera or scanner, it might have a Photoshop plug-in that enables you to open the image from within
Photoshop. Check your owner's manual.

Logically enough, Photoshop can also save documents in all the formats it can open.
Different formats have different purposes and different file sizes. Some are specifically
intended for Web use; others for printing. Choose a format based on the intended use of
the image.

The History palette saves a step-by-step list of everything you do to your picture. You
can travel backward or forward through the history list and easily undo or redo your
changes, even if you have already saved the document.

Q&A

Q When should I use Save a Copy instead of Save As?

A Use Save a Copy when you want to make a copy of the picture you are working on and then continue to work on the original, instead of the copy. Suppose I have a picture called "Roses," which I have worked on and saved. If I save a copy as "Roses copy" and then keep working, I will still be working on the original "Roses" but will also have a copy of the picture in a closed file as it was before I did the additional work.

Q What file formats should I use for images I'll be putting in my Web page?

A You should try to stick with .psd files when creating your images. This allows you to use all the powerful Photoshop 5 editing features, such as layers. Once you finish your image, save it as a .gif, .jpg, or .png for use on the Web.

Q How does color depth affect image file size?

A Simply put, the more colors that are in your image, the larger the file size is because it takes more bits to encode more colors.

Quiz

Let's see if you were paying attention to file types.

Questions

1. .bmp is

    a. a PC format, which stands for bitmap.

    b. a Mac format, which stands for bump.

    c. a UNIX code for a better management program.

2. PICTs are

    a. another name for pixels.

    b. a Macintosh graphics format.

    c. the little images used as icons on the desktop.

3. .tif stands for

    a. Tiled Image Format

    b. Tagged-Image Format

    c. Typical Information Font

2

Answers

1. a. Bitmaps are a pixel-by-pixel analysis of the picture. They're not necessarily large files.

2. b. The DOS extension for a PICT is .pct.

3. b. When you save a TIFF, you must choose whether to save it for Mac or PC.

Activity

1. Visit our Web site, www.mcp.com, navigate to the book info page, and download the photo used in this chapter. Open it and save it in different formats. See how the format affects the file size.

2. Mac users, here's one just for you. You can replace that silly "Welcome to Macintosh" message that pops up when you start your computer with a more interesting picture and/or message. Macs use a type of file called a PICT resource to create "splash screens" that you see when you start the Mac or when you start an application. Because Photoshop can save in the PICT resource format, you can make any Photoshop picture into a Startup Screen. Follow these steps:

   1. Start with any image you like. (If it's not as big as your screen, that's okay. It appears with a gray border.)

   2. Open the File→Save As dialog box.

   3. Choose PICT Resource from the Format pop-up menu and click Save.

   4. The PICT Resource dialog box opens.

   5. Name the file StartupScreen. (You must type it exactly that way, with both Ss capitalized and no space between the words.)

   6. Choose None from Compression options. Choose a bit depth: 16 bits if your monitor displays thousands of colors, 32 bits if it is a high-resolution monitor and displays millions of colors.

   7. Click OK to save the file.

   8. Drag the file to your System folder and restart. The picture appears when you start the computer.

HOUR 3

Selection Modes

Now you're making progress. You've learned how to bring images in and out of Photoshop. The next step is learning to work with images and edit them. In order to do this, you have to *select* the part of the picture to work on. Selections are just what they seem to be—portions of the image that you have *selected*.

The Selection Tools

There are several ways to select a piece of the picture. You can use any of the Selection tools: Marquee tools, Lasso tools, or the Magic Wand. You have different kinds of Selection tools because you sometimes need to make selections in a particular way, such as punching a shape out of an image, or selecting all of the sky. Photoshop's Selection tools give you the power to select the whole picture or as little as a single row or column of pixels. Just to refresh your memory, Figure 3.1 shows the Selection tools. (The rollout menus have been shifted slightly so you can see what's normally hidden.)

FIGURE 3.1.

*The Selection tools
are at the top of the
toolbox.*

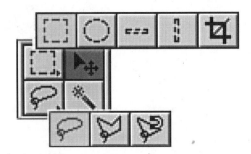

Rectangle and Oval Marquees

The Marquee tools, both Rectangular and Oval, are found in the upper-left corner of the
toolbox. To select the Rectangular Marquee, just click it or type the letter M. To select
the Oval Marquee (also known as the Elliptical Marquee), click and hold the Rectangular
Marquee in the toolbox. When the rollout menu appears, select the Oval Marquee.

Assuming that the Rectangular Marquee is the currently selected tool, you can also type
Shift-M to switch back and forth between the two. The Oval Marquee tool works the
same way that the Rectangular Marquee tool does.

To experiment with its many uses, first create a new file (go back to the first hour if you
can't remember how). Again, give yourself some room to work. Set the dimensions at six
inches square.

1. Click the Marquee tool in the toolbox.

2. As you move the tool over the canvas, the cursor appears as a crosshair.

3. While over the canvas, click and hold the mouse button.

4. Drag out a Marquee. Experiment with dragging out an Elliptical Marquee. Try to
   get a sense for how they appear. Try dragging from different directions.

If you hold the Shift key down while you're using the Marquee, you can make additional
selections. (You'll see a plus sign beneath the crosshair.) Where the selected areas overlap, they'll merge to form one larger selected shape. In Figure 3.2, I've selected several
areas with the Rectangle Marquee and the Oval Marquee to make larger shapes.

To select an area inside another area (making what graphic artists call a "knock out"),
press the (Option) [Alt] key as you drag the inner shape. (You'll see a minus sign
beneath the crosshair.) For instance, if you have a circle selected and drag another smaller circle inside it while pressing the (Option) [Alt] key, the selected shape is a donut.

The thin horizontal and vertical Marquees select a single row of pixels, either horizontally or vertically. They are often useful for cleaning up edges of an object.

FIGURE 3.2.

You can also combine square and round selections.

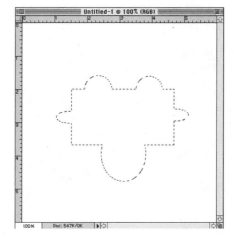

It is important to remember that when you are dealing with selections, for good or bad, only the area within the confines of the Marquee may be edited. It is, in a sense, the only active area of the canvas. Thus, after a selection is made, you can perform whatever action you desire, but before you move on, the selection must be turned off, or *deselected*, by clicking outside the selected area with one of the Marquee tools or by typing (Command - D) [Control - D]. Until you do so, you can only edit within the selection's boundaries.

If you copy or paste something onto your canvas and then try to select a different part of the picture, you may find that the Marquee tool doesn't work or you get a message saying "Could not complete your request because the selected area is empty." This is Photoshop's way of reminding you that you have added another layer to your picture by pasting into it, and the part you're trying to copy isn't on that layer. You will learn all about working with layers in Hour 11, "Layers."

Lasso

As useful as the Marquee tools and their modifier keys are, there will come times when you have to select irregular shapes. Perhaps you might need to select a single flower from a bunch or, as in this example, a person who wandered into the picture and doesn't add to it (see Figure 3.3).

FIGURE 3.3.

*Selecting an object
with the Lasso.*

Using the Lasso tool to select an object in this way requires a steady hand and good
hand-eye coordination. As with the Marquee tools, you can add to your lassoed selection
by holding the Shift key and selecting additional parts of the object.

> I've found that when I am trying to make a very careful selection with the
> Lasso tool, and when I am using Photoshop in general, it helps to slow my
> mouse down. You can adjust this in the Mouse section of your machine's
> Control Panel. Start by setting the slider just a little higher than the slowest
> setting. Experiment to see what works best for you.

To make a selection with the Lasso tool, follow these steps:

1. Select the Lasso tool from the toolbox or type **L**.

2. Click and carefully drag the Lasso tool around the piece of the image that you
   want to select. You see a blinking line. Be careful not to release the mouse. If you
   do, you lose the Marquee (it automatically closes the selection).

3. When you're close to completely enclosing the selection, you can release the
   mouse button. The two ends of the Selection Marquee that you have drawn around
   the shape automatically join together, completing the Selection Marquee.

The Polygon Lasso Tool

The Polygon Lasso tool behaves in much the same way as the regular Lasso tool. The
difference is that, as its name implies, it makes irregular *geometric* selections. It's actually easier to use when you need to make detailed selections because it can be controlled

more easily. Instead of simply dragging a Marquee line, as you do with the regular Lasso, you click the Polygon Lasso to place points and Photoshop inserts a straight-line Marquee between the points. You can place as many points as you need, as close together or far apart as necessary.

FIGURE 3.4.

The Polygon Lasso tool.

3

To use the Polygon Lasso tool, follow these steps:

1. Click the Lasso tool and hold until you see the rollout menu (or type **L**).

2. Select the Polygon tool.

3. Click once in the canvas. Now drag your mouse. Notice that a line follows your Polygon Lasso wherever you move it.

4. Click again. This draws the first line and sets another point from which you may drag. Drag another line and click again.

5. Now with two lines set, you have an option. You can either continue to select the image or you can double-click. This automatically finishes the selection for you.

6. When you near your starting point, notice that a small circle becomes appended to your cursor. This signals that if you click, the selection will be complete.

7. Click to complete your selection.

Many of Photoshop's tools, including the Selection tools, have additional options for their use. These are found on the Tool Options palette, which is a window that you can open either from the Window menu or simply by double-clicking the tool. Whenever you select a new tool, double-click it to see its options.

The Magnetic Lasso

NEW TO
VERSION 5 | The Magnetic Lasso is one of the new tools in Photoshop 5. As you drag it around any shape with a reasonably well-defined edge, it snaps to the edge. Because it finds edges by looking for differences in contrast, the Magnetic Lasso is most effective on irregular objects that stand out from the background. You can use its Options window, shown in Figure 3.5, to set the parameters. Lasso Width, the only one of these settings that isn't self explanatory, refers to how close to the edge you must be to have the Lasso recognize it.

FIGURE 3.5.

Set the edge according to the contrast between the intended selection and what surrounds it.

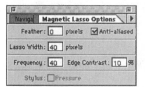

Magic Wand

The software designers at Adobe Systems must not have been able to come up with a more descriptive name for this fantastic tool, choosing instead to let it, perhaps, speak for itself—the Magic Wand. Maybe it's better that way.

The Magic Wand is a different kind of Selection tool. So far we've looked at tools that select pixels based on their placement in the bitmap (the picture). The Magic Wand selects pixels somewhat differently; it selects them based on color values. This enables you to cut foreground objects, such as the person in the art gallery, out of the background. You may need to combine several selections by holding the Shift key, as we have in Figure 3.6, to select all of the object.

FIGURE 3.6.

Selection made with the Magic Wand.

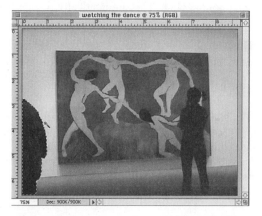

Like the tools above, the Magic Wand can make and merge selections if you press the Shift key as you click the areas to select.

The Magic Wand selects adjacent pixels based on color similarities. Its *tolerance* can be set in the Options palette. To open the Magic Wand Options palette shown in Figure 3.7, either double-click the Magic Wand in the toolbox or simply select it and then choose Window→Show Options.

 Tolerance, in this instance, refers to the Magic Wand's sensitivity to color differences.

FIGURE 3.7.

The Magic Wand Options palette.

3

The rule is easy to remember: The lower the Tolerance, the less tolerance the Magic Wand has for color differences. Thus, for example, if you set the Tolerance higher (and it ranges from 0 to 255), it selects all varieties of the color that you initially selected.

The Magic Wand is best used for selecting objects that are primarily one color, such as the person in the art gallery shown earlier. It's ideal when you need to select the sky in a landscape. In a few minutes, you'll see exactly how to do this, but first there are some other selection tricks to learn.

The Selection Menu

NEW TO VERSION 5 | You may have noticed that, in addition to the Selection tools you have just learned about, there's also a Select menu, shown in Figure 3.8. Probably the most useful commands on the menu are the top four. Select All simply draws a Selection Marquee around the entire picture. Deselect removes the Selection Marquee from the image. Reselect is a new tool in Photoshop 5. As you'd expect, it replaces the Marquee if you have accidentally deselected something. Inverse lets you select everything but an object, by selecting the object and then inverting. For instance, if I had a photo of a lemon on a plate, I could select the lemon and then invert to select the plate.

FIGURE 3.8.

The Select menu.

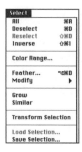

Feather

Feather lets you make selections with fuzzy, *feathered* edges rather than hard ones. It's very helpful when you want to select an object from one picture and paste it into another, because it adds a slight blur that helps the object to blend in. You can use the Feather Selection dialog box shown in Figure 3.9 to determine how many pixel widths of feathering to apply. Experiment with feathering selections to find out what works best.

FIGURE 3.9.

The Feather Selection dialog box.

To make a feathered selection, follow these steps:

1. Choose an appropriate Selection tool and use it to select a piece of the picture or an object within the picture.
2. Choose Select→Feather to open the dialog box.
3. Enter an amount in the window. Start with 5 and increase or decrease as needed.

Modifying Selections

The Select→Modify submenu gives you some other options for working with your selections. Border changes the selected area so that instead of the whole object, you have only selected a border around it. You can set the width of the border in its dialog box. Smooth is helpful when you have made a Lasso selection with a shaky hand. It smoothes out bumps in the Marquee line by as many pixels as you specify. Expand and Contract work, as their names suggest, to make your selection grow or shrink as necessary by as many pixels as you designate in the dialog box.

Tutorial: Selecting the Sky

It's often necessary to select a large part of the picture, like the sky, so that you can darken its color or otherwise change it without changing the rest of the picture. Figure 3.10 shows a picture with a lot of sky and a very complicated object sticking up into it. There are also branches, which have gaps where the sky shows through. Selecting the sky in this case requires careful clicking with the Magic Wand.

FIGURE 3.10.

Selecting just the sky will be difficult.

3

To select the sky in this picture, we'll follow these steps:

1. Choose the Magic Wand tool and double-click to open its Options palette.

2. Set the tolerance in the Options palette to 20, as shown in Figure 3.11. This allows us to select only similar shades of blue.

FIGURE 3.11.

*You can set the toler-
ance anywhere from 0
to 255.*

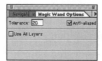

3. Click the Magic Wand on a typical piece of blue (see Figure 3.12).

FIGURE 3.12.

*You may need to make
several selections to
include all of the sky.*

4. Hold down the Shift key and select additional pieces of sky until you have gotten it all.

5. Choose Select→Feather and set the Feather amount to about three pixels, just enough to even out the selection. Figure 3.13 shows the result.

6. Now you can proceed to change the color of the sky, remove it, or do whatever else you intended.

Find a picture with a lot of sky and practice this yourself. It's not difficult. Remember, if you select more sky (or whatever) than you intended, Undo will deselect the last portion selected, leaving the rest of the selection active.

FIGURE 3.13.

The entire sky is selected.

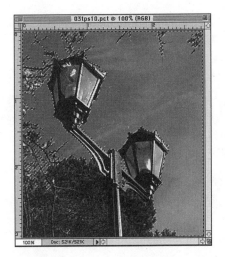

3

Cutting and Copying

If you have cut and pasted or copied in any other application, you can do it in Photoshop. The commands are identical and so are the results. You'll find the Cut, Copy, and Paste commands on the Edit menu.

Cutting, or copying, and pasting allow us to "borrow" from one picture to add to another. In the examples that follow, I'll take a seagull from one picture and add it to another. In Figure 3.14, I've selected the bird and post and set the Feather amount to three pixels. Next, I'll use the Copy command (Edit→Copy) or (Command-C) [Control-C] to copy the bird to the Clipboard.

FIGURE 3.14.

Before you can copy the seagull, you have to select it.

Now I'll open the new picture, (see Figure 3.15) and paste the gull in. Then, just for fun, I'll paint in a shadow behind the gull. Figure 3.16 shows the final result.

FIGURE 3.15.

The new picture, without the added bird.

FIGURE 3.16.

The picture is more interesting with the gull added.

Cropping

Cropping is the artist's term for trimming away unwanted parts of a picture. You could think of it as a specialized kind of selection, which is probably why the people who created Photoshop put the Cropping tool in with the Selection Marquees. The Cropping tool is shown in Figure 3.17.

FIGURE 3.17.

The Cropping tool.

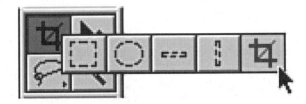

To crop a picture, follow these steps:

1. Select the Cropping tool from the toolbox. (It pops out from the Selection Marquee when you hold the mouse button.)

2. Drag it across the picture, holding the mouse button down.

3. Use the handles on the Cropping window to fine-tune the selection. You can even twist the Cropping window, by clicking the dotted line and dragging when the double-headed bent arrow appears. Figure 3.18 shows the Cropping window in use.

4. After you have the Cropping window placed where you want it, double-click inside it to delete the area outside the window.

FIGURE 3.18.

The Cropping window in use.

Open any picture and practice cropping it. Remember that, if you crop too much of the picture, you can undo. If it's too late to undo, because you have already done something else, just go back to the History palette and click the uncropped picture. You can also choose Revert to go back to the last saved version of your picture. As long as you don't close the file, you can keep cropping and using the History palette to undo as much as you want.

Summary

Some of the most powerful tools in Photoshop are the Selection tools. They enable you to edit selectively as well as create interesting effects with the Transformation tools.

Try to develop a feel for when you can use selections. They can save you a great deal of time when you need to fill a space with color or image, when you need to manipulate just a piece of an image, or when you need to extract a piece of an image from a larger work.

We will refer to selections throughout the remainder of the book, so it you need to, dog-ear a page. See you next hour.

Q&A

Q Can I combine selections made with different selection tools?

A Yes. Make a selection with one of the tools. Switch tools and then press the Shift key before you add to your selection. As long as you hold down the Shift key (making a tiny plus sign visible next to the tool), you can add to your selection as many times as you wish.

Q How can I unselect *part* of a selection?

A The easiest way to do this is to hold down the (Option) [Alt] key with the Selection tool active. You will see a small minus symbol next to the Selection tool. Select the part of the selection to unselect, and it is removed from the selection and added back to the picture.

Quiz

Test your memory on these.

Questions

1. To change Marquees,

   a. Go back to the toolbox and select a different one.

   b. Type Shift-M.

   c. Either of the above.

2. To select a single row or column of pixels,

   a. Hold down Control-C and the Return key while double-clicking.

   b. Press Return as you drag the mouse.

   c. Use the narrow Marquees.

3. What happens if you double-click a tool?

   a. Nothing

   b. You open its Options window.

   c. You undo what the tool did.

Answers

1. c. Easy, huh?

2. c. (A isn't even possible unless you have three hands.)

3. b. You can also open it by selecting it from the Windows menu.

Activity

Most pictures can be improved by careful cropping. Try this experiment. Take a sheet of white paper or cardboard and cut two L-shaped pieces from it, as shown in Figure 3.19.

FIGURE 3.19.

How to make a cropping frame.

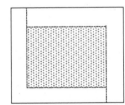 

Use them as a cropping frame and look at your snapshots or pictures in a magazine to see how different cropping affects the picture. Try finding long, narrow compositions and square ones, as well as rectangles.

HOUR 4

Transformations

It's extremely rare, if not impossible, that your pictures will always be the right size and shape for your purposes. You might need to make an object bigger or smaller as you copy it from one picture to another. You may need to straighten a tilted horizon, or even stand the Leaning Tower of Pisa upright. Perhaps you simply need to make someone face left instead of right, or turn an object upside down. You can do all this and more with just a few mouse clicks or simple commands. Ready? Let's start by looking at making the whole picture bigger or smaller.

Resizing

Photoshop makes it easy to change the size of the picture or of anything in it. You have two options: resizing the image or the canvas. Resizing the image makes the picture bigger or smaller. Resizing the canvas makes the picture *area* bigger while leaving the image floating within it. You do this if you need more space around an object without shrinking the actual image.

Image

To resize an image, open the Image→Image Size dialog box, shown in Figure 4.1. You can see the pixel dimensions in pixels (logically) or percentages. You can also see the image print size in pixels, inches, centimeters, points, or columns; percentages can also be found using the pop-up menus.

When you first open the Image Size dialog box, if you set the Width and Height Pixel Dimensions to percent, you'll see 100%. To enlarge or reduce the image, the easiest way is to make sure that Constrain Proportions is checked at the bottom of the dialog box, and then simply enter new percentages in one of the fields and click OK. As if by magic, the other numbers will change to give you the correct percentage of enlargement or reduction.

FIGURE 4.1.

The Image Size dialog box.

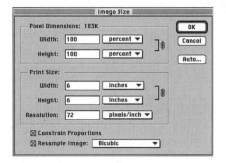

To see how changing the image size affects the file size and dimensions of the print image, reopen the dialog box. The file size is also displayed at the bottom of the image window.

Canvas

Resizing the canvas larger gives you extra work space around the image, instead of changing the size of the image. Resizing it smaller is another way of cropping the picture by decreasing the canvas area. It's not recommended because you could accidentally lose part of the picture and not be able to recover it.

To resize the canvas, open the Image→Canvas Size dialog box and specify the height and width you want the canvas to be (see Figure 4.2). You can specify any of the measurement systems you prefer on the pop-up menu, as you saw in the Image Size dialog box above. Photoshop calculates and displays the new file size as soon as you enter the numbers. Added canvas always appears in the background color.

FIGURE 4.2.

*The Canvas Size
dialog box.*

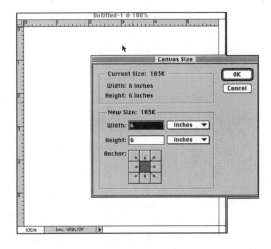

Use the Anchor to determine where the image will be placed within the canvas. Click in the middle to center the image on the enlarged canvas or in any of the other boxes to place it relative to the increased canvas area. Figure 4.3 shows the result of anchoring an image in the upper-left corner of the canvas. The image size hasn't changed, but we made the canvas bigger.

FIGURE 4.3.

*Before on the left;
after on the right.*

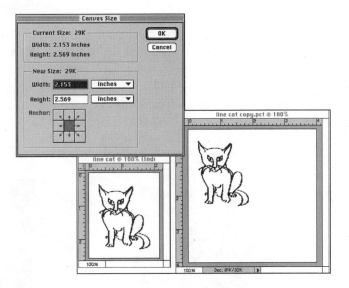

Selection

You can also resize a selected object. To do so, first select the object or a piece of an image to be resized. Use whichever Selection tool is most convenient. With the Selection

Marquee active, choose Edit→Transform→Scale. This places a window that looks like the Cropping window around your selected object (see Figure 4.4). Drag on any of the corner "handles" on the box to change the size of the image, while holding the Shift key down to maintain its proportions. If you drag on the side handles of the box, you'll stretch the selection's height or width accordingly.

FIGURE 4.4.

Resizing a selection.

Rotating

There are many reasons why you might want to, or need to, rotate an image. If you have a scanned picture or a digital camera image that should be vertical but opens as a horizontally oriented picture, rotating it 90 degrees corrects the problem. This is a common occurrence when you use a scanner, because it's usually quicker to scan with the picture horizontal, regardless of its normal orientation (see Figure 4.5).

FIGURE 4.5.

Scanned image rotated 90 degrees clockwise.

Picture in flatbed scanner　　　　　After rotation in Photoshop

NEW TO VERSION 5 If you have used a previous edition of Photoshop, you may be accustomed to looking for the Transform commands on the Layer menu. In Photoshop 5, they've been moved to the Edit menu.

90 L, 90 R, 180

To rotate the entire image, use the Image→Rotate Canvas submenus shown in Figure 4.6. Choose 90 degrees clockwise or counterclockwise to straighten up a sideways image, or 180 degrees if you somehow brought in a picture upside down.

FIGURE 4.6.

The Rotate Canvas submenu.

4

By Degrees

To rotate the canvas by something other than a right angle, choose Image→Rotate Canvas→Arbitrary to open a dialog box like the one in Figure 4.7. Enter the number of degrees to rotate. If you're not sure, guess. You can always undo or reopen the box and rotate more, or even change the direction if you need to. Click the radio button to indicate the rotation direction: clockwise or counterclockwise. Then click OK to perform the rotation.

FIGURE 4.7.

Arbitrary opens this dialog box.

Tutorial: Straightening the Horizon

Using the Arbitrary Rotation dialog box is one easy way to fix a picture that needs to be straightened. The picture in Figure 4.8 was shot just as I was about to be blown off a cliff. Fortunately, tilting horizons are an easy problem for Photoshop.

FIGURE 4.8.

Oops, the horizon's not supposed to slant uphill.

We can tell just by looking at the picture that it needs to rotate clockwise several degrees. To straighten the horizon, follow these steps:

1. Open the Image→Rotate Canvas→Arbitrary dialog box. Enter the number of degrees by which you think the horizon is "off."

2. Click the CW (Clockwise) radio button to lower the right side or the CCW (counterclockwise) radio button to lower the left side. In Figure 4.9, we've rotated the canvas by three degrees clockwise. Now the horizon is level, but the picture is twisted. Cropping squares up the corners again and improves the composition at the same time.

3. Select the Cropping tool from the toolbox or type **C**. Drag the Cropping tool across the picture to position the Cropping window. Use the handles to fine-tune your cropping. Figure 4.10 shows the Cropping window in position.

FIGURE 4.9.

You can see the background color filling in the corners of the canvas.

FIGURE 4.10.

Drag the Cropping box until you get rid of the twisted corners of the image.

4. If the horizon isn't completely straight, click the dashed line of the Cropping window. When you see a double-pointed bent arrow, you can drag the Cropping window at an angle until the horizon looks right.

5. Double-click inside the Cropping window when the picture looks the way you want it. Figure 4.11 shows our corrected horizon.

If you can't decide whether something is really vertical or horizontal, drag a guide line as appropriate from the top or left side ruler. To get rid of a guide line, use the Move tool to drag it off the screen or use View→Clear Guides.

*The horizon is level
and the composition's
better, too.*

Rotating Selections

To rotate a selected object, first select it with whatever tool works best for you. Choose
Edit→Transform→Rotate. This places a box around the selection. Rotate the selection
by dragging a corner of the box, as shown in Figure 4.12.

*The Selection Marquee
is still active inside
the box.*

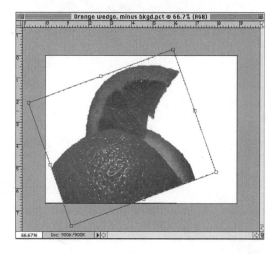

Flipping

Flipping sounds like something you'd do with a pancake, rather than a picture, but the general effect is the same. When you flip the pancake, you reverse it so the other side cooks. When you flip the image, you reverse it so you see a mirror image. You can flip horizontally or vertically. Figure 4.13 shows both. Quite often, you'll find that you need to flip as well as rotate an object to put it in the proper orientation. For comparison purposes, Figure 4.14 shows the effects of rotation. To make this composition, I typed the word "Rotate" and copied it, rotating each copy. Then I placed the rotated type over the background flower.

FIGURE 4.13.

The top pair of words has been flipped horizontally and the bottom pair flipped vertically.

FIGURE 4.14.

You can rotate an image by dragging the selection or by choosing to rotate 90 or 180 degrees.

Flipping is different from rotating because it changes the up/down or left/right orientation of the image. Of course, sometimes you may need to do both in order to get the image or selected object oriented the way you want it.

You can flip almost any object without anyone knowing, as long as there's nothing in it that would give the viewer a clue. You can't flip a picture that has type in it, obviously. You also need to be careful about flipping pictures of people who may be wearing shirts with a pocket on one side, a wristwatch, wedding ring, single earring, or other telltale item. In many cases, it won't matter, but you might find it helpful to edit out the jewelry, shirt pocket, and so on. (You'll learn how to do this in a later hour.)

Selection Transformations

Resizing and reorienting, as you've seen, can be applied either to the whole canvas or to any selected object. The Transformation methods that follow can only be applied to selections, not to the whole image (unless you start by selecting the entire image).

Skewing Selections

Skew, according to my trusty *Webster's*, means "to place at an angle." When you skew an object in Photoshop, you can do more than just slant it. You can twist, stretch, and distort it as if the object were on a sheet of rubber instead of a computer screen. The Skew command found under Layer→Transform→Skew enables you to twist your selection in all possible directions. Just click the Control boxes and drag the selection. Click the toolbox to apply the setting.

Skew may not seem like a very useful command at first glance, but if you look at the following examples, you'll see how useful it can be. In my original picture (see Figure 4.15), the books and software packages on the shelf are angled toward the right. I want them to look straight.

We'll start by selecting the whole picture. To skew the entire image, follow these steps:

1. Use Select All; (Command - A) [Control - A] to select the entire picture. (It's faster than dragging a Marquee around the image.)

2. Choose Layer→Transform→Skew to place the Skew window around the image, as in Figure 4.16.

3. Drag the corners of the window inward until the edges of the books look vertical. You'll see the background color behind the image.

FIGURE 4.15.

A messy bookshelf. Can we skew the books straight?

FIGURE 4.16.

Skewing a selection.

4

4. Click the toolbox to apply the transformation.

5. Crop the picture to remove the background. Figure 4.17 shows the result.

FIGURE 4.17.

The bookshelf looks neater.

Distorting Selections

All the Transformation tools operate very similarly. They possess subtle differences in how they can move the selection. The Distort command, Layer→Transform→Distort, moves something like the Scale command and Skew command, but instead of changing the size of the image, it crushes or stretches the image. Figure 4.18 shows an image before and during distortion.

FIGURE 4.18.

The original is on the left. On the right, we distorted it.

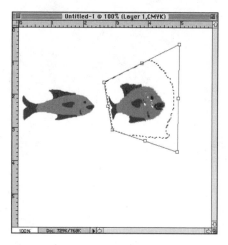

Select an object from one of your pictures and practice with skewing and distorting it. Remember that these commands are only available to you when the Marquee is blinking, indicating that there's an active selection.

Changing the Perspective of a Selection

This is one of the most useful tools in the Photoshop arsenal. When you want to create an image that appears to diminish in the distance, the Perspective tool can't be beat. Its movement is completely intuitive. The opposite corner of the one you drag becomes a mirror image—when you click on an anchor and drag the mouse away from the selection, it moves away. When you click and drag the anchor in, it, too, follows suit.

The difference between perspective and distortion is that when you apply distortion, you can do it to only one corner of the selection. Perspective automatically adjusts both corners when you drag on one.

In Figure 4.19, I'm applying perspective to the vegetable bins at the Farmer's Market. Because I shot with a wide angle lens, the picture is somewhat distorted and it looks as if the bin could tip over. A little stretching in the corners will straighten it up.

FIGURE 4.19.

Use the Perspective tool to correct tipped objects or to tip them as needed.

4

Numeric Transformations

This is probably the least intuitive of all the Transformation tools, because instead of handles appearing on your selection that you can then drag, this offers a dialog box in which you can enter numeric values for the position, the scale, the skew, and the rotation. Unfortunately, there's no way to preview these changes until you apply them. But, there's always Undo....

The Numeric Transform box (see Figure 4.20) is a great option for those of you lucky enough to be able to see numbers in your mind's eye. For the rest of us, we'll have to muddle along with the other tools, grateful once again that Adobe hasn't left anyone out.

FIGURE 4.20.

*The Numeric
Transform dialog box.*

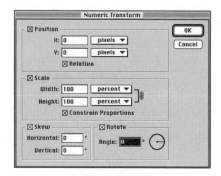

Summary

Transformations are an important function in Photoshop, especially when you're combining elements from different pictures. It's often necessary to shrink or enlarge an object or the entire image. Use the Image Size and Canvas Size dialog boxes to adjust the size of the image or work area. Photoshop also lets you transform selected objects by stretching, distorting, or applying perspective to them. You can do any of these by simply applying a menu command to place a box around the object and then dragging the sides or corners of the box. Spend some time practicing the transformations. They'll be very useful later on.

Q&A

Q How do you know when to skew, when to distort, and when to use Perspective? They all seem to do similar things.

A When you know that a transformation is needed but you aren't sure what kind, use Edit→Free Transform. You can also access it by typing (Command+T) [Control+T]. This command places a similar box around the object to be transformed, but it lets you rotate, distort, drag the object in any direction, or do whatever seems necessary.

Q What happens if I make a number of transformations and then change my mind about them later?

A Using Photoshop 5's History feature, you can now go back and undo some or all of these operations. Thanks, Adobe!

Quiz

Test your knowledge of Transformations.

Questions

1. I want the effect of a mirror to the right of an object. How can I achieve it?

   a. Copy the object to be reflected, flip horizontal, and paste. Then select the reflection and distort if needed for perspective.

   b. Select Edit→Mirror and the object.

   c. You can't.

2. How can I put more whitespace around an object?

   a. Paint the background white.

   b. Use the Canvas Size dialog box to make the canvas bigger.

   c. Shrink the object by selecting it and applying Edit→Transform→Scale.

Answers

1. a. Edit→Mirror doesn't exist (yet...).

2. b or c. Either will work.

Activity

Create a new canvas. Paint a squiggle on it and select the squiggle. Practice flipping, skewing, distorting, and rotating it. Use all the tools discussed in this chapter to find the ones you like best. See what works best for you: the visual transformations or numerical.

HOUR 5

Color Modes and Color Models

Color is all around us, a blessing few of us take time to think about or recognize. It is as common as the air we breathe, but when you become aware of its presence, you become aware of the minute variations that exist in every color. Notice the shades of green on the tree outside your window. Notice how those greens differ from the green of the grass. Watch the play of light and shadow. It becomes fascinating.

In this hour, we are going to investigate the different properties of color—both in Photoshop and in life. Some of the information at the beginning might seem a little esoteric, but in the long run, it's useful to know. After all, the more you know about color and how Photoshop addresses it, the better off you'll be. But don't worry, I'll try to be as brief and painless as possible.

Before we begin, it must be said that the best way of learning this stuff is to have Photoshop up and running on your machine. You can glean a certain amount of information from merely reading, but the real learning won't start until you start working in Photoshop. This is for two reasons:

- As we all know, you remember things better when you do them yourself.
- Photoshop's treatment of color makes it very intuitive. Keep the Color palette open at all times (Window→Show Color) and keep an eye on the sliders. Notice how they change from mode to mode, as well as the differences and similarities.

The first thing to know is that Photoshop addresses color in terms of modes and models. The models are methods of defining color. Modes are methods of working with color based on the models.

Color models describe the different ways that color can be represented on paper and on the computer screen. The color models are as follows:

- RGB (Red, Green, Blue)
- CMYK (Cyan, Magenta, Yellow, Black)
- HSB (Hue, Saturation, and Brightness)
- CIE Lab

We will examine these models for displaying and *describing* color, and then we will turn our attention to the Photoshop *modes,* which are the ways Photoshop provides for you to work with color.

Color Models

Figure 5.1 shows the Photoshop Color Picker. You can reach it by clicking either of the large blocks of color at the bottom of the toolbar. It has a graduated block of color, which you can click to select a particular shade, and windows that display the numbers for any chosen color in each of the four color models. In addition, Photoshop gives you a Color Palette, which is also shown in Figure 5.1. Open it, if it's not already open, by choosing Window→Show Color. It has a strip along the bottom that covers the full color spectrum. Clicking anywhere on it sets the Color Picker to that range of colors.

If your Color Picker doesn't look like this one, open File→Preferences→ General and set the Color Picker to Photoshop.

RGB Model

The RGB model, which computer monitors and TV screens use for display, assigns *values* on a scale of 0 to 255 for each of the three (RGB) primaries. As an example, pure Green (as you can see in the following figure) has a Red value and Blue value of 0, and a

Green value of 255. Pure White places the values of all three (RGB) primaries at 255. Pure Black places the values of the RGB primaries at 0.

FIGURE 5.1.

The Photoshop Color Picker.

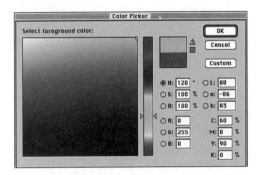

> **NEW TERM** *Value*, in this usage, means the relative strength of the color. Because the RGB model mixes colors of light to achieve white light, the full strength is 255. When you combine all three primaries at a value of 137 (half of 255), you get medium gray.

CMYK Model

The CMYK model, used for printing, defines colors according to their percentages of Cyan, Magenta, Yellow, and Black. These are the four colors of printing inks, both in your home inkjet printer and in the fancy, high-resolution color laser printers and printing presses that service bureaus and commercial printers use.

5

WHAT'S COLOR?

Back a thousand years ago when I went to grade school, every child was given a box of crayons at the start of the school year. The size of the crayon box was determined by the grade you were in. Kindergarten and first grade got flat boxes with eight big, thick crayons per box: the primaries, the secondaries, and brown and black. That was how we learned them, even back then. The primaries were yellow, red, and blue. The secondaries were what you got when you mixed any two primaries: orange, from yellow and red; green, from yellow and blue; and purple, from red and blue. Brown was the mix of all three primaries, and black was... well, black was black.

That's how we knew them, until high school. By then, we'd outgrown crayons, of course. We filed into our physics class and threw the previous nine years of learning out the window. The primary colors, according to the physics teacher were red, green, and blue. And if you mixed them you got, not brown or even the mysterious black, but... white!

Those of us still taking art classes listened to the physics lecture skeptically and went down to the art room to try mixing red, green, and blue paint. We got a sort of muddy brown, not the promised white. We asked the art teacher about this and were sent upstairs to the drama department for a demonstration. The stage lights had filters in red, green, and blue. When all of the lights were on, the result was, sure enough, white light. Why? When you're dealing with light, the drama teacher explained, colors are subtractive. They cancel each other out. When you're dealing with paint, the colors add to each other, giving that muddy brown mess. Aha! We were enlightened.

When you bought your computer system, you had to deal with this issue, whether or not you knew it at the time. Your monitor uses light to produce color. That's why it's called an RGB (Red, Green, Blue) monitor. Your printer uses ink to produce color. Not red ink, green ink, and blue ink, but a set of colors called Cyan, Magenta, and Yellow, along with our old standby Black. This color system is known by its initials, CMYK. Why K for black? Black is *still* mysterious.

HSB Model

When artists talk about color, they generally define it using a set of parameters called HSB. Photoshop also includes this color model. H stands for Hue, which is the basic color from the color wheel, for example, red, blue, or yellow. It's expressed in degrees (0-360), which correspond to the positions on the color wheel of the various colors. S is saturation or the strength of the color, and it's a percentage of the color minus the amount of gray in it. Pure color pigment with no gray in it is said to be 100% saturated. Neutral gray, with no color, is 0% saturated. Saturated colors are found at the edge of the color wheel and saturation decreases as you approach the center of the wheel. If you look at the Apple Color Picker, in Figure 5.2, it's a little easier to understand this. Brightness, the relative tone or lightness of the color, is also measured as a percentage, from 0% (black) to 100% (white). Brightness is equivalent to the value used by the RGB model.

CIE Lab

The most encompassing of these color models is CIE Lab. It defines a color gamut that is broader than any of the other models. Photoshop uses the CIE model, because its gamut is so broad, to convert from model to model. Lab color is designed to be device-independent, meaning that colors defined in this model appear and print the same regardless of whether you are seeing them on paper or on the video screen. However, this is probably not a model you will use frequently. Let's focus our attention now on what works and what you need to know to get up and running.

FIGURE 5.2.

The Apple Color Picker uses a standard color wheel.

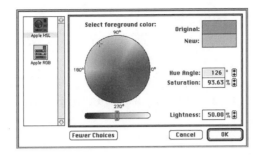

 I suggest that you work in either RGB or CMYK, depending on whether your final image will be printed or viewed onscreen as, for instance, a picture on the World Wide Web. Use CMYK for color print and RGB for video.

The Modes and Models of Color

First, forget about Lab color. It's there. Photoshop uses it in the background, but you needn't concern yourself with it. The other three models, HSB, RGB, and CMYK, will have much greater impact on your work in Photoshop. The difference between the modes and the models is simple. The models are methods of defining color. Modes are methods of working with color based on the models. HSB is the only model without a directly corresponding mode. Otherwise, the other color models, CMYK and RGB, have corresponding modes in Photoshop. There are also modes for black and white, grayscale, and limited color work.

The Photoshop modes available under Image→Modes are as follows:

- Bitmap
- Grayscale
- RGB Color
- Indexed Color
- CMYK Color
- Duotone
- Lab Color
- Multichannel

5

Bitmap and Grayscale

We'll start out here with the most basic of the Color modes available within Photoshop—Bitmap and Grayscale.

The Bitmap mode uses only two color values to display images—black and white—whereas the Grayscale mode offers 256 shades of gray that range from white to black (see Figures 5.3 and 5.4 for examples). (Because this book isn't printed in color, you'll just have to trust us when we tell you that this photo was rendered in grayscale. It's hard to see any difference, but trust us!)

FIGURE 5.3.

An image in the Grayscale mode.

Notice the vast difference in quality. The Grayscale image is clear and crisp, whereas the bitmap image is not. There are, however, a number of ways to convert to Bitmap mode, which we'll discuss later today.

There are really only four color modes that you'll use often. We've already touched on them—grayscale, RGB, CMYK, and Indexed color. Now let's take a closer look at what they do and how you can apply them.

Whenever a picture is printed in black and white or grayscale, for instance, as part of a newsletter or brochure, it makes sense for you to work on it in Grayscale mode. Doing the conversion yourself rather than sending a color photo to the printer gives you the opportunity to make sure that the picture will print properly. You can tell by looking at it whether the darks need to be lightened or the light grays intensified to bring out more detail.

FIGURE 5.4.

The same image in the Bitmap mode.

To convert a color photo to grayscale, simply choose Image→Mode→Grayscale. You'll be asked for permission to discard the color information. Click OK to confirm and the picture is converted to grays.

RGB

RGB is the color mode for working on pictures that will be viewed on a computer screen. If you are preparing pictures in Photoshop that will eventually become part of a desktop presentation, a video, or a Web page, stick with RGB for the best color rendition. If your work is only going on the Web, I still recommend doing the color adjustments in RGB and then converting the picture to Indexed Color when you save it in its final form.

Indexed Color

Indexed Color, when it can work for you, is a wonderful thing. Because of cross-platform compatibility issues, Web designers are currently limited to the 216 colors shared by Mac and PCs. Indexed Color is a palette or, rather, a collection of palettes—256 to be exact. With this mode, you know exactly what you are getting, and if you don't like any of the palettes Photoshop supplies, you can build your own.

Indexed Color is perfect for the World Wide Web. The Indexed Color mode includes a specific Web palette. Indexed Color doesn't really limit you to 216 colors though. *Dithering* takes place in Indexed Color images. Choose Image→Mode→Indexed Color to take a look at the Indexed Color dialog box (see Figure 5.5).

5

Dithering means that certain colors are *combined*; that is, adjacent pixels are blended onscreen to create a new color.

FIGURE 5.5.

The Indexed Color dialog box.

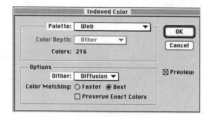

You are given a number of palette choices when you work with Indexed Color. They are as follows:

- **Exact**   This option takes the colors that are in the RGB version of the image for its palette. This only works if there are less than 256 colors in the original image.

- **System (Macintosh)**   This option uses the Macintosh System palette.

- **System (Windows)**   This option uses the Windows System palette.

- **Web**   This palette uses the colors most often used by Web browsers. If you are planning to publish your work on the World Wide Web, this is the palette in which you should do most of your work. Otherwise, you might have problems with incompatible colors dropping out when viewed with a Web browser.

- **Uniform**   The Uniform option bases the colors in the palette on a strict sampling of colors across the color spectrum.

- **Adaptive**   This is your best bet for most work in Indexed Color. During conversion, this option samples the most frequently used colors from the original. Adaptive usually provides you with the closest match to the original image.

- **Custom**   If none of the other options suit you, you can always build your own palette. See the Photoshop manual for instructions.

CMYK

As you previously saw, CMYK mode should be used when your image is printed. By working in CMYK (and being aware of gamut warnings), you can make sure your nice yellow banana or flower doesn't end up a muddy brown, or your bright blue sky doesn't print as purple.

Converting Between Modes

All you have to do to convert, at least mechanically (this is not taking image degradation or changes into account), is to select Image→Mode and then choose your poison.

Although Photoshop uses the model (Lab) with the broadest gamut of color to change Color modes (as if all of the other modes are circles that will fit with Lab color), this is no guarantee that your colors are going to turn out the same in another mode as they did in the original mode.

The rule of thumb is this and I can't stress it enough: don't work in RGB if you are going to output your images to print. Instead, work in CMYK. If you are going to publish your images on the Web, use Indexed Color (or use RGB and then convert). Knowing this will save you many hours of wondering why the Web page that looks great on the office Mac looks funky on the Windows machine you use at home, or why the yellow in your printed piece looks brownish.

But what if the color mode you want happens to not be available in the Image→Mode menu? Nothing to worry about. It is true that sometimes the mode you want will not be available, but you can always get to it by first converting to Lab Color and then to the color you want. For example, when you have created or imported an image that is in Indexed Color, the CMYK option is grayed out or not available. You actually have two choices here. Convert to Lab or RGB, and then take the image over into CMYK, but beware. Make sure that the color is the one you want.

Exercise: Getting Started with Color

Just for fun, why don't we dive in with some hands-on before we go any further? Working through this exercise will give you a better idea of the concepts and ideas that we have been talking about because the pictures in the book are in black and white. Let's look at a colorful image and examine how the modes affect the way the color appears.

1. First, find a colorful picture and open it. (You can download this one from Macmillan's Web site at www.mcp.com and find the book's info page). If yours doesn't have the letters RGB in parentheses after the title, choose Image→Mode→RGB color. This is our starting point. If your monitor is correctly adjusted, you should see very good color.

2. Select Image→Mode→Grayscale. A dialog box appears, asking if you want to discard the image's color information. Click OK. Photoshop then proceeds to examine your image and assigns all the colors to 256 shades of gray that range between white and black, inclusive (see Figure 5.6).

   Notice in the status bar at the bottom of the picture how the size of your file diminishes. This is because color is difficult for a machine to reproduce. The amount of information or data in a color image is much greater than that required to display a grayscale image (see Figure 5.7).

5

FIGURE 5.6.

Lobsterpot markers; Plymouth, Mass.

FIGURE 5.7.

Changed to grayscale. All of the color values were assigned a value of gray between 1 and 256—1 being white and 256 being black.

3. Before we move on, we need to return the image to its original RGB state. Select File→Revert. When Photoshop asks if you want to return to the last saved version of your file, click OK.

   This time, let's change our RGB image to CMYK. This process becomes enormously important for anyone who will be taking his or her images to print. RGB can display a number of colors that CMYK, by the nature of its four inks, cannot reproduce. The inks, for instance, can only approximate neon colors.

   Before we make the mode change, let's take a closer look at some of the colors in our RGB image to see if they can be reproduced in CMYK.

4. Click the Eyedropper tool in the toolbox.

5. Next open the Colors palette by selecting Window→Show Colors.

6. Use the Eyedropper to select (click) a color in the image. Try clicking a very bright one.

7. Look in the Color palette. Is there an Out of Gamut warning there? This little triangle indicates that the selected color cannot be reproduced precisely by the process colors of CMYK (see Figure 5.8).

FIGURE 5.8.

The triangle symbol means gamut warning.

To get an idea how far out of gamut your colors are, select View→Gamut Warning. This gives you an indication of the colors that will be lost or modified during the translation of RGB mode to CMYK. Figure 5.9 shows what the gamut warning looks like for this picture. Click the warning triangle to select the nearest color that can be achieved with CMYK colors.

FIGURE 5.9.

The white patches are out of gamut.

5

8. To change the mode from RGB to CMYK, select Image→Mode→CMYK.

9. After you've seen and perhaps printed the picture in CMYK mode, feel free to experiment with the other modes, too.

To change the color used in the display of the Gamut Warning, select File→Preferences→Transparency & Gamut. Click the color swatch at the bottom of the dialog box and choose a color that contrasts with the colors in the picture.

If you have a color printer, you might want to print your picture and compare it to what you see onscreen. Does it look OK? If so, you're in luck. Your monitor is accurately calibrated. If not, you need to calibrate your monitor so that the images onscreen accurately display the colors as they print. We will discuss calibration in a sidebar later on when we talk about printing.

COLOR RECOGNITION

The human eye is extremely sensitive to even the slightest variation in color. Think for a moment about something familiar: a can of Coca-Cola. I'll bet that if you were shown two swatches of red, you could, without much hesitation, select the Coke's red and differentiate it from, say, the red used on the cover of *Time* magazine. If you saw cans of Coke displayed with a slightly off-color red, you'd probably think they were either outdated, or perhaps counterfeit. Most people are very much aware of even slight color changes. That is why color becomes so important in the branding of products through advertising.

Summary

Color is fun to play with, but it's also rather complicated to understand. The world in general, and Photoshop in particular, uses color models as a way of describing colors. The four color models are HSB, RGB, CMYK, and Lab color. There are also color modes, which allow you to work with color.

In this chapter, we discussed the color modes and the specific color models in Photoshop. We also looked at a few of the more salient issues regarding converting between modes. Try, if it is at all possible, to work in the mode in which you will output your final product.

Next hour, you will delve deeper into the world of color by learning how to make tonal adjustments and general adjustments.

Q&A

Q What's Duotone and how can I use it?

A Duotones, and their cousins monotones, tritones, and quadtones, are quite simply grayscale images printed in various numbers of colored inks. The colors blend to reproduce tinted grays. There's a good reason for using duotones, rather than black ink, when you want really good reproduction of a grayscale image. The bottom line is quality. A grayscale image can have as many as 254 shades of gray, plus pure black and white. The best a printing press can do is to reproduce only about 50 levels of gray per ink. If you print in black (or any monotone color), your pictures automatically get compressed, each five steps of gray becoming one. So the image comes out looking a lot coarser than it would if two inks are used. When you convert the grayscale to a duotone, you add another 50 levels of gray and immediately your image looks better, less compressed.

Duotones can be printed with a black ink and a gray ink; but more commonly black plus a color is used, giving a slight tint to the midtones and highlights. You can also make a duotone with two contrasting colors for a more unusual and colorful effect. To create a duotone, start by converting the image to grayscale; then open the Image→Mode→Duotone dialog box and choose color(s) for the duotone. Photoshop will translate the image into duotone.

Q If I want to print my pictures *and* put them on the Web, should I be working in CMYK or RGB?

A It doesn't really make much difference. I'd do my work in RGB mode, and then save a copy in CMYK and check the gamut before printing it. Your video monitor can't show you true CMYK colors, no matter how many times you calibrate it. It doesn't display color that way.

Quiz

Questions

Try these colorful questions to see what you learned in this hour.

1. RGB, used by your monitor, stands for

   a. Raster (white), Gray, Black

   b. Red, Green, Blue

   c. Initials of Apple's new CEO

2. How many colors can a Web page display?

   a. Millions

   b. 256

   c. 216

3. Which color mode should you use for printed pages?

   a. CMYK

   b. HSB

   c. Pantone

Answers

1. b

2. c, but only because that's all Macs and PCs can agree on.

3. a

Activity

Using the Photoshop Color Picker, select a nice bright red. See how it's represented in the different color models. Click at the upper-right corner of the color square. Saturation and Brightness should be 100%, regardless of which color you have selected. Red will read 0 in the Hue window. Enter 60 in the Hue window. The color square will change to yellow. Knowing that red is 0 and yellow is 60, can you predict what number pure blue will be? Look at some other colors and see how they affect the settings. Try to see the relationship of the colors on a theoretical color wheel to the colors you see on the spectrum.

HOUR **6**

Adjusting Color

Are you one of those people who likes to play with the color adjustments on the television set? If you are, you're going to be absolutely astounded with Photoshop's color adjustment capabilities. If you haven't a clue as to what we mean by adjusting color, that's okay, too. By the end of this chapter, you'll be able to turn red roses blue, change a sky from midday to sunset and back again, bring out the detail in shadows, and manage every imaginable aspect of color manipulation.

Photoshop includes a full set of tools for making color adjustments. You can find them all on the Image→Adjust menu (see Figure 6.1). Some of these terms, like Brightness/Contrast, may be familiar to you; others may not. Don't worry. You'll learn about them all in this chapter.

FIGURE 6.1.

*The Adjust submenu
gives you all the tools
you'll need.*

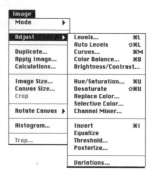

Before you start to adjust color, you need to evaluate what kind of color you have in the picture and how you'll eventually use the image. You learned about color models and color modes last hour, so you know that RGB color is the kind that is displayed on computer screens and CMYK color is the kind that is printed. If you're going to be adjusting the color in a picture, it makes sense to adjust it according to the way it will be displayed. If your picture is going on a Web page, you should work in RGB mode. If it's going to be printed in color, make your adjustments in CMYK mode. If it's going to end up in grayscale, forget about trying to make the sky a perfect blue. Change the mode to grayscale and make the contrast perfect instead. Just keep these few rules in mind and you won't go wrong.

TABLE 6.1. COLOR ADJUSTMENT MATRIX.

Adjust color in:	If output is:
RGB	Computer screen
CMYK	Color print
Grayscale	Black and white print

Adjusting by Eye

The most obvious way to make a color adjustment is to compare "before and after" views of the image. In Photoshop, the tool for doing this is called Variations. It's the last item on the Image→Adjust submenu. Variations combines several image adjustment tools into one easy-to-use system that shows thumbnail images that are variations on the original image. Simply click the one that looks best to you. You can choose variations of hue and brightness and then see the result (which Photoshop calls Current Pick) compared to the original.

If Variations doesn't appear on the Adjust submenu, it's because the Variations plug-in may not have been installed. Consult the Photoshop manual for information about using Plug-in modules.

Figure 6.2 shows the Variations dialog box. When you first open it, the Current Pick is the same as the original image because you haven't yet made changes. You can set the slider to the left (Fine) or right (Coarse) to determine how much effect each variation applies to the original image. Moving it one tick mark in either direction doubles or halves the amount. The finest setting makes changes that are so slight as to be almost undetectable. The coarse setting should be used only if you're going for special effects and want to turn the entire picture to a single color. The default (middle) setting is the most practical for "normal" adjustments.

FIGURE 6.2.

The seven left thumbnails adjust hue, whereas the right set of three adjusts brightness.

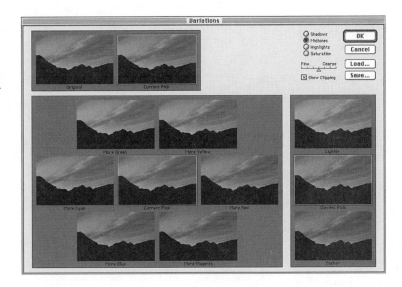

Adjusting Shadows, Midtones, Highlights, and Saturation

When you use Variations to adjust a color image, you also have the option of individually adjusting shadows, midtones, highlights, or overall color saturation. Shadows, midtones, and highlights are Photoshop's terms for the dark, middle, and light tones in the picture or what would be black, gray, and white in grayscale. Overall saturation adjusts all of them at once.

6

When you select Shadows, Midtones, or Highlights, you adjust the hue and brightness of only that part of the picture. The advantage here is that you can adjust the midtones one way and the highlights or shadows another way, if you choose. Each setting is independent of the others, and you can, for example, set the midtones to be more blue, thus brightening the sky, yet still set the shadows to be more yellow, offsetting the blueness that they possess inherently.

NEW TERM *Hue* refers to the color of an object or selection. *Brightness* is a measurement of how much white or black is added to the color.

Selecting Saturation changes the strength of the color in the image, giving you a choice simply of less or more. In Figure 6.3, I'm adjusting the saturation of this photo. Remember that you can apply the same correction more than once. If, for instance, "less" saturation still leaves more color in the image than you want, apply it again to get even less.

FIGURE 6.3.

Less saturation gives you a lighter image. More saturation gives you a darker one.

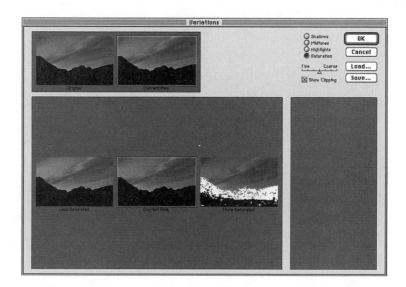

To adjust an image using the Variations command, use the following steps:

1. Open a color image. Choose Image→Adjust→Variations.

2. Set the radio buttons according to what you want to adjust: Shadows, Midtones, Highlights, or Saturation.

3. Use the Fine/Coarse slider to determine how much adjustment to apply.

4. To add color, click the appropriate color thumbnail.

5. To reduce a color, click its color wheel opposite. To reduce magenta, for example, click green.

6. To adjust the brightness, click the thumbnails for a lighter or darker image.

7. If you're not sure exactly what you need to do, simply click the image that looks most "right" to you.

8. If you think you may have overdone your corrections and want to go back to the original image, press (Option) [Alt] to change the Cancel button to Reset. This restores the settings to zero and reverts to the image saved prior to changes. (Note: This works with all Adjustment windows.)

9. Click OK when done or Cancel to undo all your adjustments.

Saving and Loading Corrections

There's one other set of buttons that appears in this window and in the other adjustment windows as well. These are the Load and Save buttons. They can save you a lot of time and effort if you have a whole series of pictures that need the same kind of corrections. Perhaps you used your digital camera to shoot several outdoor pictures in a row with the same lousy light conditions. Maybe your scanner tends to make everything a little more yellow than reality. After you determine the settings that correct one picture perfectly, you can save those settings and then load them each time you want to apply them to another picture.

Click the Save button and you'll see a typical dialog box that asks you to give your settings a name. You might call them "foggy day fix" or "scanner correction." Then when you need to apply them to another picture, use the Load button to locate and open the appropriate setting file, and your corrections will be made.

Making Other Adjustments

6

As you've seen, Variations is the quick way to adjust color, but sometimes it doesn't give you enough control. Other times you just want to experiment. Maybe you have a picture that's mediocre, but if you play with the colors in it and beef up the contrast, you can make something out of it. These are the times when you'll want to work with individual adjustment settings. Let's start with Levels and Curves.

HISTOGRAMS

There's a menu item under the Image menu called Histogram. It doesn't actually *do* anything, but if you learn how to use it, you can save lots of time.

If you ever took a course in statistics, you already know that a histogram is a kind of graph. In Photoshop, it's a graph of the image reduced to grayscale, with lines to indicate the number of pixels at each step in the gray scale from 0 to 255.

You might wonder why this is important. The main reason is that you can tell by looking at the histogram whether there's enough detail in the image so that you can apply corrections successfully. If you have an apparently bad photo or a bad scan, studying the histogram will tell you whether it's worth working on or whether you should throw away the image and start over. If all the lines are bunched up at one end of the graph, you probably can't save the picture by adjusting it. If, however, you have a reasonably well spread out histogram, there's a wide enough range of values to suggest that the picture can be saved.

The histogram has another use, which is to give you a sense of the tonal range of the image. This is sometimes referred to as the *key type*. An image is said to be either low key, average key, or high key, depending on whether it has a preponderance of dark, middle, or light tones. A picture that is all middle gray would have only one line in its histogram, and it would fall right in the middle.

All you really need to know is that when you look at the histogram you should see a fairly even distribution across the graph, if the image is intended to be an average key picture. If the picture is high key, most of the lines in the histogram are concentrated on the right side with a few on the left. If it is low key, most of the values will be to the left with a few to the right.

Levels and Curves

Levels and Curves are two methods of adjusting the brightness of an image. They accomplish essentially the same purpose, the difference being that Curves do it with more subtlety. Let's start by looking at the Levels window (see Figure 6.4). As you can see, it has a histogram, along with some controls that you can use to adjust the values.

Adjusting with Levels

The Levels window is a tool for adjusting the brightness of an image based on the information in the histogram. Setting the black point (the point at the left of the histogram that represents absolutely saturated black) to match the concentration of darkest levels in the image and setting the white point (at the right, indicating completely unsaturated white) to match the concentration of the lightest levels in the image force the rest of the levels to reassign themselves more equitably.

FIGURE 6.4.

Be sure to click the Preview box so that you can see the effect of your changes.

To adjust the brightness using Levels, follow these steps:

1. Choose Image→Adjust→Levels or press (Command-L) [Control-L].

2. Click the Preview box so that you can see your changes in the image window. If you don't check this box, everything on the desktop, including the desktop pattern and icons, changes as you move the sliders.

3. In a color image, you can adjust the composite RGB or CMYK color image, or individual colors, by using the Channels pop-up menu. For now, stay with the composite. (You'll learn more about channels later in this chapter.)

4. To set the black point in the image, move the slider at the left side of the Input Levels histogram to the point at which the dark lines begin to cluster.

5. Set the white point by moving the right Input Levels slider to the point where the light pixels begin to rise.

6. Adjust the midrange by watching the picture while you move the Input Levels middle slider left or right. Figure 6.5 shows the settings for this picture.

7. To adjust the contrast in the image, use the sliders on the Output Levels bar. The black slider controls the shadows; moving it toward the center decreases shadows. The white slider controls the highlights; moving it toward the center decreases highlights.

6

FIGURE 6.5.

Adjusting the darks helps bring out shadow detail.

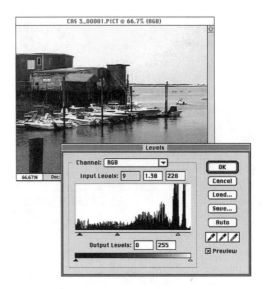

8. Click OK when you're done.

You can also use the Eyedroppers to adjust the levels. Click the white Eyedropper (on the right) and click the lightest part of your image. Then click the dark-tipped Eyedropper (on the left) to select it and click the darkest point on the image. If you have an area in the image that seems to be right in the middle, click it with the midrange Eyedropper (in the middle).

> If you click Auto in the Levels window or choose Auto Levels from the Image→Adjust menu, Photoshop adjusts the levels based on its evaluation of the tonal range. However, this is usually not satisfactory. Try it, but be prepared to undo.

Adjusting with Curves

Adjusting curves is much like adjusting levels. You can use the Curves window instead of the Levels window to adjust the brightness. The big difference is that instead of adjusting at only three points (black, middle, and white), you can adjust at any point (see Figure 6.6).

FIGURE 6.6.

On this kind of a graph, the zero point is in the middle.

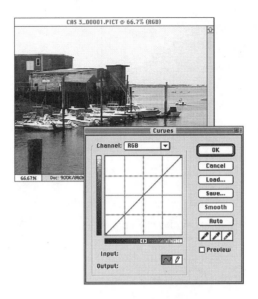

When you open the Curves window, you don't see a curve. You don't see the histogram either. Instead, you see a different kind of a graph, one with a grid and a diagonal line. The horizontal axis of the grid represents the original values (input levels) of the image or selection, while the vertical axis represents the new values (output levels). When you first open the box, the graph appears as a diagonal because no new values have been mapped. All pixels have identical input and output values. As always, be sure to check the Preview box, so you can see the effects of your changes.

As with the Levels window, you can click Auto or use the Eyedroppers to adjust the values. Because the Curves method gives you so much more control, you might as well take full advantage of it. Hold down the mouse button and drag the cursor over a piece of the image that needs adjusting. You'll see a circle on the graph at the point representing the pixel where the cursor is. If there are points on the curve that you don't want to change, click them to lock them down. For instance, if you want to adjust the midtones while leaving the darks and lights relatively untouched, click points on the curve to mark the points at which you want to stop making changes; then drag the middle of the curve until the image looks right to you. Dragging up lightens tones, whereas dragging down darkens them. Figure 6.7 shows what this actually looks like. To get rid of a point that you have placed, drag it off the grid.

6

FIGURE 6.7.

You can add up to 15 points on the curve.

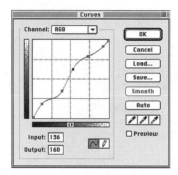

 To see the curves displayed with a finer grid, press (Option) [Alt] and click the grid.

Balance

In order to really understand color balance, you have to look at the color wheel. In case you don't remember the order of the color wheel, there's a reference in Figure 6.8.

FIGURE 6.8.

It's difficult to reproduce this in gray. Use your imagination.

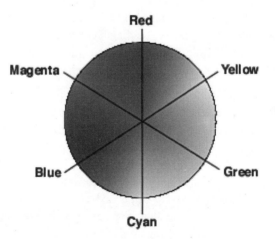

Every color on the wheel has an opposite. If you draw a line from one color through the center of the wheel, you reach its opposite. Cyan is opposite to red, green is opposite to magenta, and yellow is opposite to blue. When you use the Color Balance window to adjust colors in a picture, you're adding more of the opposite color to the one you want to reduce. Increasing the cyan reduces red. Increasing red reduces cyan, and so on around the wheel.

Figure 6.9 shows the Color Balance window. Color Balance is intended to be used for general color correction rather than correcting specific parts of an image, although you can use it that way by selecting only the part to correct. It's especially helpful if you have a scanned image that is off color, such as an old, yellowed photograph. It's very simple to apply the Color Balance tools to remove the yellow without altering the rest of the picture.

FIGURE 6.9.

Check Preserve Luminosity to avoid changing the brightness of the image.

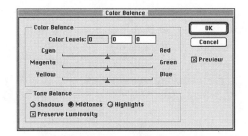

NEW TO VERSION 5 There's an updated Photoshop 5 feature in this window. In addition to Color Balance, you can use the sliders to adjust tone balance. As with the Variations window described earlier, you can concentrate your efforts on adjusting shadows, midtones, or highlights by clicking the appropriate button. (Earlier versions of Photoshop provided the buttons but didn't tell you what they were for.)

To apply Color Balance, use the following steps:

1. Select the image or portion of the image to correct. Open the Color Balance window by choosing Image→Adjust→Color Balance or typing (Command-B) [Ctrl-B].

2. Choose Shadows, Midtones, or Highlights. Generally it's advisable to start with Midtones if you are correcting the whole picture because they comprise 90% of it.

3. Check Preserve Luminosity so that you don't change the brightness of the image as you shift colors. If maintaining the brightness isn't important, don't check the check box. Be sure to select Preview so that you can see how your changes affect the image.

4. Move the sliders to adjust the colors. The numbers in the boxes change to indicate how much of a change you are making. They range from 0 to +100 (toward red, green, and blue) and to -100 (toward cyan, magenta, and yellow).

5. Adjust the shadows and the highlights; then repeat the corrections until the image looks right to you.

6. Click OK to apply the changes.

If Color Balance doesn't seem to do what you want, undo it.

6

Hue/Saturation

The Hue/Saturation window is a very powerful tool with a slightly misleading name.
Sure, it lets you adjust the hue (colors in the image) and the saturation (the intensity of
the colors), but it also gives you control over the brightness.

NEW TO VERSION 5 This window has also gone through an extensive overhaul in Photoshop 5. First,
let's look at the controls in the Hue/Saturation window (see Figure 6.10). The
first pop-up Edit menu lets you select a single color to adjust or Master, which adjusts all
the colors in the image or selection at once. For now, let's work with the Master setting.
Check Preview to see the effects of your changes on the picture you're working on.

FIGURE 6.10.

*Check the Preview box
to see the changes as
you make them.*

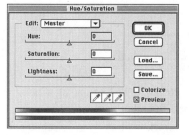

There are three sliders: Hue, Saturation, and Lightness. The Hue slider moves around the
color wheel. With Master selected, you can move all the way from red (in the middle of
the slider), left through purple to blue or blue-green, or right through orange to yellow to
green.

The Saturation slider takes you from zero, in the center, to 100% saturated (pure color,
with no gray) on the right, or 100% unsaturated (no color) on the left.

The Lightness slider lets you increase or decrease the brightness of the image, from
–100 through 0 in the center, to +100 on the right.

As you move these sliders, watch the two spectrum strips at the bottom of the window,
as well as the image itself. The upper strip represents the current status of the image and
the lower one changes according to the slider(s) you move. If you move the Hue slider to
+60, for example, you can see that the reds in the picture turn quite yellow and the blues
turn purple. In effect, what you are doing is skewing the color spectrum by that amount.
If you move the Saturation slider to the left, you'll see the lower spectrum strip become
less saturated. If you move the Lightness slider, you'll see its effects reflected in the
lower spectrum strip as well.

Lightness is technically the same as brightness. The Hue, Saturation, Brightness (HSB) color model uses these terms to define a color, as opposed to the RGB and CMYK models that define it as percentages of the component primaries, which, of course, are either Red, Green, and Blue for RGB or Cyan, Magenta, and so on for the CMYK model.

Instead of selecting Master from the pop-up menu, if you select a color, the window changes slightly. In Figure 6.11, you can see the differences. The Eyedroppers are now active, enabling you to select colors from the image, and adjustable "range" sliders are centered on the color you have chosen to adjust. You can move these back and forth to focus on as broad or narrow a range within that color as you want. This may not seem like a big deal, but it's really very powerful.

Suppose I want to change the sky from gray to blue without affecting skin tones of the people in the picture. I can set the sliders to include only the range of blues that need to be enhanced, and then make them more saturated and brighter without turning my family and friends into Smurfs.

FIGURE 6.11.

Click and drag to move the sliders.

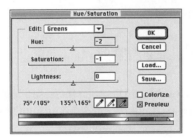

Adjusting Hue and Saturation

To adjust an image using the Hue/Saturation window, do the following:

1. Open the window by choosing it from the Image→Adjust menu or by typing (Command-U) [Ctrl-U]. Click Preview to see your changes as you make them.

2. Choose Master to adjust all the colors or use the pop-up menu to select the color you want to adjust.

3. Drag the Hue slider left or right until the colors look the way you want them to. The numbers displayed in the Hue text box refer to the degree of rotation around the color wheel from the selected color's original color.

6

4. Drag the Saturation slider left to decrease the saturation of the colors and right to increase it.

5. Drag the Lightness slider to increase or decrease the lightness of the image.

6. Click OK when done.

Brightness/Contrast

If you need to make a simple adjustment to the tonal range of an image and it scanned too dark, for example, the Brightness/Contrast window (Image→Adjust→Brightness/ Contrast) is an easy way to adjust everything at once (see Figure 6.12). Instead of separately correcting the dark, middle, and light values, it applies the same correction throughout the image.

Although the Brightness/Contrast window doesn't give you the same control that you'd have if you made the adjustments using Levels or Curves or even the Variations window, it's quick and easy. Sometimes it's all you need. Many images are improved by just raising the brightness and contrast by a couple of points. As always, be sure to check the Preview box so that you can see the effect your changes have on the image.

FIGURE 6.12.

Use the sliders to adjust the brightness and contrast.

Dragging the sliders to the right of the middle-point increases brightness or contrast. Dragging them to the left decreases it. If you're not happy with the results you get with this tool, undo your changes and use the Variations window or Levels or Curves to adjust the brightness and contrast.

Adjustment Layers

An important point to remember about color correction is that you can apply it to the whole picture, selectively to a single area, or to all but a selected area. When you apply a correction to the whole picture, it may improve some parts and make others worse, so you really need to look carefully at the end result and decide whether the good outweighs the bad.

Fortunately, there's an easy way to apply a correction and then change your mind. One of the best features of Photoshop is the ability to work in layers. Think of layers as sheets of cellophane that you place over your image and paint or paste on. If you like what you do, you can merge the layers so that the additions become part of the image. If not, you can throw them away and try again. In addition to the layers that you paint on, Photoshop lets you apply *adjustment layers*. These work like normal layers except that instead of holding paint or pasted pictures, they hold the color adjustments that you make to the image.

To open an adjustment layer:

1. Choose Layer→New→Adjustment Layer and a dialog box opens (see Figure 6.13).

FIGURE 6.13.

The New Adjustment Layer box.

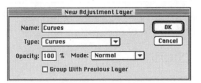

2. Select the particular kind of adjustment that you want to make from the pop-up menu. Click OK to open the appropriate adjustment dialog box.

Summary

In this hour, we looked at working with color. Variations make simple, "by eye" adjustments, letting you choose from differently enhanced thumbnails. Histograms and Curves apply adjustments more scientifically. You learned how to make the sky a perfect blue and the grass a greener green. Now you know that adjusting Levels lets you set limits for dark, middle, and light tones in an image. You have learned about Color Balance and how to apply changes to hue and saturation. You have seen how to change the brightness and contrast ratio of an image.

Color adjustment is one of Photoshop's most used features, and one that you'll rely on whenever you need to touch up a photo or a scanned image. Practice with it as much as you can, using your own favorite images.

6

Q&A

Q I have a sepia-tinted photo (brown tones) that I have scanned into the computer, but the scan came out yellow. Is there a way to get rid of the yellow cast without losing the sepia?

A The easy way is to convert it to grayscale, so you get rid of *all* the color. Then convert it back to RGB. Open the Image→Adjust→Curves dialog box. Instead of RGB on the Channels pop-up menu, select Red and drag the curve up until you have added an appropriate amount of red. Then set the pop-up menu to Green and drag the curve down until you have added enough of that color. Finally, set the pop-up menu to Blue and drag down until you have removed the blue and achieved a reasonable sepia. Experiment until you get the color you want; then click OK.

Q **If the picture's going to be printed in black and white for a newsletter, do I really need to adjust the color balance and stuff?**

A Always leave your options open. Adjust a *copy* of the picture in grayscale mode, just to make sure the contrast is good for reproduction. For that, you don't need to think about color. But keep a copy in color in case you want to put the same picture on a Web page or do something else with it later.

Quiz

You're well adjusted, but are your pictures?

Questions

1. The picture came out too green. What should you do?

   a. Open Variations and choose More Red.

   b. Open Variations and choose More Magenta.

   c. Say you took it in Ireland.

2. It was a foggy day and the colors look "washed out." Is there any way to fix it?

   a. Increase the Saturation.

   b. Lower the Lightness.

   c. Paint over the picture with brighter colors.

Answers

1. b. On the color wheel, magenta is opposite green, so adding more magenta removes excess green.

2. a. Weak colors lack saturation. Increasing it slightly brightens the picture, but don't overdo!

Activity

Download some of the photos from our Web site (www.mcp.com/info) and correct the colors. Then see how much further you can go. Turn a cloudy day into a sunny one and vice versa. Experiment. Try your hand at changing the colors by eye and then see if you can duplicate your efforts by using the Histograms.

Hour 7

Paintbrushes and Art Tools

You are already a quarter of the way through and now it's time to have some fun. Photoshop, as I'm sure you realize, is mainly an image editor. It was created for that purpose and it accomplishes its purpose very elegantly. Yet there is more to Photoshop than just editing. You can also create artwork from scratch, just as in any good graphics program. Photoshop's art tools, shown in Figure 7.1, include the following:

- Airbrush
- Paintbrush
- Eraser
- Pencil
- Line
- Gradient
- Paint Bucket
- Eyedropper

FIGURE 7.1.

Tools for painting and drawing.

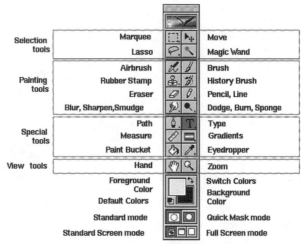

Each tool is highly configurable. You can adjust such settings as diameter, hardness, roundness, angle, opacity, and so on. It's easy, too. You'll learn about this in the next few pages.

The Brushes Palette

Before we discuss specific brushes, let's take a brief look at the Brushes palette, which is available via the menu command Window→Show Brushes and shown in Figure 7.2. Although each tool has its own set of options (available under Window→Show Options or by double-clicking the tool in question), the Brushes palette works with all the art tools, from the Airbrush down to the Dodge tool. It gives you the ability to select any of Photoshop's preset brush shapes or to create your own.

FIGURE 7.2.

The Brushes palette.

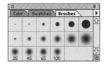

Just click to select one of the preset brush shapes. The size and shape you see in the box are the size and shape of the brush. The only exceptions are the brushes with numbers beneath, which indicate the diameter of the brush in pixels. A brush can be up to 999 pixels wide, which translates to almost 14 inches. Remember, this doesn't select a tool. You have to do that in the toolbox or by typing a letter shortcut. The Brushes palette just influences the shape of the tool you select.

Brush Options Dialog Box

Double-click a brush and the Brush Options dialog appears (see Figure 7.3). Here you can select the diameter, hardness, spacing, angle, and roundness of the brushes.

The harder a brush is (nearer 100%), the more defined the edges of paint will be. A brush with a setting of around 20% has a much more diaphanous or translucent appearance.

FIGURE 7.3.

The Brush Options dialog lets you design custom brushes.

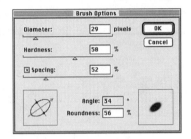

The next option is for Spacing. If left unselected, the speed of your mouse movements determine the spacing of discrete drops of paint. If you move more slowly, paint appears in a continuous line. If you move the mouse more quickly, circles of paint appear with spaces between them.

By selecting the Spacing check box, however, you are able to set a standard spacing of paint, no matter what the rate of the mouse movement is. Anything around 25% should give you a very smooth line of paint. As you move the percentage up (either by dragging the slider or entering a number into the box), the spaces increase (see Figure 7.4).

FIGURE 7.4.

Spacing set at 50%, 100%, and 200%, respectively.

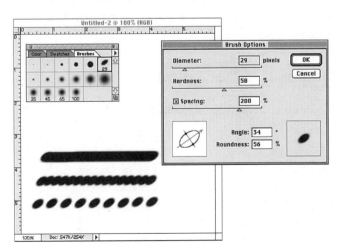

7

Finally, you also can set the Angle and Roundness of your brushes. Play around with these settings. With a little experimenting, you can end up with a brush that behaves just as a real brush does—painting thicker and thinner depending on the angle of your stroke.

To make adjustments, you can enter values into the boxes provided, or you can click and manipulate the graphic (on the lower left of the Options dialog).

When you find a brush that you are comfortable with, save it with the Save Brushes command found in the Brushes palette menu (see Figure 7.5). (Click and hold the arrow in the upper-right corner to open the menu.) Give the grouping a name and it will be available to you from then on.

FIGURE 7.5.

The menu for the
Brushes palette.

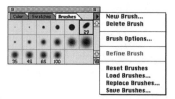

To open a set of your customized brushes, choose either Load Brushes to append brushes to the current set or Replace Brushes to replace the current set. You'll find several sets of special brushes in Photoshop's Goodies folder.

Tool Options Palette

Photoshop also includes a Tool Options palette, which you can open from the Window→Show Options menu or simply by double-clicking a tool. The tool options change according to the tool you're using at the time. Figure 7.6 shows the options for the Paintbrush tool.

FIGURE 7.6.

The Paintbrush
Options palette.

The first thing to notice in the Options palette is the slider that sets the Opacity. Click and hold the right pointing arrow next to the Opacity field to enable the slider. A low setting applies a thin layer of paint—nearly transparent. The closer you come to 100%, the more concentrated the color is.

Wet Edges creates a sort of watercolor effect when you paint. Figure 7.7 shows an example of the same brush and paint with Wet Edges on and off. Paint builds up at the edges of your brush, and as long as you are holding the mouse down and painting, the paint stays "wet." In other words, you can paint over your previous strokes, without building up additional layers of color. If, however, you release the mouse button and begin to paint again, you will be adding a new layer of paint, which creates an entirely new effect.

FIGURE 7.7.

The Wet Edges effect darkens the edge of a stroke and lightens the middle.

Fade, when used with a brush full of paint, makes the paint run out after a set number of steps. It's just as if you were painting and used up all the paint in the brush. Figure 7.8 shows this effect. You can set the fade amount from 1 to 9,999 steps. I generally start with a Fade setting of approximately 24 to get an easily controllable brush stroke, neither too long or too short. Experiment with the settings to see what works best for you.

FIGURE 7.8.

From the top down, Fades of 12, 25, and 50 steps.

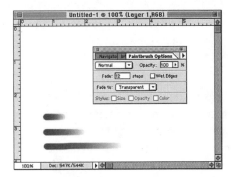

7

The Stylus Pressure options affect the way that Photoshop responds to a pressure-sensitive digitizing tablet, such as the Wacom. If you don't have one of these devices, ignore it. If you do, when you use the Tablet and Stylus, you can click the boxes to determine whether Stylus pressure affects the size, opacity, and/or color of your brush stroke. To most Tablet users, it feels most natural and logical to let the pressure affect the brush size.

Blending modes affect the way a layer of paint interacts with whatever is under it. You'll learn about them in the next hour. For now, just leave the Blending mode set to Normal.

Brushes

Now let's turn our attention to the painting tools themselves. For the rest of this hour, we'll be working with the Airbrush, Paintbrush, Eraser, and Pencil tools.

Before you go any further, why not stop and try out some of these tools? Follow these steps:

1. Open a new page, making it big enough so you have some elbow room. About six- to eight-inches square is fine.
2. Open the Brushes palette (Window→Show Brushes). On the same set of palettes as brushes, you'll see a tab for Swatches.
3. Click Swatches to open an electronic paint box. For now, just click any color you like.
4. Type B to select the Paintbrush from the toolbox.
5. Click the Brushes tab to go back to Brushes to choose a brush shape.
6. Press and hold the mouse button as you move the brush over the canvas to paint.
7. Try the Airbrush and Eraser tools, too. Type J for Airbrush and E for Eraser. See what changing the options does for each tool.

Airbrush

This tool, as its name suggests, sprays paint (or pixels) on the canvas. It's like an artist's airbrush that uses compressed air to spray paint through an adjustable nozzle. The Airbrush applies paint with diffused edges, and you can control how fast the paint is applied. You can adjust it to spray a constant stream or one that fades after a specified period. Experiment with different amounts of pressure and different brush sizes and shapes.

Remember that the longer you hold the Airbrush tool in a single spot, the darker and more saturated a color becomes. Type J to activate the Airbrush or click it in the toolbox. (This command has changed from previous versions of Photoshop. Why J? Think "jet" of paint.)

Figure 7.9 shows a drawing done with just the Airbrush. The spotty effect comes from using a Blending mode called Dissolve. (You'll learn about Blending modes later.)

FIGURE 7.9.

Varying the pressure and changing brush sizes give the picture some variety.

The Paintbrush Tool

The Paintbrush tool is the workhorse of all the painting tools in Photoshop. Type B to use the Brush, and double-click it to open the Brush Options palette if it's not already open. The Paintbrush behaves very much like the Airbrush, only paint is applied more evenly. That is to say, if you hold the mouse clicked in one area, paint does not continue to flow onto the canvas.

7

Although you can hit Caps Lock to get a precision painting cursor, there is an even better option. Instead, select File→Preferences→Display & Cursors. In the dialog box that appears, look into the Painting Cursors section. There is an option there that enables you to select from the following choices: Standard, Precise, and Brush Size. Choose Brush Size because this changes your painting cursor from a paintbrush or a crosshair to a circle that is the actual size of your brush.

If you need to paint a straight line, constrained either vertically or horizontally, hold down the Shift key as you drag the brush. To draw a straight line between two points, click once on the canvas to set the first point, and then Shift-click to mark the end point. A line appears between the two points. Figure 7.10 shows some work with the Photoshop paintbrushes.

FIGURE 7.10.

The garlic bulbs were painted with several different brushes.

Eraser

The next tool in the toolbox that we'll investigate is one that most of us, unfortunately, have to use far too often—the Eraser tool. The one nice thing about the Eraser is that it too can be undone, so if you happen to rid the canvas of an essential element that you wanted to keep, just choose Edit→Undo.

The Eraser tool is unique in that it can replicate the characteristics of the other tools. It can erase with soft edges as if it were a paintbrush painting with bleach. It can erase a single line of pixels as if it were a pencil, or it can erase some of the density of the image as if it were an airbrush. Of course, it can also act as an ordinary block eraser, removing whatever's there. The first three options are controlled via the Brushes palette—size, hardness, and so on. These characteristics are set on the Eraser Options palette, shown in Figure 7.11.

FIGURE 7.11.

The Eraser and its options.

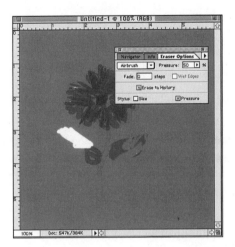

The Opacity slider (not available in all Eraser modes) controls how much is erased. This is useful for blending parts of images, and it also can create a nice watercolor effect.

The Fade option works just as the Fade option in the Airbrush tool. After a certain number of steps, which you specify, the Eraser no longer erases. This is useful to create feathering around irregularly shaped images. Set the Opacity to approximately 75% and the Fade to approximately 8 steps and then drag away from the image you want to feather.

NEW TO VERSION 5 Photoshop 5 has added one more command to the Eraser Options palette. Instead of erasing to the background, you can choose Erase to History. This command lets the Eraser work with the History palette so you are actually erasing to an earlier version of the picture. Before you begin to erase or make any other drastic changes to your picture, you can take a snapshot of it by choosing New Snapshot from the History palette.

If, for example, I painted a leaf onto the flower stem in Figure 7.11 and wanted to erase part of it to try again, I'd select Erase to History and erase the leaf without erasing the stem or the background. Experiment with this tool until you understand what it's doing. It can save you lots of time when you're trying new techniques.

7

Pencil

The Pencil tool, in large measure, works like the Paintbrush tool, except that it can only create hard-edged lines—that is to say, lines that don't fade at the edges as Paintbrush lines can. Click the Pencil tool in the toolbox. Double-click it to bring up the Pencil Options palette, shown in Figure 7.12.

FIGURE 7.12.

The Pencil tool options.

You can set the diameter of your Pencil in the Brush Option palette (Window→Show Brushes), but remember, Hardness is not an option. You *can*, however, set all the other options just as we have with all the other tools up to now—I won't bore you with a recap.

The Pencil tool does have one option, though, that you haven't seen before. In the lower-left corner of the Pencil Options palette, there is a check box for Auto Erase. When you turn on Auto Erase, any time you start to draw on a part of the canvas that already has a pencil line on it, your Pencil becomes an Eraser and will erase until you release the mouse button.

Summary

Photoshop's painting tools are easy and fun to use. In this hour, we took a look at the Airbrush, Paintbrush, Pencil, and Eraser tools. Brush shapes apply to all the tools, not just to the Paintbrush. You can alter the brush shape or its behavior by double-clicking the Brush palette to open a Brush Options dialog box. You learned to activate the Airbrush, Paintbrush, Pencil, or Eraser by typing a single letter. Double-clicking the tool in the toolbox opens its Tool Options palette. You learned about some of the tool options and how they affect the quality of the brush stroke.

Q&A

Q Can I make a custom brush that's not round?

A Sure. You can even make part of your image into a custom brush. Use the rectan-gular Marquee to select a portion of an image. (You can use the Pencil tool to draw a particular brush shape if you want.) With the Marquee active, select Define Brushes from the Palette menu on the Brushes palette. The new brush appears on the Brushes palette. Double-click it to set its Spacing option. Set Anti-aliased to make the brush blend with the background image. When you're done creating brushes, choose Save Brushes from the Brush Options palette menu to save your current brush set.

Q How do I make my brush strokes look like a watercolor?

A Easy. Just click the Wet Edges check box. If you'd rather use "Oil paint," leave the check box empty.

Quiz

Look back through the chapter if you need to "brush up" on brushes and Paint tools.

Questions

1. How do I find the Brush Options menu?

a. Double-click the brush

b. Click the Options tab and then click on the brush (or other tool)

c. Either A or B

2. What happens if I hold the Airbrush in one spot?

a. Nothing.

b. You deposit more paint in that spot.

c. The paint runs down the screen.

Answers

1. c

2. b

Activity: Painting and Erasing

Let's do some more practice with the Airbrush, Paintbrush, and Eraser. Follow along with these steps:

1. Start by opening a new page. Make it at least six inches square, so you have room to work.

2. Click the Paintbrush in the toolbox, and then double-click to open the Paintbrush Options palette. Set your opacity to 100%, choose a medium size, hard-edge brush, and draw a star.

7

3. Click the check box to turn on Wet Edges and draw another star.

4. Choose a soft-edged brush and draw another star.

5. Now turn off Wet Edges and draw another star with the soft-edged brush. Your result should look something like Figure 7.13.

FIGURE 7.13.

Four kinds of brush strokes.

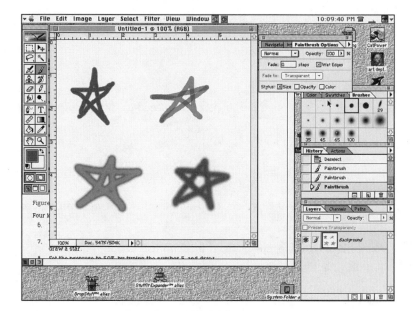

Okay, it's not great art, but you have four distinctly different brush looks.

6. Scroll to the top of the History palette and click the blank page that's labeled New. This returns you to your freshly opened page, minus stars. (It's a quick way to erase everything.)

7. Type J to activate the Airbrush. Set the pressure to 100% and draw a star.

8. Set the Pressure to 50% by typing the number 5 and draw another star. (You can change Paintbrush Opacity settings by typing a number, too.)

9. Change brushes. If you have been using a soft-edged brush with the Airbrush, try a hard one, or vice versa. Draw more stars with different brushes and Pressure settings.

10. Type E to bring up the Eraser. Set the Eraser mode to Paintbrush and the Opacity to 50%. (Type a number 5.) Try to erase one of your stars. Don't click the mouse more than once while you're erasing.

11. Change the Opacity to 100% and erase another star.

12. Experiment with different settings until you are comfortable with these tools.

HOUR 8

Digital Painting

Now that you know a little bit about brushes and painting tools, you need to know how to choose some colors to paint with. One of the nice things about digital paint is that it doesn't get under your fingernails and you don't have to clean out your paintbrushes afterward.

In this hour, we're going to learn about choosing and applying color. There are several ways of choosing colors and we'll also discuss Blending modes, which affect the way colors (and layers) interact with each other.

Foreground and Background Colors

At any given moment while working with Photoshop, you have two colors available. Only two? Don't worry—that's really kind of misleading. Perhaps it's better to say that you have two colors *active*, a foreground color and a background color. The foreground color is the one that you use to paint, to fill or stroke a selection. It's the color that's currently on your brush or pencil. (You'll learn about filling and stroking later on when we talk about paths.) The background color is the color Photoshop uses when you erase or delete a selected area on the background layer. You might think of it as the color of the canvas under your painting.

Selecting Colors

The fastest and easiest way to select color is to use the foreground or background swatch in the toolbox (see Figure 8.1). The color swatch to the upper left is your foreground color, and the one to the lower left is the background color. You can set either color by clicking its swatch.

NEW TERM   *Swatches* are those two little squares of color at the bottom of the toolbox—not trendy wristwatches.

FIGURE 8.1.

The foreground and background colors.

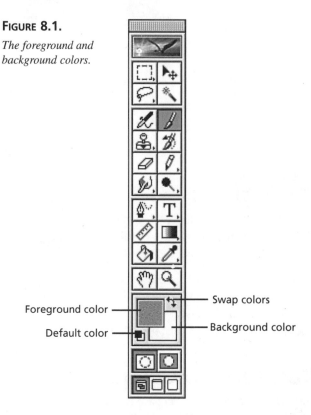

Foreground color ———

Default color ———

——— Swap colors

——— Background color

The small icon to the lower left of the swatches, which looks like a miniature version of the swatches, resets to the default colors (black and white). The little curved arrow to the upper right of the swatches toggles between background and foreground colors.

Here are a couple of quick keyboard shortcuts for you. You can reset the default colors by pressing D. Press X to toggle between the background and foreground colors.

8

To change the color of either of these swatches, click the swatch. This opens the Color Picker that you selected in the Display and Cursors preferences dialog box. If you haven't made a choice, the Photoshop Color Picker is selected by default. Your other choice is either the Apple or Windows Color Picker, depending on which operating system you use. The examples here use the Photoshop Color Picker.

The Color Picker

Photoshop's Color Picker lets you select a foreground or background color in any of several ways. Figure 8.2 shows the Color Picker window. You can click the color spectrum to select a color, or drag the triangle up or down if you'd rather. You can click the large swatch (the color field) to select a color, or you can enter numbers in any one of the color model boxes.

By default, the Color Picker opens in HSB model, which stands for Hue, Saturation, Brightness, with the Hue radio button active. This makes the color field show you all the possible saturation and brightness of the particular hue that's selected. If you click anywhere in the color field, you'll see the Saturation and Brightness numbers change, but the Hue setting remains the same.

JUST TO REMIND YOU:

Hue = Color, measured as location on the color wheel in degrees.

Saturation = Strength of the color measured as percentage from 0% (gray) to 100% (fully saturated color).

Brightness = Relative lightness of the color measured as a percentage from 0% (black) to 100% (white).

If you click the Saturation button, the color field changes to something like the one in Figure 8.3. It shows you all the possible hues at the designated saturation value. If you click anywhere in the color field, the other numbers change, but the saturation remains where it was.

FIGURE 8.2.

The Color Picker.

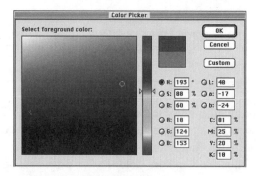

FIGURE 8.3.

Saturation Color Picker.

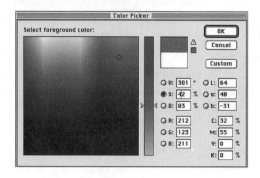

HSB mode is the one artists generally prefer because it's easy to understand. You're not stuck with it, though. Feel free to select RGB as a working mode. This is the model that governs how your computer displays color (it uses red, green, and blue, just like a projection television, for instance).

It's a little bit more complicated to choose a color in the RGB mode. When you click the Red radio button, the color that you see in the color field is just as likely to be blue or green. Here's where the spectrum slider and the numbers start to make a difference.

Remember, in this model, colors are made from three components, red, green, and blue, in amounts from 0 to 255. Pure red has a value of 255 R, 0 G, and 0 B. If you set those numbers in the Color Picker, as I have in Figure 8.4, the pure red will be way down in the lower-left corner of the color field. Colors representing mixes of green and blue with the red will fill the rest of the field.

The best way to learn this color mode is to work with it. Open up your Color Picker and click a color. Then watch the numbers as you click a different one. Explore the different radio button settings and their color fields.

FIGURE 8.4.

*The selected color is
mixed with percentages
of the other two pri-
maries.*

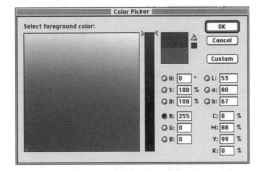

The Color Palette

The Color palette has several advantages over the Color Picker when you're working in
Photoshop. First of all, you can leave it open on the desktop, so you can change colors
without having to go through all the fuss of clicking a swatch in the toolbox, finding the
color, and then OK. For those of us who are mathematically challenged, there are fewer
numbers to contend with and the ones you see, as in Figure 8.5, are logically related to
the sliders. By default, it opens in HSB mode, but you can set it to grayscale or whichever color model you prefer to work in by using the pop-out menu as shown in the figure.

FIGURE 8.5.

*The Color palette and
its menu.*

The menu also gives you access to a dialog box, shown in Figure 8.6, which enables you
to reset the color bar at the bottom of the Color palette window, according to the color
model you are working with. If your work will be printed and you want to avoid using
colors that are "out of gamut" (or can't be achieved with CMYK inks), you can set the
color bar to the CMYK Spectrum and know that any color you click will be printable.

FIGURE 8.6.

*If you're using your
pictures on the Web,
stay with the HSB or
RGB color bar.*

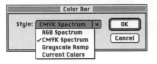

The Swatches Palette

Remember I said at the beginning of the hour that Photoshop gives you several ways of choosing colors? Well, here's the easiest one of all. The Swatches palette (shown in Figure 8.7) works like a child's box of watercolors on your screen. You simply dip your "brush" in a color and paint with it. To choose a foreground color, click the one you want. To choose a background color, Option-click (Mac) or Alt-click (Windows) the color you want to use.

FIGURE 8.7.

The Swatches palette and its pop-out menu.

The Swatches palette, by default, opens with the current System palette. You can choose colors from the Color Picker to add to the Swatches palette, or you can select a color system, such as PANTONE, Focoltone, Trumatch, or Toyo, and have an additional 700 to 1,000 or more *Process Color* (printing ink color) swatches appended to the palette. You can also add custom color to it using the Eyedropper tool described in the next section.

To add new colors from the Color Picker onto your palette, use the following steps:

1. Click the foreground color swatch in the toolbox.
2. Use the Color Picker to select the desired color and click OK.
3. Open the Swatches palette (Window→Show Swatches).
4. Using the tab in the lower-right corner of the Swatches palette, drag the window out so that it resembles the one in Figure 8.8.

FIGURE 8.8.

Adding a new color to the Swatches palette.

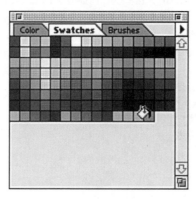

8

5. Move your cursor into the space below the existing swatches. It changes into the Paint Bucket tool.

6. Click and the new color is added.

7. If you press Shift, you can add the new color anywhere you like, replacing whatever swatch you click.

If you use a lot of the same colors over and over, and they are not represented in any of the palettes that ship with Photoshop, just elect to save a palette. Choose Save Swatches from the Swatches palette menu. This saves you time and the headache of having to reselect all your favorite colors each time you open Photoshop.

The Eyedropper Tool

You've seen the Eyedropper appear when you moved the pointer over a color swatch or over the color bar in the Color palette window. Its function, quite obviously and intuitively, is to pick up a bit of whatever color you touch it to, making that the active color. What's neat about this tool is that it works in the same way on a picture—you can pick up a bit of sky blue, grass green, or skin and not have to try to identify a match for it with the Color Picker.

The Eyedropper tool is extremely helpful, especially when you are retouching a picture and need to duplicate the colors in it. Click it on any spot in the image and the color underneath its tip becomes the new foreground color. Use (Option-click) [Alt-click] to select a background color instead. If you drag the Eyedropper across an image, the swatch color changes each time the Eyedropper touches a new color.

Remember that the Eyedropper, like all the tools, is active only at its "hot spot," in this case right at the tip.

The Eyedropper Options palette, shown in Figure 8.9, lets you decide how much of a sample to pick up with the Eyedropper. You can take a single pixel sample, or average a 3×3 or 5×5 pixel color sample.

You can convert any other Painting tool (except the Eraser) into an Eyedropper to change foreground colors on-the-fly by pressing (Option) [Alt] while you're working.

FIGURE 8.9.

The Eyedropper Options palette.

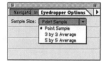

To choose a foreground or background color with the Eyedropper and save it as a swatch, follow these steps:

1. Click the Eyedropper tool or press I to select it.
2. Click the image at the spot where you want to capture the color. If you're saving a background color, (Option-click) [Alt-click] the color you want.
3. Open the Swatches palette, if it's not already open. Put the Eyedropper on any empty (gray) space in the Swatches palette. It turns into a Paint Bucket.
4. Click once to put a swatch of the selected color into the palette.
5. Choose Save Swatches from the palette's pull-out menu.
6. Follow the usual procedure to name your Swatch file and save it in Photoshop Goodies or whatever folder is convenient for you.

To load a saved Swatch file, use the Swatches palette's pull-out menu. Select Load Swatches. Locate the Swatch file you want to use, as in Figure 8.10, and click OK.

FIGURE 8.10.

The swatches are identified with Swatch icons.

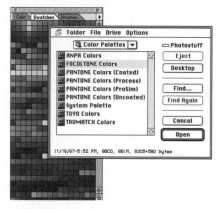

Exercise: Using the Eyedropper and Paintbrush

Let's take a few minutes to do some practicing with the Paintbrush and Eyedropper. Pick out a picture that has lots of color and open it in Photoshop. Then do the following steps:

8

1. Before you begin, choose Save a Copy from the File menu and save a backup copy of your picture, just in case you accidentally save a messed-up version.

2. Open the Brush palette and choose a medium-size brush shape. Type B to activate the Paintbrush tool.

3. Put the Paintbrush on an area of dark color in the picture, as I have in Figure 8.11. Press Option (Mac) or Alt (Windows). The Paintbrush turns into an Eyedropper and copies the dark color to the foreground.

FIGURE 8.11.

Click to copy the color.

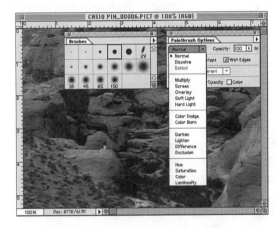

4. Paint on the picture with the color you just picked up. I added another tree to the picture above.

5. Open the Color palette (Window→Show Color) if it's not already open. Put your Paintbrush onto the Color bar at the bottom of the palette. It turns into an Eyedropper.

6. Choose another color and add something else to your picture. Use the same Paintbrush or switch to the Pencil (type P) or Airbrush (type A). Experiment with colors and brushes until you feel comfortable with them.

7. If you run out of space to paint, choose File→Revert to go back to the original version of the picture and start over.

CAN YOU DRAW WITH A BAR OF SOAP?

As you get more used to using Photoshop, or any other graphics program for that matter, you'll begin to realize that drawing with a mouse isn't really the best way to do it. As for the trackball and touchpad—well, they're even more difficult. They simply weren't designed for artwork.

The natural way to draw is to pick up a pencil or pen or brush and some-thing to draw on. People have been doing it for thousands of years, all the way back to the ancient Sumerians who used a stylus and slab of wet clay, and the Egyptians who wrote and drew with squid ink and feathers on papyrus.

Today we have something much better—graphics tablets that work with Photoshop and programs like it. These consist of a flat drawing surface, tethered to the computer by a cable, and a stylus about the size and weight of a ballpoint pen. The drawing surface is sensitized to "read" the motion and pressure of the stylus and sends the input to the screen. A tablet like the Wacom ArtPad II or Calcomp's Drawing Slate costs approximately $150 and will save you a good deal of time and frustration. Try one at your friendly local computer store and you'll be sold on it too.

Blending Modes

In the real world, when you place a second brush full of paint over one that's already there, different things happen, depending on the color of the paint you're applying, how opaque it is, whether the first layer is wet or dry, and so on. In Photoshop, you can control all of these factors by applying *Blending modes*. You'll find them on a pop-up list in the Paintbrush Options window. As you can see in the following figures, there are quite a few different ones. Let's take a quick look at the Blending modes and how they work.

FIGURE 8.12.

Normal: This is the default mode. The blend color replaces the base color.

Let's suppose that we're working with only two colors. One is the *base* color, the one that's already in place. The second is the *blend* color, the one that we apply with each Blending mode enabled. We get a third color, a *result* that varies according to how we blend the first two.

Here's what happens when you choose these options:

FIGURE 8.13.

Dissolve: A random number of pixels are changed to become the blend color. Gives a splattered or "dry brush" effect.

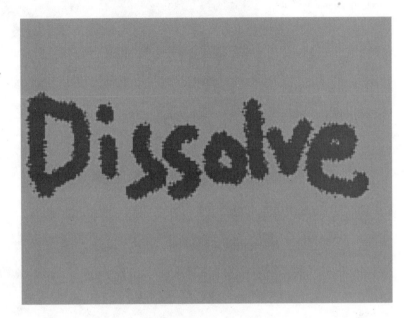

- **Behind:** Works only on transparent parts of a layer. You appear to be painting on the back of a sheet of acetate laid over the picture (not available if nothing is transparent).

FIGURE 8.14.

Multiply: Multiplies the base color by the blend color, giving you a darker color. The effect is like drawing over the picture with a magic marker.

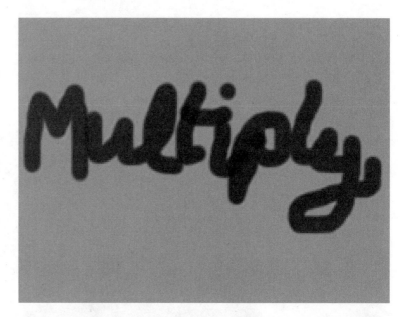

FIGURE 8.15.

Screen: Multiplies the base color by the inverse of the blend color, giving you a lighter color. The effect is like painting with bleach.

FIGURE 8.16.

Overlay: Either multiplies or screens, depending on the base color. Preserves the highlights and shadows of the base color.

FIGURE 8.17.

Soft Light: Darkens or lightens, depending on the blend color. The effect is similar to shining a diffused spotlight on the image. With a light blend color, it has very little effect.

8

FIGURE 8.18.

Hard Light: Multiplies or screens the colors, depending on the blend color. The effect is similar to shining a harsh spotlight on the image.

FIGURE 8.19.

Color Dodge: Brightens the base color to reflect the blend color.

FIGURE 8.20.

Color Burn: Darkens the base color to reflect the blend color.

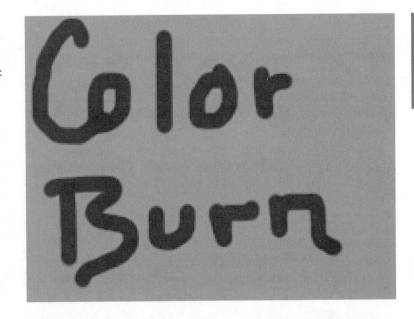

8

FIGURE 8.21.

Darken: Evaluates the color information in each channel and assigns either the base color or the blend color, whichever is darker, as the result color. Lighter pixels are replaced, but darker ones don't change.

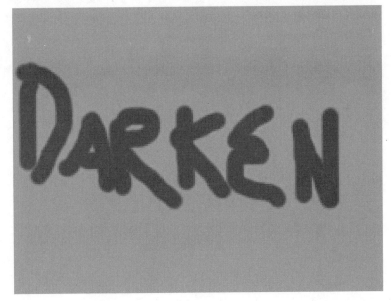

FIGURE 8.22.

Lighten: Evaluates the color information in each channel and assigns either the base color or the blend color, whichever is lighter, as the result color. Darker pixels are replaced, but lighter ones don't change. This is the exact opposite of Darken, above. (Had to switch background and foreground colors to show this effect.)

FIGURE 8.23.

Difference: Compares brightness values in base and blend, and subtracts the lighter from the brighter.

FIGURE 8.24.

Exclusion: Similar to the Difference mode, but with a softer effect.

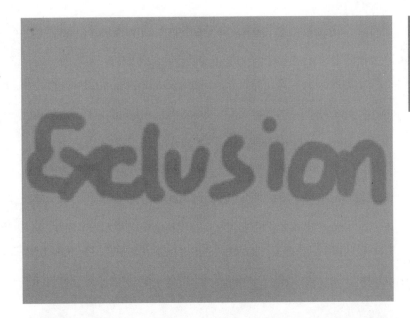

FIGURE 8.25.

Hue: Gives you a result combining the luminance and saturation of the base color with the hue of the blend color.

8

FIGURE 8.26.

Saturation: Gives you a color with the luminance and hue of the base color and the saturation of the blend color.

FIGURE 8.27.

Color: Retains the luminance of the base color with the hue and saturation of the blend color. Useful for coloring monochrome images as it retains the gray levels.

FIGURE 8.28.

Luminosity: Gives a result color with the hue and saturation of the base color and the luminance of the blend color. Opposite effect to Color Blend mode.

8

Summary

In this very full Hour, we covered the different ways that Photoshop gives you to choose and apply color to a picture. First you learned the difference between the foreground color, which is the color that's on your brush or pencil, and the background color, which is the color of the canvas under the painting.

The Color Picker, Color palette, and Swatches palette all contain colors that you can paint with. The Color palette and Swatches palette are easier to use than the Color Picker because you can leave either one of them open on the desktop as you work. You learned to use the Eyedropper tool with the Paintbrush to choose colors from the palette or from the picture itself.

Finally, we covered Blending modes, the way that two layers of paint or image interact with each other.

Q&A

Q The Color Picker has too many buttons and numbers in it! Which ones should I use if I want to change colors?

A If picking colors by numbers is difficult for you, as it is for me, use my solution. Forget the numbers and click directly on the color you like. Either click on the

color bar at the bottom of the Color palette, or click on a swatch to open the Color Picker.

Q **What happens when I have the Eyedropper set to sample a 5 × 5 pixel area and there is more than one color there?**

A Photoshop takes an average of all 25 pixels in the square and makes that the selected color.

Quiz

So you think you've got it? Try to answer these questions.

Questions

1. Blending involves

   a. Taking paint and mixing it in a bucket.

   b. Using home appliances.

   c. Being able to blend colors in different ways in Photoshop.

2. How many *active* colors do you have to work with in Photoshop?

   a. 16 million

   b. 256

   c. 2

Answers

1. c. Photoshop can blend colors much like you would on a canvas with real paint.

2. c. Remember, your foreground and background colors are the active colors, not the total number of colors available.

Activity

Because this Hour covered picking Color and Blending modes, fire up your Web browser and visit the Museum of Modern Art (www.moma.org). Navigate to the painting and sculpture section and look through their collection. Pay special attention to their use of color and blending effects. (Click on the small images on the index page to see larger versions.)

Compare and contrast the use of color and blending in Van Gogh's *Starry Night* and Rousseau's *The Dream*. See if you can duplicate Van Gogh's brush strokes. (Wet edges are part of the secret.)

Hour 9

Moving Paint

Did you ever wonder why artists always have those paint-soaked rags lying around, and why they always have paint on their hands, under their fingernails, and all over their clothes? It's because you don't just paint with a brush, you sometimes paint with your finger, or with a piece of cloth or with some other tool that will help you blend the paint, or lighten it or darken it just a little bit. In this hour, you will learn the tricks that painters and darkroom technicians have been using ever since their respective media were invented.

Smudges

Smudge is the artist's term for blending two or more colors. In Photoshop, there are, naturally, several ways of doing it. There are several ways of doing virtually anything in Photoshop. Be that as it may, the Smudge tool is the most obvious and the quickest way to blend something into its background.

Using the Smudge Tool

The Smudge tool looks like, and works like, a finger. It's in the same toolbox compartment with the Blur and Sharpen tools. The Smudge tool picks up color from wherever you start to drag it, and moves it in the direction in which you drag. Honestly, nothing could be much simpler. You do, however, have to use the Smudge Tool Options window to set the pressure of your smudging finger. At 100% pressure, the finger simply wipes away the paint. At 50%, it smears it. At 25%, the smear is smaller. Figure 9.1 shows these different smear pressures. Photoshop considers the Smudge tool to be a brush, so you can set the width of the "finger" by choosing an appropriate brush size from the Brush palette.

FIGURE 9.1.

Smudges at different pressure settings.

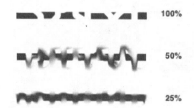

You can also use the Smudge tool to mimic finger painting. This option starts each stroke with the foreground color. You'll find it quite handy if you need to blend some color into an existing picture, perhaps to hide something that's part of the original photo but that you'd rather do without. Figure 9.2 shows an example of finger painting. We used a small brush and made sure the strokes followed the same direction as the water.

FIGURE 9.2.

We needed to hide the bushes, so we smudged them out.

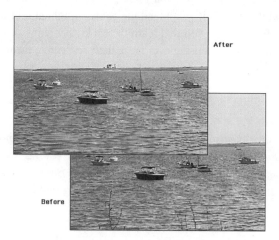

Setting Smudge Options

Pressure and finger painting options are set in the Smudge Options palette, shown in Figure 9.3. Click and hold the arrow next to the pressure setting to access the setting slider, and drag the slider to set the pressure or type a single digit to set it to a multiple of 10. For instance, type 4 to set to 40.

FIGURE 9.3.

The Smudge Tool Options palette.

Check Finger Painting if you want to use the Smudge tool to add some smudged color as you drag. Otherwise leave the checkbox empty. (Press and hold (Option) [Alt] to temporarily enter the Finger Painting mode.)

The Blending modes are on a pulldown menu. This tool doesn't give you all the Blending mode options that you learned about in the last hour, but you can choose—aside from Normal—Darken, Lighten, Hue, Saturation, Color, or Luminosity. Of these, Darken and Lighten are obviously the most useful. The Darken and Lighten modes only affect pixels that are lighter or darker, respectively, than the beginning color. The Darken mode changes lighter pixels and the Lighten mode affects darker pixels.

If the Smudge tool doesn't achieve the effect you intended, there's also a Smudge stick filter, which you'll learn about in Hour 15, "Filters to Make Your Picture Artistic." Filters, in case you haven't encountered the term before, are tools that apply special effects to your picture. Photoshop has ninety-nine different filters.

Focus Tools

Now we turn our attention to the Focus tools. These tools, Blur and Sharpen, are great for touching up an image, fixing tiny flaws, and bringing items into sharper contrast. They can't save a really bad photo, but they can do wonders for one that's just a little bit "off." Sharpen can bring up the contrast to create the illusion of sharper focus, while Blur is most useful to rid the background of unwanted clutter and to de-emphasize parts of the picture that you don't want viewers to notice.

The Blur Tool

The Blur tool, simply put, creates blurs in images. By blurs I mean a softening or evening out of pixel values. Select the Blur tool from the toolbox (see Figure 9.4). Double-click it to invoke the Options palette (see Figure 9.5). When you are working with the Blur tool, you can temporarily select the Sharpen tool (and vice versa) by pressing (Option) [Alt].

FIGURE 9.4.

The Blur tool.

FIGURE 9.5.

The Blur tool's Options palette.

Options for the Blur and Sharpen tools are much the same as those for the Smudge tool described above. You have the same choices of Blending mode and the same Pressure settings.

Figure 9.6 shows a close look at the Blur tool's effect. The picture of a ramshackle shed had a fence running right through the middle of it. A minute with the Blur tool merged the fence into the weeds and put the emphasis back on the shack. Figure 9.7 shows the picture before and after retouching.

FIGURE 9.6.

The Blur tool in use.

FIGURE 9.7.

Before and after blurring.

Make sure that as you blur you cover the entire area that you intend to blur. A missed spot stands out very conspicuously. Also don't forget that you can change the size of your Brush tool by choosing a different brush from the Brushes Options palette. For the Blur tool, I recommend using a brush with a soft edge, but not for the Sharpen tool. When sharpening, I prefer to use a small brush with hard edges, so that I know exactly where I am. You'll also find it helpful to work on a magnified view of your picture, just so you have a little better control of the tool.

Can You Believe Your Eyes?

One of the things you'll begin to notice as you become more accustomed to working with Photoshop is the use of image manipulation techniques in advertising and even in magazine and news editorial photos. You'll begin to recognize—in magazines and other printed pieces—pictures that betray the work of a digital retoucher. You should also begin to examine them for technique and skill. Take note of the next automobile advertisement you see in a flashy, four-color magazine or brochure. Note the foreground. Check the highlights. Examine the reflections in the headlights. Do they look good? Too good? Almost all advertising images are retouched (mainly in Photoshop) and the people doing this are incredible professionals. Learn from them. Notice how the backgrounds fade or the trees blur or how the highlights appear. Not to foster any conspiracy, but evidences of Photoshop are all around you. Just keep your eyes open....

The Sharpen Tool

The Sharpen tool is the exact opposite of the Blur tool. Where the Blur tool softens pixel values, the Sharpen tool hardens them and brings them into greater relief by increasing the contrast between adjacent pixels. Because of their equal but opposite relationship, they share a space on the toolbox, with a pull-out that lets you choose either one. You can also activate the Blur and Sharpen tools by typing R (for Retouching?). Type it a second time to toggle between the two. Figure 9.8 shows the shed again with some sharpening applied to the structure. Compare it to the "before" picture in Figure 9.7.

FIGURE 9.8.

Applying the Sharpen tool.

Figure 9.9.

Too much sharpening.

Sharpening is best done in very small doses. If you go over a section too much or have the pressure set too high, you can end up burning the color out of an image, which will probably make it look worse than it did initially. See Figure 9.9 for an example of over-sharpening.

Remember, too, that not even the magic of Photoshop can put back what wasn't there originally. Always work with the clearest, sharpest pictures you can manage. Rather than trying to salvage a bad scan, do it again. If your photo is fuzzy all over, instead of trying to sharpen it, set it aside until we start working with filters (see Hour 15, "Filters to Make Your Picture Artistic").

Exercise: Using the Focus Tools

Let's take a quick break here and try out these tools. Open any convenient picture in Photoshop and follow these steps:

1. Click once on the Magnifying Glass to zoom in on your picture. This gives you a magnification of 200%.
2. Choose a soft-edged brush from the Brush palette (Window→Show Brushes).
3. Double-click the Focus tools in the toolbox to open the Options palette.
4. Click the Options palette and type 5 to set the pressure to 50%.
5. Make sure the Blur tool is selected and drag it across the picture. Notice the effect (see Figure 9.10).
6. Switch to the Sharpen tool by typing Shift+R. Choose a hard-edged brush. Drag it over a different part of the picture. Try to drag it along the edge of an object and note the effect (see Figure 9.11).

FIGURE 9.10.

Blurring the shadowed area with the image (and tool) enlarged.

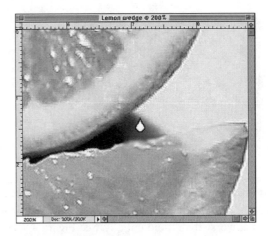

FIGURE 9.11.

Sharpening is more obvious than blurring.

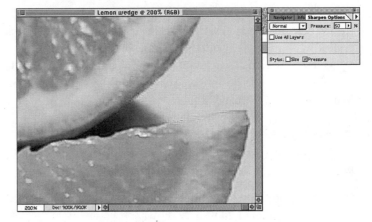

7. Try sharpening the area you previously blurred. Can you restore it to its previous appearance? (Probably not.)

8. Now, just for fun, switch to the Smudge tool and see for yourself the difference between Blur and Smudge.

9. Practice with these tools at different pressure settings and with different brushes. Use Revert (File→Revert) to restore the picture if you run out of practice room.

The Toning Tools

Photoshop is primarily a digital darkroom program, so it makes sense that some of its most useful tools mimic the darkroom techniques that photographers use to lighten and darken portions of an image or to brighten colors. The Toning tools include the Dodge,

Burn, and Sponge tools. Dodging and Burning are opposites, like Sharpen and Blur, but instead of affecting the contrast between adjacent pixels, they either lighten or darken the area to which the tool is applied.

Dodge and Burn Tools

Dodging, in the photographer's darkroom is accomplished by waving a dodging tool, usually a cardboard circle on a wire, between the projected image from the enlarger and the photographic paper. This blocks some of the light and makes the dodged area lighter when the print is developed. It's also called "holding back" because you effectively hold back the light from reaching the paper. Photoshop's Dodge tool, shown in Figure 9.12, looks just like the darkroom version.

FIGURE 9.12.

The toning tools: Dodge, Burn, and Sponge.

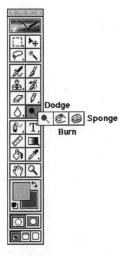

Burning has the opposite effect to dodging—instead of lightening a small area, it darkens the area. In the darkroom, burning in is accomplished either by using a piece of cardboard with a hole punched out (the opposite of the Dodge tool) or by blocking the enlarger light with your hand, so it only reaches the area to be burned. Photoshop's Burn tool icon is a hand shaped to pass a small beam of light.

Notice the drop-down menu in the Tool Options palette. (Double-click the tool to open it, if it's not already open.) It gives your three choices:

- Shadows
- Midtones
- Highlights

These options indicate the types of pixels that the tool will affect. If you want to adjust the shadows, such as making them lighter and leaving the lighter pixels untouched, select Shadows. The default option for the Dodge tool is Midtones. This is a good choice when you want to affect the midtone pixels or when you are unsure of how to proceed. Select the Highlights when you want to lighten already light-colored areas, leaving the darker areas untouched. Figure 9.13 shows the effects of dodging and burning on a typical picture.

FIGURE 9.13.

From the top: Original, Dodging applied to the rocks, Burning applied to the rocks.

Sponging

Surprisingly enough, sponging is also a darkroom trick. When a picture in the developing tray isn't turning dark enough or looks to be underexposed or weak in color, the darkroom technician can often "save" it by sloshing some fresh, full-strength developing chemical on a sponge and rubbing it directly on the wet print in the tray. The combination of the slight warmth from the friction of the sponge and the infusion of fresh chemical can make the difference between a useless picture and an okay one. It's no substitute for a proper exposure, of course.

Photoshop's sponge does much the same thing. On a color image, it subtly increases (or reduces, versatile tool that it is) the color saturation in the area to which you apply it. On a grayscale image, it increases or decreases contrast by moving the grayscale level away from or toward middle gray. When you use the sponge you also need to adjust its setting in the Options palette to determine whether it intensifies color (saturates) or fades it (desaturates). Figures 9.14 and 9.15 show before and after views of a woodland scene with the sponge applied. You can't truly appreciate this one in black and white. Check it out at our Web site (www.mcp.com/info).

FIGURE 9.14.

Before...

Have you ever wondered what's meant by "middle gray"? If you consider the grayscale as going from 0% (white) to 100% (black), middle gray is the tone that's exactly 50%. In practice, highlights are anywhere from 0 to about 20 to 25%. Shadows are 70 to 100%. So anything between a 25% gray and a 70% gray is considered a midtone.

These tools are great for fine-tuning images and creating shadows or highlights. Use them in small doses to enhance the appearance of your images.

For this sort of precision work, I strongly recommend that you change your cursors to Brush Size in the File→Preferences→Display & Cursors dialog box (see Figure 9.16). This permits you to see exactly what you are doing when using these precision tools. Enlarging the picture is also helpful.

FIGURE 9.15.

After the Sponge,is used, the colors are much brighter.

FIGURE 9.16.

Setting the cursor to show the brush size.

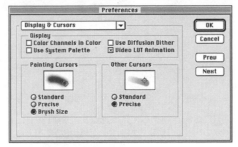

Summary

Photoshop provides several different ways to move paint around, once you have applied it. The Smudge tool is useful for blending small areas of color. It has the same effect as dragging your finger through wet paint. Blur and Sharpen are two sides of the same coin, so to speak. One increases the contrast between adjacent pixels, while the other diminishes it. The Toning tools, Dodge, Burn, and Sponge, are the digital darkroom equivalents of real darkroom tools and procedures. They can darken or lighten an image or change the color saturation, either adding more color or removing some. These tools are mostly used for retouching pictures that you have scanned or shot digitally, rather than for creating your own art.

Q&A

Q What's the difference between Smudge and Blur?

A The main difference is in the way you apply them. Smudging, because you're moving the pixels from point A to point B, tends to show the direction of the move. Blurring decreases the contrast between adjacent pixels, so they seem to blend together visually but with no hint of movement.

Q I keep running the Sharpen tool back and forth over the same section of the picture, and it doesn't change. Why not?

A As long as you keep your finger on the mouse button, you're making a single pass with the tool. To build up layers of sharpening, or of paint or anything else you apply with the mouse, release the button between strokes.

9

Quiz

Test your knowledge with these questions.

Questions

1. What effect does 100% pressure have on the Smudge tool?

    a. None.

    b. It turns the smudges black.

    c. Rather than smudging, it erases.

2. If you sharpen a piece of the picture too much, what happens?

    a. It turns into a random collection of black and colored pixels.

    b. It turns white.

    c. It turns black.

Answers

1. c.

2. a. This effect is not recommended.

Activity

Using the Toning Tools

Find a photograph that has a good range of dark and light tones, or download this one and work along with us. Open it in Photoshop and prepare to use the Toning tools on it.

1. Click the Dodge tool and then double-click to open its Options window.

2. Set the intensity to somewhere around 30% and choose a small, soft-edged brush, as we have in Figure 9.17.

FIGURE 9.17.

This picture needs lightening in the shadow areas, and darkening where there is too much light.

3. Find a dark area in your photo. Apply the Dodge tool. Press the mouse button and hold as you move the tool.

4. If one step wasn't enough, press the mouse button again and reapply the tool. Remember that the effects are cumulative: Each time you press the mouse button you remove more of the dark tone. Don't overdo it.

5. If you find that you have dodged too much and left a light spot, undo your last pass with the Dodge tool. If there's still a light spot, use File→Revert and start over. Lower the intensity and try again.

6. Now find a light spot and type the letter **O** to toggle to the Burn tool.

7. Using the same method you used above to dodge, try darkening a light area. If you overdo, undo.

8. Type **O** to toggle to the Sponge tool. Set the pulldown menu in the Options window to Saturate. Find an area in your picture that could use more intense color and apply the Sponge.

FIGURE 9.18.

We brought out the detail on the balcony and enhanced the people on the dock.

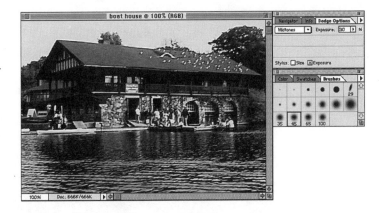

9

9. Set the Sponge to Desaturate on the Options window pulldown menu. Now find an area that could use *less* color and use the Sponge tool to remove some. Again, if you go too far, use Undo or Revert, if necessary.

10. Continue to experiment with these tools until you understand what they do and how to control them by changing the brush size and intensity.

HOUR 10

Advanced Painting Techniques

Digital paint is so much easier to work with than the real kind. It doesn't smell, it never spills on the table, and there are no messy brushes to wash out when you're done. It doesn't get all over you and you don't even have to wait for it to dry. In Photoshop, you can either paint a picture from scratch, starting with a blank page and using it as if it were any other graphics program, or you can take an existing image and convert it into a painting. In the course of this Hour, we'll explore both ways of working.

When we talk about "paint" in the digital realm, we're talking, of course, about image manipulation that mimics "real-life" painting techniques. Because we're imitating real life, you might think that we'd be limited in the number of painting techniques that we can use—but this isn't the case. We're not just limited to watercolor or oil paint, for instance. Under the broad category of painting, we can include colored pencil drawing, pastels, chalk, charcoal, and even neon tubing, as many of today's artists and art students are doing. Even though digital painting is the most spectacular part of Photoshop, as well as the most fun, you'll be amazed at how easy it is.

More important, mastering Photoshop's painting tools will take you a long way toward becoming a more proficient digital artist.

Using Photoshop as a Graphics Program

Quite honestly, Photoshop wasn't designed to be a graphics program. It lacks some of the tools that you'll find in Adobe Illustrator, CorelDRAW, or Fractal Painter (to name just a few of the very best programs). However, it can be used very effectively for many kinds of graphics. Because of its plug-in filters, which you'll learn about later on, it can do some very remarkable things with graphics, most of which would be way beyond the capability of an ordinary painting or drawing program. Should Photoshop be your *only* graphics program? Probably not, if you need to do a lot of drawing. Its vector drawing tools are non-existent. But for painting and digital darkroom work and retouching, nothing can top it.

Simulating Different Media

One of the remarkable "tricks" Photoshop can do is to simulate the appearance of other media. The effect can be achieved through the use of a filter (we'll jump ahead a little in this Hour and introduce you to some of Photoshop's "artistic" filters). It can also be achieved through the use of the Smudge and Blur tools, or by choosing custom paintbrushes and carefully applying paint with a particular Blend mode. You can either create a picture "from scratch," or you can start with a photograph and make it look like a watercolor, an oil painting in any of a half dozen different styles, or a construction of neon tubing. Whatever the method, the results will amaze you.

Watercolors

Artists who work in conventional media have a great deal of respect for those who choose watercolors. It's probably the most difficult medium of all to handle. You have to work "wet" to blend colors, but not so wet that the image turns to mud. Doing it digitally is much easier. Photoshop has a watercolor *filter* that converts a picture to a watercolor version of itself. You can find the filter in the Filter→Artistic submenu, as shown in Figure 10.1.

NEW TERM   Filters, in Photoshop terminology, are instructions built into the program (or "plugged-in" as added features) that apply specific effects to your pictures. For instance, one of Photoshop's filters converts your image to a pattern of dots. Another simulates flames shooting out of a selected object. Dozens of filters are available. Some come with the program, while others are sold by third-party vendors or distributed as shareware or freeware. In Hours 14 through 16, we'll talk more about what kinds of filters you can get and where.

FIGURE 10.1.

Watercolor is one of fifteen "artistic" filters.

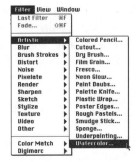

The Watercolor filter works most effectively on pictures that have large, bold areas, and not a lot of detail. Because it also tends to darken backgrounds and shadows, it's best to start with a picture that has a light background. The photo in the figures that follow is a digital photograph of the ladder that encircles a water tank.

When you select the Watercolor filter (or virtually any other Photoshop filter, for that matter), you open a dialog box like the one shown in Figure 10.2. It has a thumbnail view of your picture and sliders that allow you to set the way in which the picture is converted. If you click and drag on the thumbnail image, you can slide it around to see the effect of your settings on different parts of the photo. Most Photoshop filters have dialog boxes and settings very much like this one. After you have tried even one, the rest will be just as easy.

FIGURE 10.2.

Use the + and - symbols to zoom in and out on the thumbnail.

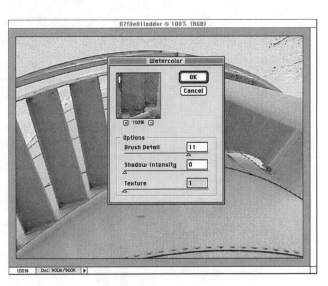

Filters can take anywhere from a few seconds to a minute or more to apply. If you don't see the effects of the filter on the thumbnail view immediately, look for a flashing underline beneath the percentage number under the thumbnail window. It flashes to tell you that the computer is calculating the Filter effect. When the underline disappears, the filter is applied.

Brush detail varies from 1 to 14, with 14 giving you the most detail and 1 being a sort of Jackson Pollock splatter effect. Depending on the nature of the picture you are converting and your own preferences, you may want to start experimenting with settings around 9 to 12. Shadow intensity can be adjusted from 0 to 10, but unless you are looking for special effects, leave it at zero. The Watercolor filter darkens shadows too much, even at the 0 setting. By the time you move it past 3 to 4, the picture's gone almost totally black. Texture settings vary from 1 to 3. These are actually quite subtle and you may wonder if they have any effect at all. They do but are more noticeable combined with less detailed brush settings. In Figure 10.3, I've gathered samples of different brush detail and texture settings so you can see the differences.

FIGURE 10.3.

All three texture settings have been applied to each sample brush setting.

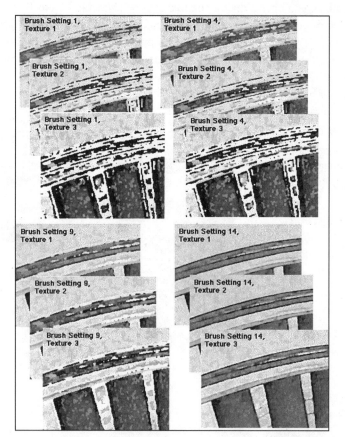

Converting a Photograph to a Watercolor

You might not want to convert all your photos into imitation watercolors, but some look really good with this treatment.

1. Find a picture that you think might look good as a watercolor, or download this one from our Web site. Open it in Photoshop and make any color adjustments you think necessary. (If you've forgotten how, turn back to Hour 6, "Adjusting Color," to refresh your memory.) Remember not to let the colors get too dark before you start applying filters. Photoshop filters, in general, tend to add more black to the image.

2. Then, choose Watercolor from the Filter→Artistic submenu.

3. In the Watercolor filter window, shown in Figure 10.4, use the sliders to choose a combination of texture and brush detail that you like. Move the thumbnail image to check details.

10

FIGURE 10.4.

We've set the Brush to 12 and Texture to 1.

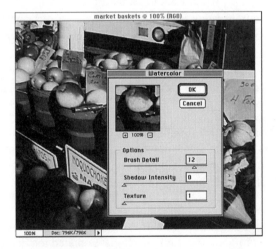

4. Set the Shadow Intensity to 0, unless you want a lot of black in the image.

5. Click OK when you're done to apply the changes.

Watercolors from Scratch

Sometimes you either don't have a photo of what you want to paint, or you just want to do it yourself. Perhaps you want a different style of watercolor than what's possible with the filter. If you work patiently and with some forethought, you can produce watercolors that you'd almost swear were painted with a brush on paper. Let's open a new page in Photoshop and do some painting.

You learned about working with the Paintbrush tool in Hour 7, "Paintbrushes and Art Tools." As you remember, you can leave the Brushes and Options windows open while you work, so you can switch from a large brush to a small one or change the Opacity with just a click. I also like to open the Swatches window and use it as a paint box to select colors, rather than going to the Color Picker each time. Please feel free to flip back if you need to refresh your memory about any of these things.

If you drag on the tabs at the top of the palettes, you can move them around so you can use the brushes, colors, and swatches all at once, or whatever combination of palettes you need. Close the ones you aren't using to make more room. (Figure 10.5 shows my usual painting setup.)

Transparency is one of the distinguishing features of "real" watercolor. In order to make a "synthetic" watercolor, you'll want to set the Brush Opacity at no more than 75%. This means that because transparent is the opposite of opaque, your paint will be 25% transparent, which is about right for watercolors. Try out the brush on a blank page and you'll notice that, as you paint over a previous stroke, the color darkens. Click the "wet edges" checkbox for even more authentic brush strokes. This option adds extra color along the edges of a stroke, making it look as if the pigment gathered there, as it does when you paint with a very watery brush.

Watercolor artists painting on paper often start with an outline and then fill in the details. Figure 10.5 shows the beginnings of a watercolor painting of a flower. We've drawn the flower and its stem and leaves, and now we're working on filling in the leaves with a small brush. It's often easier to work in a magnified view when you're doing small details like this.

Another useful "trick" for creating a watercolor is to use the Eraser as if it were a brush full of plain water to lighten a color that you have applied too darkly. Use it at a very low opacity to lighten a color slightly, and at a high opacity to clean up around the edges if your "paintbrush" got away from you. Don't forget that the Eraser always erases to the background color. If you have been changing colors as you paint, make sure to set the background color to what you want to see when you erase.

For this kind of task, a pressure-sensitive graphics tablet, though not an absolute must, is certainly helpful. Drawing with a stylus is far more natural than drawing with a mouse or trackball, and the pressure-sensitive function permits you to make brush strokes that trail off like the real ones.

FIGURE 10.5.

Use the brushes with soft edges.

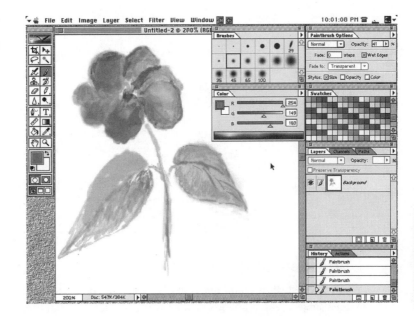

Most real watercolors are painted on a heavily textured watercolor paper. If you would like yours to have the same grainy character, you can use the Texturizer (Filter→Texture →Texturizer) filter to add the watercolor paper texture to the picture after your painting is completed. Don't apply it until everything else is done, though, because any further changes you make will alter the texture. Figure 10.6 shows the Texturizer filter being applied.

The Canvas texture comes the closest to replicating watercolor paper, especially if you scale it down some. I like to set it at about 70 to 80% with a relief height of 3 or 4. Use the sliders to set relief and scaling. I find that applying the same texture a second time with the light coming from the opposite direction gives me the best imitation of textured paper.

Oil Painting

Oil paint has a very different look from watercolor, and it's a look that Photoshop duplicates particularly well. The qualities that distinguish works in oil are the opacity of the paint, the textured canvas that adds a definite fabric grain to the image, and the thick, sometimes three-dimensional quality of the paint. In order to get the full effect in Photoshop, you may have to combine several different techniques. We'll start, as artists do, with underpainting.

10

FIGURE 10.6.

The direction of the light affects the shadows that make up the texture.

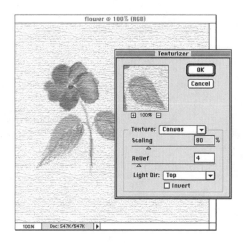

Underpainting

When an artist starts an oil painting of a landscape or a seascape, she usually sketches out the subject with a few lines, often working with charcoal or a pencil to locate the horizon and major land masses. Then she dips a big brush in thinned-out paint and begins the process of underpainting. This blocks in all of the solid areas; the sky, the ground, the ocean, and any obvious features like a large rock, a cliff, or whatever else may be included. Underpainting builds the foundation of the picture, establishing the colors and values of the different parts of the image. It's kind of like building the foundation and framework of a house before you start stacking up bricks to make the walls. Underpainting lays down the basic structure of the picture. Then you go over it and add the details.

Photoshop's Underpainting filter looks at the image that you're applying it to and reduces it to the same sort of solid blocks of color. In Figure 10.7, we've applied it to a photo of a beach with some nice rocky cliffs in the background.

Using the Underpainting filter requires making some settings decisions. The Texture settings are exactly the same as in the Texturize filter we used on the watercolor. Here, though, we want to bring out more of the canvas, so we would use a higher relief number, and possibly a larger scale on the canvas. You can also paint on burlap, sandstone, or brick, or on textures that you import from elsewhere. The Brush size setting ranges from 0 to 40. Smaller brushes retain more of the texture and detail of the original image. Larger brushes give a somewhat spotty coverage and remove all the detail. Texture coverage also ranges on a scale from 0 to 40. Lower numbers here reveal less of the texture, higher numbers bring out more of it. In underpainting, the texture is revealed only where there's paint, not all over the canvas.

10

FIGURE 10.7.

Underpainting gives you the basic elements of the picture, minus the details.

To turn a scene into an oil painting, follow these steps:

1 As always, start by preparing the picture. Adjust the colors if necessary and crop as needed.

2. Open the Underpainting filter (Filter→Artistic→Underpainting).

3. Set the Brush size to 3 and the Texture coverage to 3. These settings will retain most of the detail in the picture.

4. Set the Texture to Canvas and Scaling to 65%. You want to keep the texture small so it doesn't interfere with the detail you will be adding to the picture later on.

5. Set the Relief to 8 and the Light direction to Top. This shows just enough texture to establish that your painting is on canvas rather than stone.

6. Click OK to apply the filter. Figure 10.8 shows the result so far.

FIGURE 10.8.

The scene with just the underpainting applied.

Overpainting

The Underpainting filter leaves us with a somewhat indistinct picture, fine for some purposes but definitely unfinished. An artist would proceed to go back and overpaint the areas that need to have detail, so that's what we'll do to complete this seascape.

Dissolve may be the most useful mode for working into our seascape. Use it, as shown in Figure 10.9, to stipple colors into the underpainting. Vary the Brush size and Opacity to add more or less paint with each stroke.

FIGURE 10.9.

We've added white to the surf and greens to the shrubbery.

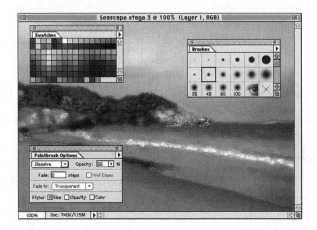

You can go on painting into this picture until it looks exactly like an oil painting, or you can use it as a basis to experiment with other filters and effects. In Figure 10.10, we've taken the seascape and applied the Smudge Stick filter (Filters→Artistic→Smudge Stick) to it. This filter, when used with a short stroke length, gives a nice paint-like texture to the picture. It does, however, also darken it quite a bit, so you may want to go back and adjust the curve again to bring back the sunshine. You can also increase the intensity to keep the picture from turning dark. This, however, changes the Smudge effect as well. Experiment with the settings until you find a combination that works with the image you're using.

Pencil and Colored Pencil

The Pencil tool has been part of every graphics program since the very first ones. It's an extremely useful tool when you know how to use it properly. The first thing to learn about it is that by holding down the Shift key as you drag, you can draw neatly constrained straight lines; vertical, horizontal, or at a 45 degree angle. The second thing is that it can also serve as an eraser if you click the Auto-Erase function in its Options window. With Auto Erase enabled, when you click the Pencil point on a colored pixel, you erase it. Use this feature to clean up edges or to erase in a straight line.

FIGURE 10.10.

The Smudge Stick adds texture to large, flat areas like the beach sand.

Pencils are great for retouching and drawing a single pixel-width line, but difficult to use for an actual drawing. The Pencil is easier to use if you zoom in to 200% so you can see individual pixels. Opening the Control Panel and setting the mouse acceleration to Slow will also help, but it's even better to use a graphics tablet instead of a mouse.

If you want to get the look of a pencil drawing, without all the effort, try the Colored Pencil filter (Filters→Artistic→Colored Pencil) or the Crosshatch filter (Filters→Brush Strokes→Crosshatch). The Colored Pencil filter, which is shown in Figure 10.11, gives you a light, somewhat stylized drawing from your original image. The Crosshatch filter, applied to the same image in Figure 10.12, retains much more of the color and detail, but still looks like a pen and ink drawing.

FIGURE 10.11.

The Colored Pencil filter adds a light, airy feel.

FIGURE 10.12.

Crosshatching uses a different, more detailed drawing style.

Chalks, Pastels, and Charcoal

Chalk and charcoal drawings date all the way back to prehistoric times. When the cave dwellers at Lascaux decided to decorate their walls, they used colored clays, chalk, and charcoal, with animal fat as a binder.

Artists today use almost the same medium, except that the chalks are now compressed so well they don't need tallow. Natural birch charcoal is still considered the best of its kind. Chalk drawings in the real world can be found on virtually any surface, from grained paper, to brick walls and sidewalks. Chalk drawings in Photoshop let you take advantage of the capabilities of the Texture filters. Place your drawing on sandstone, burlap, or on a texture that you've imported from another source.

Chalk and charcoal are linear materials, which is to say that they draw lines rather than large flat areas like paints. Choose your subjects with that in mind. You can, of course, apply shading as a pattern of lines or a crosshatch, and you can smudge to your heart's content. If you're drawing from scratch, start with a fairly simple line drawing and expand on it. If you're translating a photo or scanned image into a chalk or charcoal drawing, choose one that has strong line patterns and well-defined detail.

Chalk and Charcoal Filter

When you apply the Chalk and Charcoal filter, which is found on the Filter menu (Filter→Sketch→Chalk and Charcoal), you'll see that it reduces your picture to three colors, using a dark gray plus the foreground and background colors that you have set in the tool window. Chalk uses the background color and Charcoal becomes the foreground color. Areas that aren't colored appear in gray. You will probably want to do some experimenting to find the "right" colors. It's a little bit counterintuitive, because the foreground color is usually the lighter one, and this filter applies it to the darker areas of the image.

Figure 10.13 shows the Chalk & Charcoal dialog box, which controls how this filter works. In it you can set amounts for the chalk and charcoal areas. These sliders have a range from 0 to 20. Start somewhere in the middle and adjust until you get a combination that works for your picture. The stroke pressure varies from 1 to 5. Unless you want the picture to turn into areas of flat color, keep the setting at 1 or 2. Intensity builds up rather fast with this filter.

FIGURE 10.13.

Move around in the preview window to see the filter's effects on different parts of the image.

To convert a photograph to a chalk and charcoal drawing, follow these steps:

1. Open the image and then the Chalk & Charcoal filter dialog box (Filter→ Sketch→Chalk and Charcoal).

2. Set the Charcoal and Chalk areas to 10 or less. When you work with a filter for the first time, always start in the middle of the settings range and increase or decrease as necessary.

3. Set the pressure to 1 or 2. Click OK if you like the view in the Preview window, or experiment with other numbers.

4. Click OK to apply the filter. Figure 10.14 shows this filter applied to a yellow chrysanthemum.

5. Study the result. Decide what areas need touching up.

6. Select the Eraser tool and erase to bring up more of the background color.

7. Select the Paintbrush tool to apply more of the foreground color.

8. Use the Eyedropper to select the gray tone, if you need to apply more of it.

9. When you're satisfied with the drawing, save it.

FIGURE 10.14.

*Smudging the chrysan-
themum.*

The Smudge tool works nicely with chalk and charcoal. Use it exactly as you would
to soften a line or blend two colors using your finger or hand on paper. Photoshop's
Blur and Sharpen tools can also be used to define edges or to soften a line without
smudging it.

After you apply the filter to the picture, you can go over it with the Paintbrush and
Eraser tools, adding back important detail that was lost in translation or touching up as
necessary. You can use the Eraser tool to apply the background color and the Paintbrush
to apply the foreground color. In order to add more of the gray tone, however, we have to
sample it with the Eyedropper tool so that we can paint it in. The gray is an arbitrary
color used by this filter and can't be adjusted.

Photoshop 5.0 includes nearly 100 different filters! If you master one each
week, within two years you'll know them all.

Charcoal

Use the Charcoal filter (Filter→Sketch→Charcoal) to convert an image to a good imitation of a charcoal drawing. Because charcoal doesn't come in colors, your charcoal
drawings will be most successful if you set the foreground to black and the background
to white, or to a pale color if you want the effect of drawing on colored paper. The
Charcoal filter dialog box is shown in Figure 10.15. You can adjust the thickness of the
line from 1 to 7 and the degree of detail from 0 to 5. The Light/Dark Balance setting
ranges from 0 to 100 and controls the proportion of foreground to background color.

FIGURE 10.15.

Experiment with these settings. Every image is different.

Figure 10.16 shows before and after versions of a portrait converted into charcoal and lightly retouched with the Paintbrush, Blur, and Sharpen tools. Using a graphics tablet instead of a mouse makes it easier to reproduce the filter's cross-hatched lines.

FIGURE 10.16.

Retouching brought back the details that were lost in translation.

Before   After

Summary

Whew! This has been a very full and intense hour. Spend some time trying out these techniques before you move along further.

In this Hour, you saw that digital painting is an area where Photoshop truly excels. You can either work "from scratch" or convert images that you have uploaded as digital photos or scans or have created in some other compatible program. Once you have the image in Photoshop, the various filters and brushes enable you to turn your work into a good imitation of an oil painting, watercolor, or drawing. The "artistic" filter set includes filters that can do much of the work of conversion for you. For best results, though, you'll want to go in and touch up the picture after the filter has done its work. Choose tools and colors that are appropriate to the medium you're trying to imitate.

Experiment, and if you find a technique or filter combination that works especially well, make notes on it. Yes, you can even write in this book! (Well, not if it's a library book...)

Q&A

Q How do you know which pictures will make good digital paintings?

A For digital watercolors, look for photos with large plain areas, and not a lot of detail. In general, try lighter colored pictures, because the Watercolor filter tends to darken images. Almost any "non-descript" picture makes a good oil painting. It helps if the subject is interesting or if there's a good deal of color.

Q Can I use more than one filter on a picture?

A You can, and many times you may want to use a combination of several filters to achieve a particular effect.

Q Why do some filters have ellipses after their names while others don't?

A There are two kinds of native Photoshop filters. The ones with an ellipsis...open a dialog box with parameters to set before the filter is applied. The filters with no ellipsis are one-step filters. You have no control over the way the filter is applied. When you select a one-step filter from the menu, it's applied. Period. You can apply it a second time to double the effect.

Quiz

See what you know about art techniques and artistic filters.

Questions

1. The Watercolor filter works best on pictures with

    a. large flat areas.

    b. lots of detail.

    c. dark backgrounds.

2. Oil painting and watercolor look

    a. very different.

    b. very similar.

    c. a lot like colored pencil.

3. Charcoal comes in many colors.

   a. true

   b. false

   c. only in Photoshop

Answers

1. a

2. a

3. c. You want pink charcoal? Go for it.

Activity

Find a picture with a good range of light and dark colors and moderate detail, or download the picture called Market Baskets from our Web site at www.mcp.com/info. Apply the filters we've discussed in this chapter to the picture, and be sure to experiment with different background and foreground colors as well as with various settings for brush width, pressure, and so on.

10

HOUR 11

Layers

You're almost halfway through. You've already learned a great deal about Photoshop, but there is, as always, more to learn. From this point on, most of it's fun stuff, too. Right now, we are going to discuss one of the most important aspects of Photoshop—layers.

At first, layers might seem confusing, even daunting, but don't worry—they're not as bad as they sound. In fact, they are exactly what their name implies—layers within one image—and each layer can be adjusted and edited separately from the others. That's what makes this feature so cool.

If it helps, think of it this way: Consider a Bugs Bunny cartoon. Imagine Bugs walking through the woods. The artists at the Warner Bros. studios created the backdrops and then drew Bugs on pieces of transparent cellophane, which they laid over the background. They often put his body on one layer, his arms and legs on another, and as they cycled through the several sets of arms and legs, they made the animated Bugs appear to move through the woods or chase Elmer Fudd, who was on yet another layer or two of cellophane. There were limits, though. Too many layers and the background turned gray, or the paint on the top cell cast shadows on the bottom ones.

Photoshop has a capability similar to this animation technique, and you can create as many layers as you need, up to 100. You can hide layers while you work on others. You can link layers together. You already learned how to use adjustment layers that enable you to make color and tonal corrections in your images. Now, you'll learn the rest of the story about layers.

Using the Layers Palette

Step one is to open a new page, and then to open the Layers palette. Just select Window→Show Layers. The Layers palette (see Figure 11.1) is where you control your layers' behavior—creating, adding, deleting, hiding, and showing. Think of the Layers palette as "command central" for working with layers. The small versions of your images on the left of the palette are called *thumbnails*. Each of these small rectangles displays a separate layer. For the moment, because we have not combined any images, you should have only one blank thumbnail in the Layers palette.

FIGURE 11.1.

The Layers palette.

If the thumbnails are too small for your liking, select the Palette Options command from the palette's menu (the arrow in the upper-right corner) and check out Figure 11.2.

FIGURE 11.2.

Optional thumbnail sizes.

You can choose from three different sizes or no thumbnail image at all. Remember that every image on your screen consumes a certain amount of the RAM available to run Photoshop. So if you can get by with the smallest thumbnail, try to. The smaller the thumbnail, the less space the palette will take up on your desktop. This is an advantage as you begin to work with three, four, five, and more layers at a time.

Creating a New Layer

Now let's make some layers. First of all, let's put something on the background layer, just so we'll know where it is. Follow these steps:

1. Using the Airbrush and your biggest brush shape, choose any light-to-medium color and spray paint a large patch of color on the canvas.

2. Look at the thumbnail called Background. (It's the only one on the palette.) It should look something like Figure 11.3.

FIGURE 11.3.

A colored background.

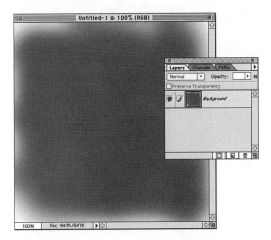

11

3. Click the small page icon at the bottom of the Layers palette. You've just added a layer! Now your palette should look like Figure 11.4.

FIGURE 11.4.

Adding a layer.

Let's pause here for a moment and take a close look at the new layer's thumbnail. Compared to the background layer, it has a thicker black frame around it. The thick frame indicates that this is the *active* layer. You will notice a box that contains a paintbrush. This also indicates the active layer—or the layer on which you can work. Paint all you want, but only the layer with the paintbrush receives the paint.

To change the active layer, click in the white space to the right of the icon (see Figure 11.5). If you try to click in the empty box where the Paintbrush icon should appear, you end up with a Chain icon, which indicates that the layers are linked. We'll look at this option in just a few pages, but for now it is not what we want. (Click on the chain to make it go away.)

FIGURE 11.5.

Changing the active layer.

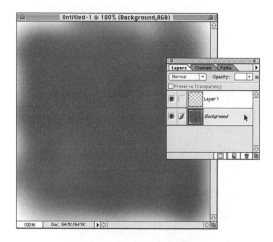

Try changing the active layer to the background layer.

1. Click in the space to the right of the background thumbnail. Notice that the active layer frame turns black and the Paintbrush icon moves down.

2. Now change the active layer back to Layer 1, by clicking next to its thumbnail. Let's put something on this layer.

3. Choose a medium paintbrush and a color that contrasts with the background. At the left side of the canvas, write a letter A (see Figure 11.6).

4. Use the Layer→New menu to add Layer 2. (This is just a different way to do it.) For now, make no changes in the dialog box (see Figure 11.7). Just click OK to add the layer.

5. In the middle of the canvas on Layer 2, use your brush to paint a letter B.

FIGURE 11.6.

Working in the active layer.

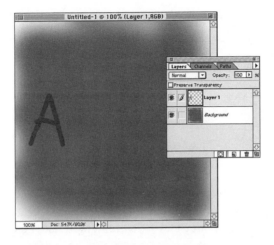

FIGURE 11.7.

Adding a layer from the New Layer dialog box.

11

6. Use the Layers palette's pullout menu to add Layer 3. Figure 11.8 shows the menu. The dialog box looks the same as the previous one. Click OK to add the layer.

FIGURE 11.8.

Adding a layer from the Layers palette.

7. Paint a C on Layer 3. Your screen should look something like Figure 11.9. You may have to expand the Layers palette to see all four layers.

FIGURE 11.9.

Adding layers is as easy as ABC.

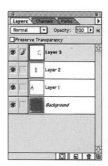

You can move, add to, or erase anything on the active layer, but doing so doesn't affect layers above or below it. For instance, if you make Layer 2 the active layer, you can use the Move tool to slide the B around, but you can't move the A or C.

Moving Layers

You also can change the order of the layers. You might want to do this if one is supposed to look as if it's on top of another, but wasn't created in that order. To do so:

1. Click to the right of the thumbnail of the active layer and hold. The active layer becomes highlighted with an outline.

2. While still holding the mouse button down, drag the layer up to the top of the stack. It then becomes the topmost layer.

Hiding/Showing Layers

Another great feature of layers is that when you want to concentrate on one part of your image, you can hide all the other layers. To the left of the thumbnails, you will notice small icons that resemble eyes (see Figure 11.10). These indicate that a layer is visible. If you see the eye, you can see the layer. If you click the eye, however, the eye disappears and the layer becomes hidden.

FIGURE 11.10.

Only the background and Layer 3 are visible.

Let's try it. Click the eye icons next to Layers 1 and 2. They disappear, as will the corresponding layers. Click again and the icon reappears—with the layer.

Removing Layers

The simple way to remove a layer is to click to make it active and then click the small trashcan icon at the bottom of the palette. You can also select Delete Layer from either the Layers menu or the Layers Palette pullout menu. When you do this you'll see a warning box asking if it's really OK to delete the layer. If you (Option-click) [Alt-click], you can skip the warning. Undo brings back the layer, if you have done nothing else in the meantime. If you have, then use the History palette to return to a previous state.

Working with Multiple Layers

You have seen how to create, move, and remove layers, but we still haven't really addressed the question of what they're good for. You will use layers in many different situations. Whenever you are combining two or more images (in Photoshop terms, *compositing*), the elements you paste over the background image are added on separate layers. You can use the Layers palette to control precisely how these elements are combined. You can control the opacity of objects you paste onto a layer or the paint that you apply to it. (The layer itself is transparent, even if you set the paint on it to 100% opacity.) You can also control the Blending modes that affect how one layer appears on top of another, just as you could when painting over an image or background.

Opacity

The Opacity slider at the top of the Layers palette controls the opacity of the active layer (see Figure 11.11). Make it active by clicking the triangle to the right of the Percentage window. It can be adjusted from 0 to 100% by dragging the slider or by entering a value by typing 0 for 100%, 1 for 10%, 2 for 20%, and so on.

FIGURE 11.11.

The Opacity slider.

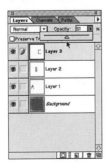

Let's give the Opacity slider a try. You should still have the ABC document open on your desktop. Make Layer 3 active and drag the Opacity slider (by clicking and holding down on the arrow key to make it appear) to about 50% (refer to Figure 11.11). Can you see the background through the C? Drag the slider down to 10% and then to 0. Then move it back to 100% again. Pretty cool, huh?

The background cannot be affected by the Opacity slider. It always remains at 100% opacity. There is, however, a way around this. There is a difference between the background of your image and what Photoshop sees as the *background* to your layers.

You can create a transparent background by opening a new canvas and selecting Transparent as the contents, as we have in Figure 11.12. When the canvas opens, you'll see a checkerboard pattern as a placeholder, indicating that there's nothing on the background layer. Now anything we copy from another source and paste in will go on a new layer that can also be made transparent. (If you don't see the checkerboard pattern, open File→Preferences→Transparency and Gamut, and change the Grid Size from None to Small.)

FIGURE 11.12.

Making a transparent background.

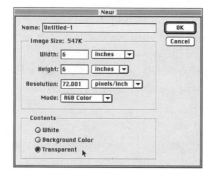

If I drag the background and some of the letters from the previous experiment into this new document, I'll be able to make the airbrushed background 50% transparent, because Photoshop will see it as just another layer, and not as a background. The advantage to this is that I can then arrange them so that one layer is on top of the semi-transparency and not affected by it, and the other layer is beneath it and is changed by it. In Figure 11.13, the layers are stacked with B on the top, then the background at 50% transparent, and C on the bottom.

FIGURE 11.13.

Each layer can have a different transparency.

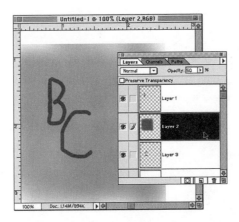

 Use the Layer→Arrange submenu to bring a layer forward or send it behind another. This menu also has Transform commands to flip, rotate, scale, and distort a single layer.

Layer Blending Modes

In Hour 8, "Digital Painting," you learned about Blending modes and how they affect the way paint goes on. The same modes are available to you for blending layers, and they produce the same general effects, but only on the layers beneath the one to which you have applied the blending mode. The layer in this case is the Blend color, and the image below is the Base color. As with the painting tools, the Layer Blending modes are found on a pulldown menu on the Layers palette.

Just as a reminder, the Blending modes are:

- Normal
- Dissolve
- Multiply
- Screen
- Overlay
- Soft Light
- Hard Light
- Color Dodge
- Color Burn
- Darken
- Lighten
- Difference
- Exclusion
- Hue
- Saturation
- Color
- Luminosity

11

Linking Layers

If you click in the box on the Layers palette next to the eye icon, on any layer that's not the active layer, you'll place a piece of linked chain in the box. This indicates that the layer is linked to the active layer, meaning that if you move the contents of the active layer, the linked layers move with it. Figure 11.14 shows the Layers palette with linked layers.

FIGURE 11.14.

Layers linked to the active layer move with it. In this case, all three letters move if you move one.

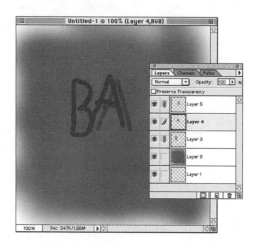

Merging Layers

The more layers you add to an image, and the more effects that you add to those layers, the larger your image file will become. If you have a large capacity hard drive and can back up to removable media, size isn't a problem.

It does, however, make a big difference if you want to use your files for anything else, such as publishing in print or on the Web. The only format in which you can save a multi-layered image is the Photoshop native format, which is great for Photoshop, but bad for other uses. For the Web, you need to save images as either GIF or JPEG files. For print, you probably will need to save as TIFF. That's why you need to either merge layers or flatten the image when you're done working with it.

Here's the difference between merging and flattening:

- Merging groups of layers without flattening the entire image conserves memory space but still enables you to work on the layers that you haven't yet finished. Merging Down merges a layer with the one directly below it. You also can merge just the visible layers, just the linked layers, and a clipping group by choosing the appropriate Layer→Merge command.

- Flattening, on the other hand, compresses all visible layers down to one layer. Any layers that you have made invisible at the time of flattening are lost. To flatten an image, simply choose Layer→Flatten Image, but make sure that you are done. At this point, all the layers are reduced to one.

You can use either the Layer menu or the Layers palette menu to merge or flatten layers, or you can use the keyboard combination (Command+E) [Control+E]. Figure 11.15 shows the Layer menu with the Flatten Image command highlighted.

FIGURE 11.15.

This compacts all the layers to one.

Summary

In this hour, you learned the mechanics of working with layers. You saw how to use the Layers palette and how to create, delete, and move layers. Layers are an important part of the Photoshop interface, and knowing how to apply them will help you a great deal, especially when you work with type and composite images later on.

Q&A

Q How can I convert a background to a layer?

A The easy way is to rename it. If you double-click the background layer in the Layers palette, you open up its dialog box. By default, it appears as Layer 0. If you click OK, it is renamed and won't be a background layer.

Q Can I add a background layer to a page that doesn't have one?

A Yes. Use Layer→New→Background to add a background layer.

11

Quiz

Test your reading comprehension with these questions.

Questions

1. How many layers can you have?

   a. 10

   b. 100

   c. It depends on how much RAM you have.

2. The active layer is

   a. the layer on top.

   b. the layer with a black line around it in the Layers palette.

   c. the layer with an eye icon.

3. To hide a layer

   a. drag it to the trashcan.

   b. press H.

   c. click the eye icon to close it.

Answers

1. b (at least theoretically). c is probably also true.

2. b

3. c

Activity

Let's do some more experimenting with layers. First, click the background color swatch and choose a medium light color for a background. Then open a new document. Be sure to click the button to use the background color. Choose a contrasting foreground color, make a new layer, and use a medium brush to write the number 1. Add layers, with a number on each, until you have about 10. Then, starting with the first one, apply different Blending modes. Try changing the transparency of a layer. Move the number 5 to the upper-left corner of the screen. Merge Layers 2 and 3. Play around until you understand how the layers are working.

Hour 12

Using Masks

Masks can be your best friends when you're working on a complicated picture. They can also be a darned nuisance, simply because there are several different kinds of masks that you can apply to your image, and they do somewhat different things. So you not only have to create a mask, you have to know ahead of time what you want the mask to do for you, and then you have to apply the right kind of mask.

NEW TERM So, what exactly *is* a mask? In a sense, any selection that you make is a mask, because it permits you to do something that affects only the selected area, effectively masking anything that's not selected. Masks can let you change one part of a picture, without changing all of it.

You can select a single flower from a picture of a garden, for instance, and change its color, without changing everything else. You can also delete the selection, which permanently masks it. Masks can cover the part of the picture you don't want to change, much like masking tape covers the woodwork you don't want to paint when you're painting the walls.

The confusion about masks comes from there being so many different types. You can have Layer masks, Mask channels, Transparency masks, Clipping paths, and Clipping groups; and there's also Quick Mask. All can be used to isolate an area that you want to protect while you make changes to the rest of the picture.

Applying Masks

Masks can hide either a selected object or the background, and can be opaque or semi-transparent. (If the mask is totally transparent, it isn't a mask.) In Figure 12.1, if I want to change the background color, I need to mask the flower. The easiest way to do this is to use the Magic Wand to select the background. By selecting the background and not the flower, the flower is masked. If I wanted to change the color of the flower, I could use the Magic Wand to select the background and then invert the selection (Select→Inverse).

FIGURE 12.1.

Selecting the back-ground.

This is the most basic kind of masking. It's not always perfect, though. In Figure 12.2, you can see that the Magic Wand didn't really give us a very smooth mask. The space between the flower petals isn't fully selected and the edges aren't very smooth. What's needed is a way to edit the mask.

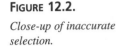

FIGURE 12.2.

Close-up of inaccurate selection.

Using Quick Mask

Photoshop provides a very quick and easy way to make a temporary mask that can, in fact, be edited. It's called Quick Mask, and one of its advantages is that you can see both the image and the mask at the same time. You can start with a selected area and use the Paintbrush tool to add to it or take away from it, or you can create the mask entirely in Quick Mask mode. Let's apply a Quick Mask to the flower.

To create a Quick Mask, follow these steps:

1. Using whatever Selection tool seems appropriate, select the part of the image you want to change. It's okay if your selection isn't perfect.

2. Click the Quick Mask button at the bottom of the toolbox (see Figure 12.3).

3. You see a color overlay indicating the mask on the protected area, which is to say, the area *not* selected. (By default, the mask is 50% opaque red, imitating a piece of the rubylith film that artists use to mask photos for retouching.)

4. If the mask needs editing, as this one does, select an appropriate Paintbrush size from the Brush palette and click the Paintbrush, or type B to activate it.

5. Painting with black adds to the mask. Painting with white (or erasing) takes it away. You will notice that the foreground and background colors change to black and white when you enter Quick Mask mode. (If for some reason they didn't, type D for Default.) Painting with gray gives you a semi-transparent mask. Figure 12.4 shows the edited mask.

12

FIGURE 12.3.

The Quick Mask button.

FIGURE 12.4.

The mask, touched up and ready to use.

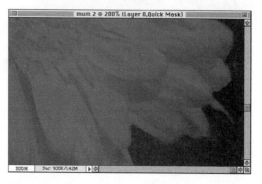

6. When the mask is edited to your satisfaction, click the Standard mode button in the toolbox, (to the left of the Quick Mask button) to return to your original image. The unprotected area (in our case, the background) is surrounded by a Selection marquee. Now we can apply any change we want to make to this area, without affecting the area that we masked (see Figure 12.5).

FIGURE 12.5.

I added a texture and changed the background color.

7. When done making changes, type (Command-D) or [Control-D] to deselect the area and get rid of the mask.

> If you need a straight edge on your mask, use the Line tool to draw a single pixel line. It appears in the Mask color, as long as you are in Quick Mask mode when you draw it.

Chroma Graphics recently introduced a plug-in tool for Photoshop called MagicMask. It includes more sophisticated Selection tools and Mask Display options. We'll discuss it in depth in Hour 19, "Photoshop Plug-ins and Add-ons."

Layer Masks

Layer masks enable you to hide and reveal parts of layers, as well as to apply special effects, such as filters, in a controlled and precise manner. Layer masks, like Quick Masks, can be edited.

To make a Layer mask, select an area of the image to mask and click the New Layer icon at the bottom of the Layer palette to make a new layer. Then click the Layer Mask icon (the left-most icon at the bottom of the Layers window) to make the new layer into a mask. When you do, you see a Layer mask thumbnail next to the image thumbnail. Figure 12.6 shows an example. Black indicates the portions of the layer that are covered and white shows the parts that are revealed. If the mask is made to be semi-transparent, the partially masked areas would be shown in gray.

12

FIGURE 12.6.

Layer 1 masks everything but the sky and Layer 2 masks everything but the boat hull.

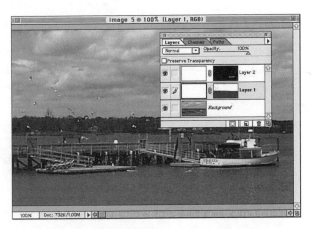

Notice the links between the two thumbnails, indicating that the mask is linked to the layer. After you create the mask, you can edit it simply by making the Mask layer the active layer. The foreground and background colors revert to the defaults, and you can apply black to add to the mask or white to remove parts of it. To see the actual size and shape of the mask as you're working, select the part of the image to be masked, and then go to the Layer menu. Select Layer→Add Layer Mask and choose either Hide Selection or Reveal Selection, depending on whether you're masking the area around the selected piece of image or the image itself. Figure 12.7 shows the menu for this.

FIGURE 12.7.

The Layer menu.

Hide Selection hides the area that you have selected, so that you can work on the rest of the image. If you look at Figure 12.8, you can see a Layer mask for the sky in the boat picture. The black section of the Layer mask is the actual mask.

FIGURE 12.8.

Black is masked; white is editable.

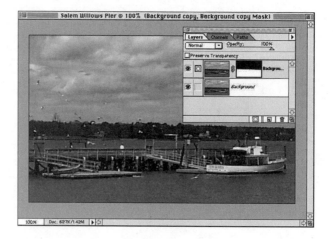

With this mask, we can protect the sky and work on the rest of the picture. Reveal Selection obviously does just the opposite of the first command, Hide Selection. This command hides everything on a layer *except* that area within the Marquee selection. The other commands, Hide All and Reveal All, work a little differently. These, as the names suggest, are based on the entire layer.

 Each layer can have only one layer mask. If you need to do additional masking, activate the layer and apply Quick Mask.

The business of making masks can seem very confusing, so let's take the process step-by-step. To add a mask to a layer:

1. Open the Layers palette, if it's not already active.
2. Select the layer to which you want to add a mask.
3. To hide the entire layer, choose Layer→Add Layer mask→Hide all.
4. To make a mask that hides or reveals a selected area, first make the selection on the active layer.
5. Choose Layer→Add Layer mask→Hide Selection *or* Layer→Add Layer mask→Reveal Selection, whichever is appropriate for your needs.

Take some time now to open a picture and practice applying masks. Try Quick Mask first, and then make a selection and turn it into a Layer mask. If you practice these skills while they're fresh in your mind, you'll remember them later on when you need to do a quick color change, or preserve an object while changing its background.

Editing Masks

If you click the Layer Mask thumbnail in the Layers palette to make it active, you will see the Mask icon appear in the small square to the left of the layer thumbnail. This indicates that the mask is active. Select a Paint tool and paint the mask with black to add to it. Paint with white to subtract from the mask, or paint with gray to make the layer partially visible, and the mask thumbnail displays your changes. Figure 12.9 shows a mask being edited. I switched the view to the larger thumbnail to make it a little easier to see what I was doing. Just as a reminder, you can do this in the Layers palette Options dialog box, which is reached from the Palette pullout menu.

12

Figure 12.9.

*I've painted white over
part of the black mask
to make an A.*

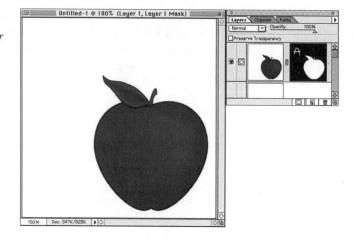

To edit the layer instead, either click its thumbnail or go to the Layer menu and select
Disable Layer Mask. This option puts a large X through the mask thumbnail so you
know it's inactive (see Figure 12.10).

Figure 12.10.

*The mask is temporari-
ly disabled.*

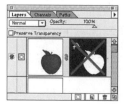

Using Layer→Disable Layer Mask allows you to get rid of the effects of the
layer mask temporarily. When you want it back, just hit Layers→Enable
Layer Mask and you are back in business.

Removing the Layer Mask

There are two ways for you to get rid of the Layer mask when you are done with it or
you want to start over. The first way, possibly the easiest, is simply to drag the Layer
Mask icon found in the Layers palette onto the small Trash Can icon at the bottom of the
window (see Figure 12.11).

You also can get rid of a layer by selecting Layer→Remove Layer Mask. Whichever way
you prefer, you are presented with the following box in which you are prompted to apply
the effects of the mask or discard the mask without applying it (see Figure 12.12).

FIGURE 12.11.

Trashing a layer.

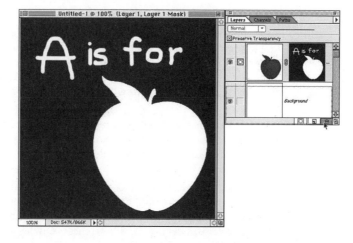

FIGURE 12.12.

Apply, Discard, or Cancel.

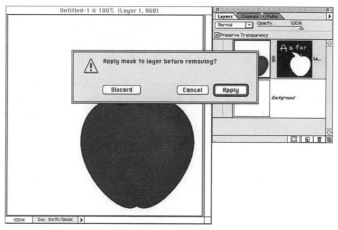

Channels Demystified

Even though a detailed explanation of channels and how to use them is somewhat beyond the scope of this book, a few words about channels may prove helpful to you at this point. Photoshop creates Color Information channels when you open a new image. An RGB document starts with four channels, one for each color and the composite that merges them. These are akin to the color separations used in four-color process printing. You can also create additional channels, called *alpha channels* in Photoshop parlance, which hold information about the masks you create for the image.

12

Channel thumbnails can be viewed in the Channels palette, which shares
a window with the Layers palette. Click the Channels tab to open it. The
composite is listed first, then the Color channels, and finally the Masks or
alpha channels show up at the bottom of the list. If you have made several
layer masks, you may need to use the scroll bars or resize the palette to see
them all.

As with the Layers thumbnails, you can increase the size of the Channels
thumbnails to see them more easily. You can also click the eye icons in the
Channel palette to hide or show single channels in the image window. This
is the function of the Channel palette that you will use most.

It's often helpful to arrange the Channel palette so that you view the Mask
and the Color Composite (RGB or CMYK) channels together. By default, individual channels display in grayscale, but you can change this to see them in
their own color by opening File→Preferences→Display & Cursors and check-
ing Color Channels in Color.

Masks and the Channels Palette

The mask that you add to an image creates a new channel in your image. Channels are
Photoshop's way of storing color and mask information. (See the sidebar for more infor-
mation about channels.) If you add a mask to a layer and select Window→Show
Channels, you will see something like the example in Figure 12.13.

FIGURE 12.13.

*The Channels palette
with a Layer mask at
the bottom.*

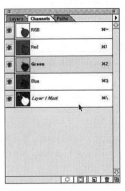

Click the eye icon to the left of the mask in the Channels palette and the mask appears as
red, representing rubylith, a carry-over from the old days when this stuff was done in the
real and not the cyber world. The main reason for displaying the mask this way is that
you can now edit it full screen, rather than by poking around and trying to see what you
are doing in a tiny thumbnail. Figure 12.14 shows edits to the mask as an alpha channel.

FIGURE 12.14.

*Use the Brush and
Eraser to edit the
Channel mask.*

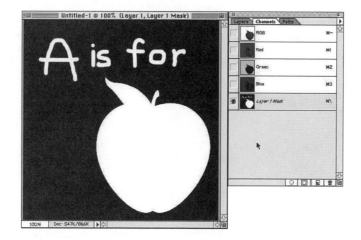

Summary

In this Hour, we looked at using masks. Masking allows you to apply changes selectively, while protecting parts of the picture that you don't want to change. You learned about the Quick Mask function, and how to edit a mask with the Paintbrush and Eraser. Then you learned about Layer masks and how to turn a layer into a mask.

Q&A

Q My picture has a lot of red in it and the red mask is hard to see. Is there a way to change it to some other color?

A Of course. If you're working in Quick Mask mode, double-click the Quick Mask icon on the toolbox to open the Quick Mask options dialog box. If you're working on a Layer mask, (control+click) [right-click] on the Layer mask icon in the Layers menu to open a context menu that gives you access to the Layer Mask Display Options dialog box. In either one, you can set the color and amount of opacity for your mask. In the Quick Mask box, you can also set a radio button to determine whether the selection or the mask is indicated by the colored area.

Q If I'm doing catalog photos of small objects and want to mask the backgrounds, is it easier to select the background or to select the object and invert the selection?

A That depends on how complicated and/or how coloful the object is. If it's all one color, then you can probably select it with one Magic Wand click, and invert it to make your mask in a couple of seconds. If the background is simple and the object isn't, then select the background.

12

Q **The selection tools missed some of the petals on the flower I'm trying to mask, but my hand's not steady enough to draw them in. What can I do?**

A Enlarge the image to 200% or even more. Then you can see what you're doing and draw or erase more precisely.

Quiz

Who *was* that masked image? Take off your mask and answer these questions.

Questions

1. A mask can hide

   a. an object.

   b. the background.

   c. either the background or an object.

2. Masks can be either opaque, semi-opaque, or transparent.

   a. True

   b. False

3. Masks are saved with the picture and, therefore, increase file size. To save disk space, always:

   a. discard the masks after you're done with them.

   b. flatten the image.

   c. hide the Layer masks.

Answers

1. c
2. b (If the mask is transparent, it's not hiding anything.)
3. a

Activity

Find a picture with several similar objects in it. Mask them separately and experiment with changing the colors of the objects, one at a time, without changing the background.

HOUR 13

Paths

Congratulations! You're halfway through, which is to say that you've seen only half of what Photoshop can do.

Early on you learned about selections and how selecting part of an image isolates that part, so that you can work on it and not the entire image. Last hour you learned about converting selections to masks in order to protect the parts of your image that you don't want to work on.

The problem with selections is that as soon as you remove the Selection marquee, it's gone. The only way to reselect something is to use the appropriate tools (Marquee, Lasso, or Magic Wand) and make the selection all over again, or use the History palette to revert back to the last Selection tool used. This, however, means that you lose whatever you did to the selection.

Paths solve this dilemma. With paths (also called Clipping paths), you can create and save specific selections for future use. The paths get saved right within the Photoshop file, very much like a layer is. Also, paths can be useful when you want to create complex shapes by using the Pen tool.

Let's start by exploring the two different ways to create paths, and then go into techniques for editing and using them in Photoshop.

Creating Paths

There are two paths you can take for creating paths (sorry, I couldn't resist):

- Create the path directly from a selection you've already made.
- Create the path from scratch by using the Pen tool and drawing the path by hand.

Paths Via Selections

Depending on the image at hand, this can be the easiest and quickest way to create a path. You simply make a selection and convert it to a path.

Let's look at an example. Figure 13.1 shows our test image, a lemon, sitting on a dark-colored towel.

FIGURE 13.1.

Our test image. We want a Clipping path that outlines the lemon.

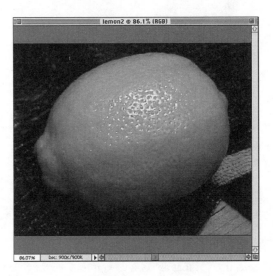

As you remember, selecting can be accomplished by using a number of tools. For this image, the Magic Wand is perfect because the subject is mostly one color. Simply set the Magic Wand Tolerance to about 25 (so you're sure to get most of the yellow pixels), and select the lemon (see Figure 13.2). If there are highlights that the Magic Wand ignores, use Select→Feather to feather the edges of the selection by two to three pixels. This is usually enough to pick up highlights and edges.

FIGURE 13.2.

The lemon is now selected.

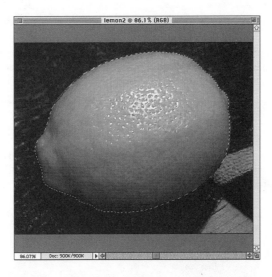

Now that you have a selection, follow these steps to convert it to a path:

1. Make sure that the Paths palette is visible. If not, choose Window→Show Paths.

2. Select Make Work Path from the pop-out menu at the upper-right of the Paths palette (see Figure 13.3).

FIGURE 13.3.

The pop-out menu of the Paths palette.

3. The only thing to set in the Make Work Path dialog box is Tolerance (see Figure 13.4). Tolerance refers to how closely Photoshop follows the outline of your selection in creating the path. The smaller the Tolerance, the more exact the path will be.

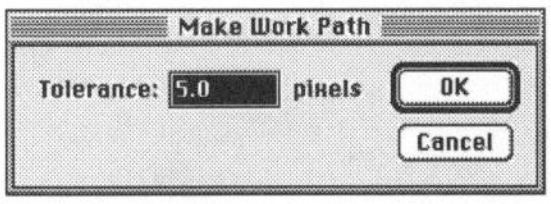

13

FIGURE 13.4.

The Make Work Path dialog box.

> Be aware that complex paths can be resource intensive. More complexity means more points, angles, curves, and so on. The result can mean slower processing of the image, bigger files, and possible problems when printing. It is definitely something to be aware of.

For this image, I first tried a Tolerance of 5 pixels. As Figure 13.5 shows, the results were unacceptable. Photoshop was too flexible and approximate in creating the path at this setting. You can see that the smoother line of the path does not follow the outline of the lemon closely enough.

FIGURE 13.5.

When the path doesn't match the selection to your satisfaction, Tolerance is set too high.

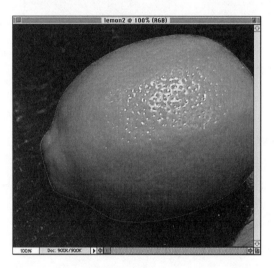

When this happens, simply reach for my favorite Photoshop command: Undo. Undo the path conversion and try a lower Tolerance setting. After some experimentation, I found that a value of one pixel works quite well (see Figure 13.6).

4. Note how the path also appears in the Paths palette. Photoshop has named it "Work Path." You can rename the path by simply double-clicking it in the Paths palette. In the Save Path dialog box that appears, simply type the new path name and click OK (see Figure 13.7).

FIGURE 13.6.

When Tolerance is set correctly, the path matches the selection satisfactorily.

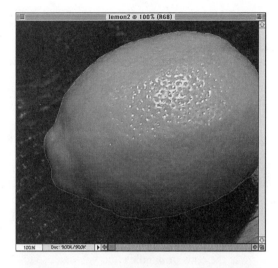

FIGURE 13.7.

Rename paths by using the Save Path dialog box.

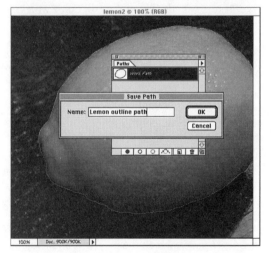

13

Although renaming paths isn't required, it's a good idea, especially if your Photoshop document will eventually have multiple paths in it. If you don't rename a path and then create a second path, the second path *replaces* the first path in the Paths palette. Don't worry: Both paths will still exist, and you can still recover the first path by selecting it and choosing Save Paths from the Paths palette pull-down menu. But if that seems like too much hassle and confusion to you, simply rename each path as you create it!

Paths Via the Pen Tool

Sometimes making a selection is too difficult or requires too much work on a particular image. In that case, consider using the Pen tool and drawing the path by hand.

If you've used vector-based illustration programs, such as Adobe Illustrator or Macromedia FreeHand, you already know about Bézier-based drawing tools like Photoshop's Pen tool. If you haven't used these kinds of tools before, you should know right up front that it takes a little practice, but the payoff is worth the effort.

NEW TO VERSION 5 And there's more good news in Photoshop 5. The new Magnetic Pen tool (available through the Pen Tool pop-out menu) makes drawing around a complicated object much easier, and the Freeform Pen tool gives you the power to draw any kind of line you want—straight, curved, squiggily—and turn it into a path.

NEW TERM A *Bézier curve* is a curve defined by three points: one on the curve and two outside the curve at the ends of handles that you can use to change the angle and direction of the curve. If this sounds like gibberish, don't worry; you'll see some examples.

The best way to learn how to use the Pen tool is simply to play around with it in a new Photoshop document, so that's what we're going to do in this tutorial:

1. First create a new Photoshop document big enough to move around in. Six × six inches sounds good, and a plain white background looks good.

2. Select the Pen tool. (It looks like a pen point.) Also make sure that the Paths palette is visible.

3. Click somewhere near the left edge of the image. This is where your path begins. (Notice that Photoshop immediately creates a path called "Work Path" in the Paths palette. This path can be renamed the same way as in the previous section.)

4. To draw a straight line, simply move your cursor and click somewhere else. You've just created a *Corner point*, which means that Photoshop connects the two points with a straight line (see Figure 13.8).

5. To continue the path but now with a curved line, move your cursor to the middle bottom of the window and then click and drag left. You'll see a curve immediately appear and change as you drag it (see Figure 13.9). You've just created a *Smooth point*, which means that Photoshop creates a smooth curve where two curved line segments meet.

FIGURE 13.8.

*A simple click creates
a Corner point and a
straight line.*

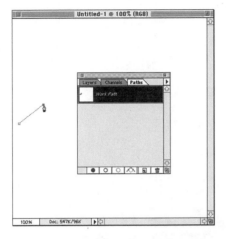

FIGURE 13.9.

*A click-and-drag
action creates a
Smooth point and a
curved line.*

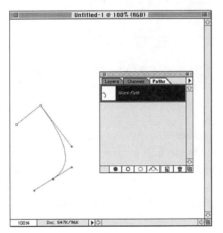

6. To make this clearer, draw another smooth curve. Move your cursor to the center
   of the window; then click and drag to the right and a bit down. Again a smooth
   point and a curve are created (see Figure 13.10).

   Notice the point you created in step 5. It creates a nice smooth curve between the
   point you just created and the point you created in step 4. That's what a Smooth
   point is all about.

   As you have no doubt noticed, creating Smooth points also results in the appearance of two *handles* for each point. These handles can be used to change the angle
   and direction of a curve after you've initially established it. You'll learn more about
   them in the "Editing Paths" section later in this chapter.

13

FIGURE 13.10.

*Click and drag to cre-
ate another Smooth
point on the same
path.*

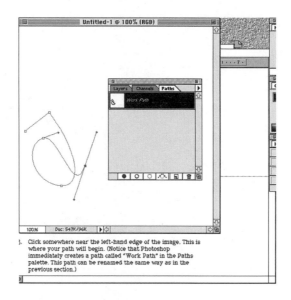

3. Click somewhere near the left-hand edge of the image. This is
   where your path will begin. (Notice that Photoshop
   immediately creates a path called "Work Path" in the Paths
   palette. This path can be renamed the same way as in the
   previous section.)

Okay, that's the basics: straight lines via Corner points and curved lines via Smooth
points. But there's more that you have to know about each one to use them effectively.

Corner Points

Corner points are easy. No matter what kind of line is coming into a Corner point, the
result is always an angle, not a curve. If a curved line comes into a Corner point, it's the
Smooth point at the other end of that line that affects the line's angle (see Figure 13.11).

FIGURE 13.11.

*Corner points surround
Smooth points.*

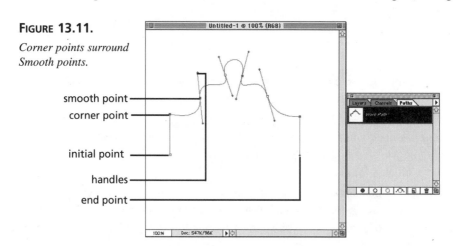

smooth point
corner point

initial point

handles

end point

If you want to constrain Corner points so they appear only at 45- or 90-degree angles, hold down the Shift key while you click to create the point.

Smooth Points

As you saw in the first Pen tool example, the behavior of Smooth points is a bit more complicated and takes some getting used to. A Smooth point always tries to create as smooth a curve as it can between two meeting lines (see Figure 13.12).

FIGURE 13.12.

Smooth points do their utmost to create curves out of any situation.

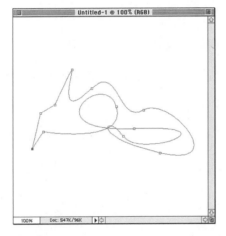

There is a less smooth kind of curve you can create when you need it. It's called a *Sharp curve*, and here is how you create one:

1. In a new Photoshop document, begin a path with an initial point.

2. Create a Smooth point as you normally would, making one curve.

3. Move the pointer so that it's exactly over the Smooth point you just created. Hold down (Option) [Alt] while you click and drag the mouse in the direction of the bump in the new curve. Release the key and mouse button. Your screen should now look something like what you see in Figure 13.13.

4. Move the cursor to where you want the line to end; then click and drag in the opposite direction you dragged in step 3. Figure 13.14 shows the resulting Sharp curve.

13

FIGURE 13.13.

Creating a Sharp curve. The rightmost line is what I just created by using the Option (or Alt) key.

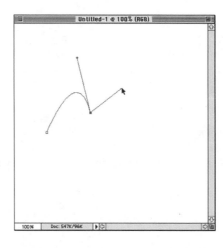

FIGURE 13.14.

The final Sharp curve.

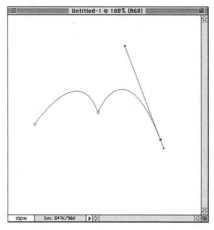

Previewing the Path

When you're creating all these points and lines, there's a preview feature that can be very helpful. Double-click the Pen tool in the toolbar to bring up the Pen Tool Options palette. The only option here is called Rubber Band. Activating this feature enables you to preview both straight lines and curves before you click to create them. Experiment to see this feature at work.

Completing the Path

To complete a path, you have two choices: "close" the path by connecting the final point to the initial point, or leave the path "open."

A closed path means you have created a "loop," so the final path has no beginning or end. To close a path, use the following steps:

1. Create a path by using whatever points you need.

2. After the last point, move your cursor so that it appears on top of your initial point. You'll see a small circle next to the Pen pointer.

3. Click to create a final corner point, or click and drag to create a final curve (see Figure 13.15).

FIGURE 13.15.

Closing a path with a final corner point click.

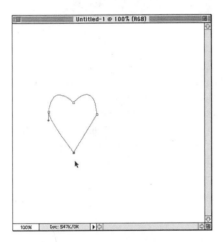

An open path means the path has a beginning and an end. Figures 13.8 through 13.14 have all been open paths. To end a path that you want to keep open, use the following steps:

1. Create a path by using whatever points you need.

2. After the last point, simply click the Pen tool icon in the toolbar. The path now has an end.

   The next time you click in the image, you'll be starting a new path instead of continuing your previous path.

Another Way to Make Paths

There's also another way to create a path from a selection. Make a selection and then simply click the Make Work Path button at the bottom of the Paths palette (see Figure 13.16). Photoshop creates the path automatically by using the existing Tolerance setting. Don't forget to rename the path using the Save Path dialog box!

13

FIGURE 13.16.

Here I'm creating a new path around the flower. Photoshop will use the same 1-pixel setting I used earlier.

Saying that you've created a "path" is a little misleading. Actually, the path that you see consists of a number of subpaths that Photoshop has created, but for our purposes, they act as a single path. One thing to remember is that any path you create is not really *part* of the image. That is, you aren't changing the actual image at all. Think of it as adding a new layer to an image, like a layer of clear acetate that helps you manipulate an image better but doesn't necessarily alter it in any way.

Editing Paths

Most of the time, the initial path you create, whether produced by converting a selection or drawing with the Pen tool, won't be perfect. It's often too difficult to get the selection just right or the lines and curves perfectly placed on the first try. You have probably already realized this while following the previous steps in this chapter.

Fortunately you can easily alter paths after they are created and, once again, you use the Pen tool (and its associated tools) to do this.

The Path Tools

First, let's look at the various Path tools available in Photoshop. Click and hold on the Pen tool. (see Figure 13.17):

- **Pen tool**: You already know this tool intimately. It's used to create new paths.
- **Magnetic Pen tool**: This is a new improved Pen tool that makes it easier to trace edges of an object by seeking out contrasts in pixel color. Use its Options box to set path width, edge contrast, and so on.

FIGURE 13.17.

Photoshop's Path tools.

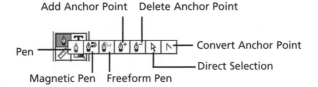

- **Freeform Pen tool**: As the name suggests, you can use this tool to draw a freeform path in any shape or direction. Photoshop will add the necessary points and handles as you go, so you can adjust any part of your path that's not quite what you had in mind.

- **Add Anchor Point tool**: Use this tool to add points to a path.

- **Delete Anchor Point tool**: Use this tool to cut points from a path.

- **Direct Selection tool**: This is the tool to use for selecting and moving points and handles. Hold down (Command) [Control] while using any other Path tool, and this tool replaces the other as long as the key is held down.

- **Convert Anchor Point tool**: Yes, you can even change the *type* of point after you have initially created it. For example, you can turn a Corner point into a Smooth point, a Smooth point into a Sharp curve, and so on. You'll learn more about this tool in the next section.

NEW TERM You can switch between these tools in one of two ways: either by clicking and holding down over the Pen tool in the toolbar, so the other Path tools appear, or by pressing Shift+P on the keyboard, which cycles through the three Pen tools. Pressing the plus sign brings up the Add Anchor Point tool, and pressing the minus sign turns the Pen into the Delete Anchor Point tool. Pressing Shift+A gives you the Direct Selection tool, as does pressing (Command) [Control] while using any other Path tool.

Basic Path Techniques

You've probably already figured these out on your own, but just in case, here are a few basic techniques for navigating among and using paths:

- To select a path, simply click its name in the Paths palette, just as you'd click a layer to activate it. Selected paths show up in your image, as you'd expect.

- To deselect a path, click another path name or click elsewhere in the empty area of the Paths palette. This makes the path disappear from the main window.

- To delete a path, select the path in the Paths palette and drag it to the Trash Can button at the bottom of the palette, just as you'd delete a layer.

13

- To create a new path, you can do one of three things: simply start drawing the path in the main image window; choose New Path from the palette's pulldown menu; or click the Create New Path button at the bottom of the palette.

- To duplicate a path, select the desired path in the palette and drag it to the Create New Path button. This works in the same manner as duplicating a layer does.

Using Paths

So what can you do with paths after you've gone to all the trouble of creating them? Well, a lot of things. In Photoshop, you can use paths to remember selections that you want to use repeatedly. You can also fill a path area or define the color, border, and so on of the outline of the path. Paths indicate selections or lines, but they don't actually appear on your canvas unless you add some paint to them to make them show up. You can fill a path or stroke it, or both. Stroking adds a stroke of paint over the path. Fill places a color or pattern inside the path. Figure 13.18 shows freeform paths that have been stroked with black and filled with gray.

FIGURE 13.18.

Filled and stroked paths. The leaf has not yet been stroked.

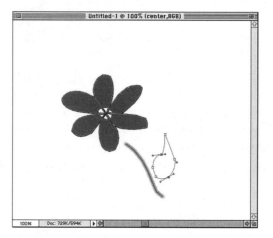

When you fill a path, you are adding pixels to the active layer of your picture. Make sure that the layer you want to put the paint on is the active one.

Turning Paths into Selections

In Photoshop, paths are most useful as permanently saved selections. This can be incredibly helpful when you think you might want to reuse a specific selection later. When in doubt, create a path so that the selection will always be available.

You already learned how to convert a selection to a path. Here's how to convert a path into a selection:

1. Create a path through whatever means suit your fancy.
2. Activate the path you want to convert by clicking it in the Paths palette.
3. Choose Make Selection from the pulldown menu at the top-right of the Paths palette.
4. In the Make Selection dialog box that appears, you can set the Tolerance of the selection that Photoshop creates (see Figure 13.19). The higher the Feather Radius setting, the less exact the selection will be.

FIGURE 13.19.

The Make Selection dialog box.

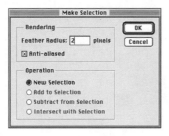

Click OK and you'll see the path turn into a selection.

Filling a Path

Filling a path means just what you'd expect. Select a path, choose Fill Path from the pulldown Palette menu, and you'll get the same kinds of options you get for filling a selection (see Figure 13.20). In the Fill Path dialog box, you can choose a color, a pattern, or a snapshot to fill the area with. You can also choose a Blending mode, opacity percentage, optional transparency, anti-aliasing, and a Feathering value (everything you already learned about in Day 2).

Stroking a Path

Stroking a path means affecting the outline of the path, not the entire area enclosed within a path. Select a path and then choose Stroke Path from the pulldown Palette menu. The dialog box enables you to choose the tool you want to use, from Pencil and Paintbrush to Blur and Sponge.

13

FIGURE 13.20.

The Fill Path dialog box.

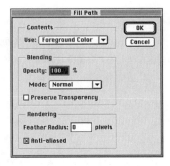

Whatever tool you pick, Photoshop uses that tool's current settings to create the result. So, for example, if you want to airbrush the path outline with only 60% pressure, make sure that value is set in the Airbrush Options palette *before* you select Stroke Path (refer to Figure 13.21).

FIGURE 13.21.

Stroke Path dialog box.

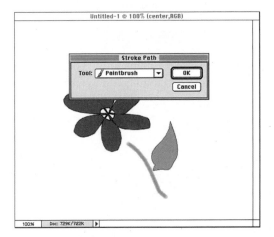

By the way, there are shortcuts for filling and for stroking. Hold your mouse pointer over the buttons at the bottom of the Paths palette, and you'll see the options.

Summary

The path is a magical Photoshop feature that has many applications in your daily Photoshop existence. You can use paths as permanent Photoshop selections that can be reused anytime, as methods to fill or stroke part of an image, as a way to convert areas of an image or work on an image in Illustrator, or as Clipping paths to be exported into a page layout program. Photoshop provides an array of tools and options for creating paths: you can do so by converting a selection you have already made, or by drawing a path from scratch by using the Pen tool. You can also edit existing paths with the assorted Path tools.

Q&A

Q How can I use paths to draw shapes onto my pictures?

A Select the appropriate Pen tool and draw the path you need. If you need a geometric shape, remember that pressing the Shift key will constrain the path to a 90 or 45 degree angle. Once you have placed the path, stroke it or fill it as necessary to create an outline or filled shape.

Q What does the Magnetic Pen do that the others don't?

A The Magnetic Pen bases its selection on contrast. This automates path creation to some degree, as you don't have to rely on your own hand-eye coordination to follow a complex path.

Quiz

Let's see how well you've followed the path of knowledge...

Questions

1. What does it mean to "stroke" a path?

   a. Using the points and Bézier handles to refine its shape.

   b. Adding a color to it so it becomes a line.

   c. Painting over it with short strokes.

2. How do you turn a selection into a path?

   a. Select it and press Command-P.

   b. Select Make Path or Make Work Path from the Paths pop-out menu.

   c. Line it with bricks.

13

Answers

1. b
2. b

Activity

Start a new page and use the Pen tool to draw a star-shaped path and a freeform path with lots of curves. Stroke both of these paths with a color. Then use the Magnetic Pen tool to trace around them. Notice that, as long as you stay fairly close to your original line, the Pen tool places a path right at the edge of the line. Fill these shapes with a color. Draw two more paths inside these shapes, and fill them with a different color. Practice with the Pen tools, adding points and refining your paths until you're comfortable with the Path tools.

HOUR 14

Filters That Improve Your Picture

I'm not sure whether Photoshop's creators pioneered the idea of plug-in filters or just took the ball and ran with it. In either case, they've given us a wonderful tool for altering the all-over appearance of a picture. Some of Photoshop's filters are strange. Some are beautiful. Some are merely useful, and those are the ones we'll look at in this Hour.

The title for this Hour's lesson doesn't really tell the story. Presumably you wouldn't apply a filter that *didn't* improve your picture. What would be the point? It might be more correct to say that the filters we'll be looking at will fix common photographic problems.

Sharpen Filters

One of the most common problems photographers face is the out of focus picture. There are many reasons why a picture might be fuzzy. Either the subject or the photographer might have moved slightly. Perhaps the camera wasn't focused correctly, or possibly the picture was taken by an inexpensive camera with a poor quality plastic lens. Some of these problems are easier to compensate for than others.

If a photo is way out of focus, there's not much that can be done to bring it back. If it's just a little bit soft, Photoshop can at least create the illusion of sharper focus. It does this with a set of filters called Sharpen. Like all the filters described in this chapter, they're found on the Filter menu (see Figure 14.1).

FIGURE 14.1.

The Filter menu.

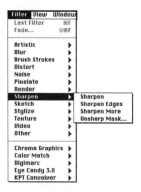

Sharpen, More

The first two Sharpen filters, Sharpen and Sharpen More, provide different amounts of the same function. They work by finding areas in the image where there are significant color changes, such as at the edges of an object. Whenever such an area is found, Photoshop increases the contrast between adjacent pixels, making the lights lighter and the darks darker. Figure 14.2 shows three views of a slightly fuzzy picture of a bowl of mushrooms. The first example is before sharpening. The second example has had Sharpen applied, and the third Sharpen More.

If you don't enlarge the picture too much, the effect looks quite good. If you take a close look, as we have in Figure 14.3, you can see that it's really quite artificial looking.

By the way, Sharpen More is the same effect as applying the Sharpen filter twice to the same picture. Keep in mind that you can do this anytime a filter has less than the desired effect. The easy way to apply the same filter again is to press (Command-F) [Control-F]. This keyboard shortcut applies whatever filter and filter settings (if any) you applied last.

Try the Sharpen filter on one of your own fuzzy pictures and see what you think. Does it help? Try the Sharpen More filter also. These are great for adjusting slightly out of focus photographs or scans, but don't rely on these filters too much. They can only do so much. They can't add what is totally missing from the image—namely, focus and good contrast. They can, however, help bring back a photo that's just a little bit off.

FIGURE 14.2.

Before and after sharpening.

Original

Sharpen

Sharpen More

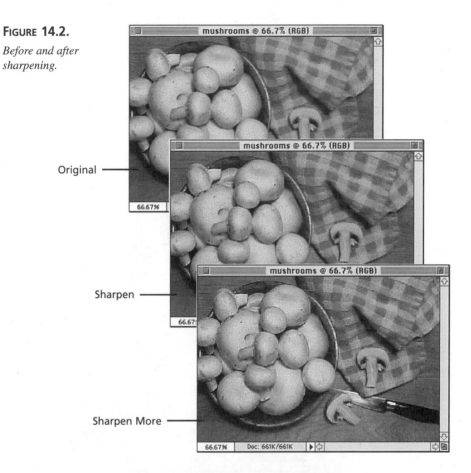

FIGURE 14.3.

Sharpen More magnified to 200%.

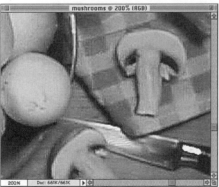

14

Sharpen Edges

Sharpen Edges is a truly useful filter. It doesn't affect the whole image, so you don't get as much of a sense of that harsh blocky effect as with Sharpen More, but it sees and enhances the contrast at whatever it perceives to be an edge. Figure 14.4 shows a before and after version of our mushrooms. Sharpening the edges has a slight but noticeable effect on the quality of the photo.

FIGURE **14.4.**

Sharpen Edges filter.

Unsharp Mask

Unsharp masking is a traditional technique used in the printing industry for many years. It is probably your best bet for precision sharpening. It corrects blurring in the original image or scan as well as any blurring that occurs during the resampling and printing process. The Unsharp Mask works by locating every two adjacent pixels with a difference in Brightness values that you have specified, and increases their contrast by an amount that you specify. It allows you to really control the sharpness of an image.

Set the amount in the dialog box for the level of sharpening you need. Figure 14.5 shows the Unsharp Mask dialog box. The Radius control sets the number of surrounding pixels to which the sharpening effect is applied. I suggest that you keep the radius fairly low—around 2.0. The Threshold setting controls how much alike the pixels must be in order to be sharpened. The lower the setting, the more similar the pixels have to be. The higher the setting, the greater Photoshop's tolerance of difference. (Of course, as always, feel free to go wild and try all the settings. That is the best way to learn.)

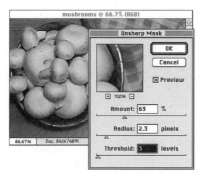

FIGURE 14.5.

The window lets you see what effect your settings have.

Many Photoshop experts recommend always applying the Unsharp Mask filter to every image that you process, whether it's going to be printed or used on the Web. (I personally don't like to say "always" or "never" because there can be exceptions to any rule.) You should probably *try* it on every image, to see whether you like the effect.

> Photoshop filters aren't restricted to Photoshop. Other Adobe products, such as PageMaker and Illustrator, can use them also. Even Macromedia's Director can employ many Photoshop filters. If you find particularly useful or interesting filters or filter combinations, try using them with other Photoshop plug-in compatible programs.

Blur Filters

The Blur filters (Filter→Blur) are useful tools when you want to soften the effects, either of a filter you have just applied or of brushstrokes in the painting. Blurring can gently smooth a harshly lit portrait or, when used on a selection instead of the whole image, can throw an unwanted background out of focus, making it less obtrusive. The Blur filters include:

- Blur
- Blur More
- Gaussian Blur
- Radial Blur

14

- Smart Blur

- Motion Blur

Blur, Blur More

There are two basic Blur filters: Blur and Blur More. They do exactly as their names suggest. Blur is very subtle. Blur More is only a little less so. Figure 14.6 shows a comparison of the two, against a non-blurred original. As you can see, the changes are minor. Blurring doesn't make much difference, but it can smooth out wrinkles in a portrait or soften a hard edge.

FIGURE 14.6.

You have to look carefully to see the effect.

No blur

Blur

Blur More

Gaussian Blur

You can apply the blur filter several times in order to get the effect you want or you can move on to Gaussian Blur (Filter→Blur→Gaussian Blur), which is a more controllable one. It uses a mathematical formula (the Gaussian Distribution Equation or bell curve) to calculate the precise transition between each pair of pixels. The result of this is that most of the blurred pixels end up in the middle of the two colors or values, rather than at either end of the spectrum, producing a generalized blur that neither darkens or lightens the image.

The Gaussian Blur dialog box, shown in Figure 14.7, lets you determine exactly how much Blur to apply by setting a Radius value from .1 to 255. You can also use it to anti-alias the edges of an object, and to blur shadow areas when you want to create a drop shadow effect. Even at fairly small settings, it has quite a dramatic effect. Anything over

5.0 would make the image incomprehensible. Notice how the subject's eye wrinkles, obvious in the large picture, are almost gone in the Blur Preview window.

FIGURE 14.7.

Smaller numbers give you less blur.

The Gaussian Blur is a useful retouching tool when applied to an area within the picture that you want to de-emphasize. The photo in Figure 14.8 was shot at a wildlife park in Canada. The tiger looks very happy, lying in his patch of sunshine, but we can also see the chainlink fence behind him and the wire-wrapped tree he's leaning against. The picture would be nicer if we got rid of these reminders of civilization. Obviously, we don't want to blur the tiger's stripes. So rather than applying Blur to the whole image, we need to select the fence and tree. Clicking the Magic Wand tool on the area in question selects it, and then we can adjust the Blur radius until the fencing disappears.

FIGURE 14.8.

Selective blurring can hide flaws, too.

14

Careful inspection shows that while the Blur filter took out most of the fence, there are still a few spots on the tree where we can see chain links. A quick application of the Blur tool, with Pressure set to 75%, blends these in and the tiger appears to be back in the wilderness again.

> Use the Blur filters when you have a large area to blur. Use the Blur tool when you just want to soften a small area. It's more controllable in terms of the degree of focus change it applies.

Radial Blur

The Radial Blur filter can be interesting if you carefully choose how to apply it. It gives you two choices: Spin and Zoom. Spin mode gives you a blur that looks as if the image is spinning around its center point. Zoom mode theoretically gives you the effect of zooming the camera into or away from the image.

Figure 14.9 shows the Radial Blur dialog box. In it, you can set both an amount for the Blur effect (from 1 to 100) and a Quality level (Draft, Good, or Best). Amount apparently refers to the distance that the pixels are moved to created the Blur. You can see the difference in the window as you set the Blur amount. You can use the same window to determine a center point for the Blur effect.

FIGURE 14.9.

The same dialog box applies both Zoom and Spin.

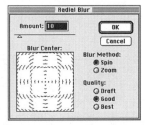

The Quality setting determines the manner in which the Blur effect is calculated; you can choose Draft, Good, or Best. There's very little difference in quality between Good and Best. The biggest difference, in fact, is not in the image quality, but in how long it takes Photoshop to compute and apply the Blur in each mode. Best can take quite a long time if the image is complex and your computer is an older model.

In Figure 14.10, I've applied Spin and Zoom blurring to a picture of a Fuji chrysanthemum. The original image is shown at the top left, then the Spin, and finally Zoom. After experimenting with the settings, I used 10 as the amount to spin and 65 as the Zoom setting.

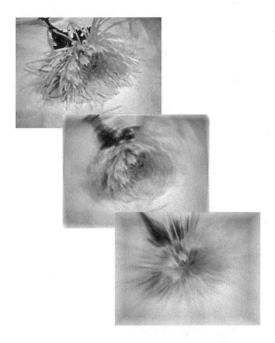

Smart Blur

The Smart Blur filter (Filter→Blur→Smart Blur) is probably the most useful one of the
bunch, especially for image editing and photo repair. It blurs everything in the image, or
selection, except the edges. Smart Blur calculates the differences between color regions
to determine boundaries, and it maintains these boundaries while blurring everything
within them. It's the perfect filter when you need to take 10 years off a portrait subject's
face, smooth out teenaged skin, or get rid of the texture in a piece of cloth without losing
the folds.

Figure 14.11 shows the Smart Blur filter dialog box and Figure 14.12 shows before and
after views of the filter applied to a portrait. You can set the Radius and Threshold to
determine how much blur is applied, and also the Quality, as above, to determine how
the effect is calculated.

14

FIGURE 14.11.

The Smart Blur filter dialog box.

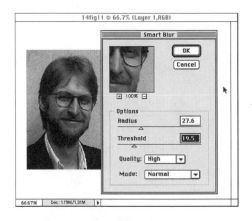

FIGURE 14.12.

On the left: before; on the right: after. Notice how the Smart Blur has despotted the background, too.

The Smart Blur filter has three modes:

- In Normal mode, the Preview window shows the effects of the blurring.
- Edge Only shows you the outlines that Smart Blur is working with.
- Edge Overlay shows the outlines as black lines on top of the image.

You can use Edge Overlay or Edge Only to help you determine what Threshold to set. Convert the mode back to Normal before you click OK to apply the effect.

Motion Blur

When we see lines drawn behind a car, a cat, or a comic strip character, we instinctively know that it or he is supposed to be in motion. Those lines represent "motion blur," which is actually a photographic mistake caused by using a slow shutter speed on a fast subject. The image appears blurred against its background because it actually travels some distance during the fraction of a second that the camera shutter was open.

In the early days of photography, motion blur was a common occurrence, simply because shutter speeds were slow and film sensitivity was not very great. Today motion blur is unusual unless the photographer is planning to try to capture the subject this way on purpose, by using the least sensitive film available and/or using a small lens opening and a correspondingly slower shutter. If you want to try to approximate the effect of motion blur, however, Photoshop gives you a tool that can do it.

The Motion Blur tool (Filter→Blur→Motion Blur) can add the appearance of motion to a stationary object by placing a directional blur for a predetermined distance. In the Motion Blur dialog box shown in Figure 14.13, you can set both the distance and direction of the blur according to how fast and in what direction you want the object to appear to be traveling. The distance sets how much of a blur is applied—or how far the original image is "moved." The angle sets the direction of the blur. To adjust, drag the Radius icon or enter precise values into the field next to it. The trick, however, is to select the right area to which to apply it. To get a convincing blur, you need to blur the space where the object theoretically was, as well as where it theoretically has moved to.

FIGURE 14.13.

Using the Motion Blur is tricky at best.

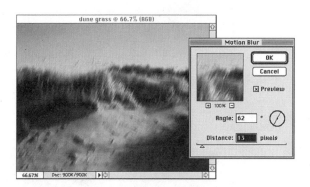

The Motion Blur filter doesn't do much for most pictures. After all, the blur caused by the camera shaking is the kind of thing we try to avoid, not add. But for some special effects, and for doing tricks with type, it has interesting possibilities. Figure 14.14 shows one possible use. Adding Motion Blur gave us a much zoomier Zoom, but we could take this even further.

This time I took the word apart, cutting and pasting each letter to a different layer. I then applied a different (increasing left to right) number of pixels to each Motion Blur, from 6 pixels on the Z to 24 pixels on the M. The resulting Zoom almost seems to be sliding into the screen, shown in Figure 14.15.

14

FIGURE 14.14.

You can't Zoom standing still.

FIGURE 14.15.

Using layers lets you apply different filters or different degrees of filter to the same image.

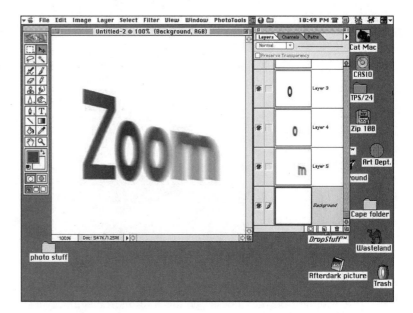

The type used in this exercise was generated with Adobe Type Twister, a wonderful little program that lets you do all sorts of strange and occasionally beautiful things to typography. If you do any Web publishing or desktop publishing, you ought to have it available. You can buy it from your friendly software dealer and it's often bundled with Adobe fonts or drawing programs.

Fading Filters

Filters are cool, but sometimes they just do a little too much to the image. Many, like the Motion Blur filter, are variable. You can set their effects to be as subtle or dramatic as you wish. Others, like the basic Blur and Sharpen, don't have dialog boxes and don't give you the opportunity to apply any less than the full amount of effect that Photoshop thinks is right. Well, Papa Photoshop *doesn't* always know best, but you do have an option.

You can apply a filter and then open Filter→Fade to fade the effect anywhere from 1 to 99%. You can also use the Fade box to set a Blending mode for the Fade effect. Even more important, in the same dialog box, shown in Figure 14.16, you can fade whatever you last did. You painted something but the color was too strong? Fade it 50%. That's quicker than redoing it with a different color. You overdid an image color adjustment? Fade it. Experiment with this feature. It can save you tons of time.

FIGURE 14.16.

The Fade dialog box.

To fade a Filter effect or color adjustment:

1. Apply the Filter or make the color adjustment (Image→Adjust...).
2. Choose Filter→Fade. If you're working on a selection, rather than the whole image, don't deselect it.
3. Set the Preview option so you can see the effect of the fade.
4. Drag the slider to adjust the opacity.
5. Choose a Blending mode other than normal, if you want a particular effect.
6. Click OK. Deselect the selection to merge it.

Summary

Photoshop's filters are the tools that make the program a "must have" for anyone working with photos. In this Hour we looked at the Photoshop filters that can help you "rescue" a bad photo or bad scan. The Sharpen filters can restore the apparent focus of out of focus photographs by increasing the contrast between adjacent pixels. The most useful of these is the Unsharp Mask filter, which allows you to set the parameters for how it finds and adjusts contrasts.

14

Blur filters come in several varieties and are most useful for putting unwanted parts of the picture out of focus and for softening hard edges. Motion Blur filters let you create the illusion of movement in stationary objects and can do interesting things to type.

Fade works with filters and with other Photoshop tools to decrease the effect of your action by a percentage you can set.

Q&A

Q. What's the difference between the Blur filter and the Blur tool?

A. You can apply the Blur tool as if it were a paintbrush to as small an area as you want. The Blur filter blurs the entire image or selection evenly.

Q. If I change my mind about applying a filter, can I stop the process?

A. To cancel the filter as it's being applied, press (Command-period)[Esc]. To undo a filter, use the Undo command: (Command-Z) [Control-Z]. If it's too late to undo, use the History palette to revert to a stage before you applied the filter.

Quiz

Were you paying attention?

Questions

1. Sharpen More applies _____ as much correction as Sharpen.

   a. exactly

   b. twice

   c. half again

2. Gaussian Blur uses a _____ to determine how blur is applied.

   a. mathematical formula

   b. random memory algorithm

   c. prismatic crystal filter

3. Many experts advise applying which filter to every photograph you bring into Photoshop?

   a. Sharpen

   b. Gaussian Blur

   c. Unsharp Mask

4. Fading a filter has this effect:

   a. It fades an action such as applying a filter according to a percentage you determine.

   b. It applies the filter at half strength.

   c. It applies a 50% gray tone over the filter.

Answers

1. b
2. a
3. c
4. a

Activity

Find or shoot a picture of yourself or a friend, and load it into Photoshop. (If you don't have a digital camera or scanner, download a newsphoto from the Web, or a portrait from our Web site.) Use the Blur and Sharpen filters to improve it. Find and remove wrinkles, eye bags, uneven complexions, and any other flaws. Save your work—we'll come back to it later.

14

Hour 15

Filters to Make Your Picture Artistic

In Hour 10, "Advanced Painting Techniques," you saw how Photoshop's filters can help imitate other media. You looked specifically at the Watercolor, Colored Pencil, Charcoal, and Underpainting filters. But those are still just the tip of the iceberg. Under the general heading of Artistic and Sketch filters, Photoshop offers approximately thirty different filters that you can apply alone or in combinations to turn your so-so picture into a masterpiece. In this Hour, you run through the alphabet of the artistic, brush stroke, and sketch effects. You will be amazed, boggled, confounded, delighted, ecstatic....

I've deliberately left out the step-by-step instructions in this chapter. You apply all of these filters in the same way: Filter→ Artistic→ and so on. Use the dialog box and its preview window to judge the effects of the filters as you change the settings. The key to success with any of these filters is to experiment until you get the effect you want. If you don't like what you see when you apply a filter to the whole picture, Undo or Revert.

Artistic Filters

Artistic filters apply a certain amount of abstraction to your image. How much depends on the kind of filter and to an even greater degree on how you set the filter's variables. Many of these filters ask you to set brush size, detail, and texture. Brush size affects the thickness of the line. Detail determines how large a "clump" of pixels must be, so that the filter will, in effect, notice it and apply its changes. Texture, not to be confused with the Texturizer filter, simply adds a random smudge here and there in your image.

Most of Photoshop's filters have a preview window, in which you can see the effects of changing the settings before you actually apply the filter. To move the image inside the preview window, click on it. The cursor turns into a hand, enabling you to slide the picture around to see the effect on specific parts of the image. If you change settings and the preview doesn't change right away, you see a thin line between the plus and minus symbols, beneath the magnification amount number. This line tells you that Photoshop is calculating the changes to apply. Click the plus or minus symbol to see a reduced or enlarged view within the preview window.

For the sake of consistency, let's apply all of the "artistic" filters to a picture of the Eastham windmill on Cape Cod. See Figure 15.1 for the unfiltered view.

Colored Pencil

The Colored Pencil filter goes over the photo with a sort of cross-hatched effect (see Figure 15.2). It keeps most of the colors of the original photograph, though any large, flat areas are translated to "paper" color, which you can set to any shade of gray from black to white. The filter's Options box, shown in Figure 15.3, asks you to choose a Pencil Width and Stroke Pressure as well.

FIGURE 15.1.

*Basic, non-artistic
photo.*

FIGURE 15.2.

Colored Pencil filter.

Using a narrow pencil (low number) gives you more lines. Greater Stroke Pressure picks up more detail from the original picture. In Figure 15.2, we used a small pencil and heavy pressure. In Figure 15.4, we reversed these, using a Pencil Width of 22 and a Stroke Pressure of 2. As you can see, the result is quite different.

FIGURE 15.3.

Colored Pencil filter settings.

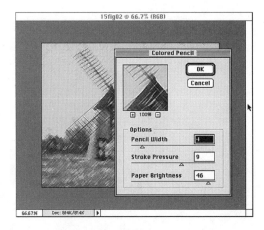

FIGURE 15.4.

More pencil, less pressure.

Cutout

The Cutout filter is one of my favorites. It can reduce your picture to something resembling a cut paper collage or a silk-screen print. The Cutout filter does this by averaging all of the colors and shades and converting them to just a handful. You can decide how many by setting a number of levels from 2 to 8 in its Options dialog window. You can also set Edge Fidelity (1–3) and Edge Simplicity (1–10) in the dialog box, which is shown in Figure 15.5.

FIGURE 15.5.

Cutout filter dialog box.

Low Simplicity and high Fidelity settings produced the picture in Figure 15.6, which seems to be the most pleasing variation for this filter and photo combination. It's important to experiment with different settings every time you apply a filter to a new photo. What works with one picture might be totally wrong for another that is more, or less, complicated. In one combination or another, this filter manages to make almost any picture look good.

FIGURE 15.6.

Cutout filter applied.

Dry Brush

Dry brush is a term used by watercolor painters to denote a particular style in which the brush is loaded with heavily concentrated pigment and dabbed, rather than stroked, on the paper. Figure 15.7 shows the Dry Brush Options box with a small Brush Size and a high Brush Detail. You can see the result in Figure 15.8.

FIGURE 15.7.

*Dry Brush filter
dialog box.*

FIGURE 15.8.

*The Dry Brush filter
can look very cool
when applied to the
right picture.*

Film Grain

One of the reasons that many commercial photographers are turning to high resolution
digital photography is to get away from the problems caused by film grain. Film grain is
the inevitable result of applying a layer of chemicals to a piece of plastic. When a picture
is enlarged a great deal, you see the graininess of the chemicals as specks in the picture.
Why Photoshop's creators decided this was an effect worth achieving is beyond me. But
it can add an interesting texture quality to your pictures, if you apply it carefully. Apply
the Film Grain effect to selections, rather than to the whole photo. Figure 15.9 shows
what happens when it's misapplied.

15

FIGURE 15.9.

Bad use of the Film Grain filter.

Notice how the Film Grain filter picks up the shading in the sky. It makes the picture look gritty. A better use is shown in Figure 15.10, where the grain is applied just to the background, keeping the shiny peppers free of it. The contrast in textures makes the picture more interesting. This used the following settings: Grain –4; Highlight area –2; Intensity –8.

FIGURE 15.10.

Better use of the Film Grain filter.

Fresco

Fresco is an Italian term for a mural painting done on a wet, freshly plastered wall. Photoshop's Fresco filter has little resemblance to the classical fresco works by such artists as Botticelli or Michaelangelo. However, it's an interesting filter—and possibly useful. You need to be careful not to let the picture get too dark, because the Fresco filter adds a good deal of black to the image in the process of abstracting it. Figure 15.11 shows an example.

FIGURE 15.11.

A fresh approach—but not exactly a fresco.

Neon Glow

It's hard to understand how the Neon Glow filter got its name; it has no resemblance to neon. As you can probably tell in Figure 15.12, the Neon Glow filter reduces the image to a single color negative and adds white highlights around the edges of objects. You can choose a color in the dialog box and specify the width of the "glow." If you use a very light color or gray, it can produce an interesting watermark effect.

The Neon Glow filter, more than most, should be applied only to certain kinds of pictures. Although it might give you an interesting spaced-out, surrealist landscape, it does nothing at all for portraits.

FIGURE 15.12.

Neon Glow (?) filter.

15

Paint Daubs

The Paint Daub filter adds a square or wavy crosshatch texture to the image (see Figure 15.13). You can set Brush Size and Sharpness, and choose from several brushes. Shown here is the Dark Blurry brush. Experiment with the settings for this filter; some settings work much better than others. This one, although it darkens the picture a great deal, gives it a texture reminiscent of Van Gogh. (Of course, the subject matter helps, too.)

FIGURE 15.13.

Paint Daub filter.

Palette Knife and Plastic Wrap

When a painter uses a palette knife, the result is large areas of smudged color, blending interestingly at the edges. The Palette Knife filter, alas, doesn't do that. Instead, it reduces the picture to blocks of color by grouping similar pixels and averaging them. The result is not very interesting and not worth reproducing.

Plastic Wrap is another filter that probably should have been left in the bit bucket (the programmer's trash can). It places a gray film over the whole picture and then adds white "highlights" around large objects. The Plastic Wrap filter is supposed to look as if you covered the scene with plastic film. Instead, it looks more like you poured liquid latex over it. Again, this is a filter not worth bothering with.

Poster Edges

Here's a filter that *is* worth playing with (see Figure 15.14). Poster Edges locates all of the edges in your image, judging by the amount of contrast between adjacent pixels, and posterizes them, placing a dark line around the edges. Unfortunately, the Poster Edges filter also breaks up large flat areas, such as the sky in the sample picture. For best results, use it only on selected areas.

FIGURE 15.14.

Poster Edges filter.

Rough Pastels

Rough Pastels is a terrific filter with an interface that's a little bit more complicated than the others because you can specify Texture as well as the Stroke Length and Detail. Figure 15.15 shows the Rough Pastels dialog box. Choose from the textures supplied or import one from another source. (You can create textures and save them as Photoshop documents; then you can open them and apply them as textures through this dialog box or the Texturizer filter dialog box.)

FIGURE 15.15.

Rough Pastels filter dialog box.

The Stroke Length and Detail settings seem to give the best results in the middle of their respective ranges, but as always, experiment to see what works best for your image. Figure 15.16 shows the Rough Pastels filter applied to our windmill picture.

FIGURE 15.16.

Rough Pastels filter on Sandstone.

Smudge Stick

This is a tricky filter. On light colored areas, the Smudge Stick filter adds a subtle, rather spotty texture that can be quite nice. On dark areas and lines, it adds a smudge, making the lines heavier and the edges blurry. Figure 15.17 shows an example.

FIGURE 15.17.

Smudge Stick filter.

Sponge

Have you ever tried painting with a sponge? It's a technique that's taught in some of the finer preschools and kindergartens. Basically, you dab a sponge into poster paint and then dab it on the paper. The results can be very nice, especially if you skip the poster paint and go straight to Photoshop's Sponge filter. On large flat areas, the Sponge filter gives a good imitation of a coarse, natural sponge (the kind they sell in the Sponge Market in Key West). In areas of detail, the sponge is a smaller one. You can, in fact, set the Brush Size, Definition, and Smoothness in the Sponge filter dialog box. One possible result is shown in Figure 15.18.

Underpainting

The Underpainting filter, which you saw in Hour 10, the chapter on imitating media, reduces everything to a somewhat grayed out, paler, and soft-focused version of itself. Use it as an intermediate filter on the way to an effect, rather than by itself.

FIGURE 15.18.

Sponge filter.

15

Watercolor

In Hour 10, you learned ways to make a photo look like a watercolor. Unfortunately, applying the Watercolor filter isn't necessarily one of them. Figure 15.19 shows this filter applied to the sample image. The look isn't really watercolor, but it might have some uses. If you like the general effect of the Sponge filter, but it distorts your picture too much, try the Watercolor filter instead. It has the same "clumping" effect, but with smaller clumps.

FIGURE 15.19.

Watercolor filter.

Brush Stroke

For reasons known only to the folks at Adobe, the Brush Stroke filters aren't part of the "artistic" set. Artists use brushes, don't they? However, Photoshop's creators isolated these eight filters as the Brush Stroke set. What do they do? Let's take a look. Figure 15.20 is a picture of a rock formation in the aptly named Red Rock Canyon National Wilderness, near Las Vegas, NV.

FIGURE 15.20.

Red Rocks.

Accented Edges

Best if applied subtly, the Accented Edges filter enhances the contrast of edges. The dialog box enables you to choose Edge Width, Edge Brightness, and Smoothness. Figure 15.21 shows the filter applied.

Angled Strokes and Crosshatch

These filters give a crosshatched effect, similar to but darker than the one applied by the Colored Pencil filter. The Angled Strokes filter is less dramatic than the Crosshatch filter. Figure 15.22 shows both.

FIGURE 15.21.

Keep Edge Width small for best results.

15

FIGURE 15.22.

The Angled Strokes filter applied on the left and Crosshatch filter applied on the right.

Dark Strokes

You can only use the Dark Strokes filter with many images if you set the Black Intensity to 0 and the White Intensity to 10 in the dialog box. Otherwise, it tends to turn the whole picture black. Even with a relatively light picture, you need to keep the Black number low and the White setting high. Figure 15.23 shows a carefully balanced application of Dark Strokes.

FIGURE 15.23.

Dark Strokes filter.

I haven't found very many situations in which I'd choose the Dark Strokes filter. Perhaps you'll like it. As they say, "Different strokes for different folks."

Ink Outlines

The Ink Outlines filter first places a white line and then a black line around every edge that it identifies (see Figure 15.24). You can set Stroke Length and Intensity in the dialog box.

Applied to a still life or landscape, the Ink Outlines filter can give you the look of an old woodcut or steel engraving. If you use it on a portrait, however, it adds warts, blobs, and other potentially undesirable effects.

Spatter

The Spatter filter did nice things to the rocks in the sample picture but thoroughly messed up the edges where the mountain meets the sky (see Figure 15.25). This is a filter that's potentially useful but needs to be applied to selections rather than to the whole picture.

FIGURE 15.24.

Ink Outlines filter.

15

FIGURE 15.25.

Spatter filter.

Sprayed Strokes

Sprayed Strokes looks like spatter—but less messy. The interesting thing about the Sprayed Stokes filter is that you can control the direction of the spray. Figure 15.26 shows what it does to our picture. The settings for this variation were: Stroke Length and Spray Radius, both 14; Direction, Right Diagonal.

FIGURE 15.26.

Sprayed Strokes filter.

Sumi-e

Sumi-e is Japanese for brush painting, but the result of the Sumi-e filter looks like the work of a crazed Sumo wrestler, rather than a Zen master. This filter turns any area with any sort of detail almost completely black, even at the lowest settings. Forget this one.

Sketch Filters

Photoshop has fourteen different filters lumped under the Sketch heading. Some, such as Bas Relief, must have landed there by default. They have little or nothing to do with the process of sketching. Others, such as Conte Crayon or Chalk and Charcoal, are definitely sketch media. Figure 15.27 shows the sample image for these filters.

FIGURE 15.27.

*Fishing boat,
Plymouth, Mass.*

15

Bas Relief

The Bas Relief filter uses the foreground and background colors to create a low relief rendering of your picture. If you choose colors carefully, it can look like copper foil, hammered metal, or carved stone. Figure 15.28 shows the result.

FIGURE 15.28.

Use a dark background color for best results.

Chalk and Charcoal

With the Chalk and Charcoal filter, which reduces the image to three tones, you need to set the foreground to a dark color and the background to a light one. The third color, by default, is medium gray, so choose colors that work with it. This filter can produce really beautiful drawings. Figure 15.29 shows the filter applied; notice how nicely it retains the "wetness" and reflectivity of the water.

FIGURE 15.29.

Chalk and Charcoal filter.

Charcoal

The Charcoal filter does much the same thing as the Chalk and Charcoal filter, but uses only the foreground and background colors. It's more difficult to control because there are only two colors. Experiment until you are satisfied.

Chrome

The Chrome filter appears to be a close relative to the Plastic Wrap filter previously described. It's only slightly more successful. As you can see in Figure 15.30, any resemblance to real metal is purely coincidental. The Chrome filter removes the color from the image as part of its process.

FIGURE 15.30.

Chrome filter.

Conte Crayon

I *love* this filter—it's done good things to every picture I have ever used it on. Conte Crayon works like the Chalk and Charcoal filter previously described but with the addition of background textures, using the same interface you saw in the Rough Pastels dialog box. Figure 15.31 shows the boat rendered in Conte Crayon on a canvas background.

Graphic Pen, Halftone Pattern

These two filters do very similar things. Both reduce the image to whatever foreground and background colors you set. Graphic Pen then renders the image in slanting lines, whereas Halftone Pattern renders it in overlapping dots. Neither is particularly useful.

FIGURE 15.31.

Conte Crayon filter.

Note Paper, Plaster

I don't understand the name of this effect. I'd have called it Stucco, or maybe Flocked Wallpaper. See for yourself in Figure 15.32. The Note Paper filter uses the background and foreground colors, plus black for a shadow effect. Interesting, but...note paper? The Plaster filter is very similar but smooth instead of grainy, with the look of wet, runny, freshly poured plaster.

FIGURE 15.32.

Note Paper filter.

Photocopy, Reticulation, Stamp, Torn Edges

These four filters can be grouped together. They all, like many of the filters in this set, convert the image to a two-color copy of itself. The Stamp filter loses most of the detail, attempting to replicate a rubber stamp—not very successfully. Photocopy keeps most of the detail, giving the somewhat confusing image in Figure 15.33. Reticulation adds dot grain to the Stamp filter, so it looks as if you stamped the picture on coarse sandpaper. Torn Edges is the Stamp filter again, only with the edges of the image roughened.

FIGURE 15.33.

Photocopy filter.

Water Paper

The last one in the Sketch set is a strange filter. Once again, I don't know how they named it. To me, the Water Paper filter looks more like needlepoint, at least in the background. Unlike most of the filters in the Sketch set, Water Paper keeps the colors of your original picture, adding a vertical crosshatching in the background and softening what it identifies as the subject of the picture. Figure 15.34 shows this filter applied to the boat.

FIGURE 15.34.

Water Paper filter.

Summary

None of the filters described this Hour can produce a work of art from a lousy photo. The old proverb about silk purses and sow's ears applies. However, these filters can, when carefully and thoughtfully applied, elevate an ordinary picture to something quite extraordinary. Photoshop's filters are well worth taking the time to master. Spend some time with this Hour's Activity to work through the filter sets, so you can see—in color and enlarged—exactly what they can do.

Q&A

Q How do you decide what filter to try?

A As you've seen, you can't always judge a filter by its name. If you want an "art" effect, decide first whether you want full color or limited color. For the latter, look at the Sketch filters. Consider how abstract you want to get.

Cutout and Conte Crayon are both successful with most pictures.

Q Are the filters that come with Photoshop 5 all there are?

A Nope! There must be literally thousands of filters that have been created by individuals or companies. You can locate them by searching for "Photoshop filters," or try out these Yahoo! pages:

www.yahoo.com/Computers_and_Internet/Software/Graphics/
Titles/Adobe_Photoshop/

www.yahoo.com/Computers_and_Internet/Software/Graphics/
Filters_and_Plug_ins/

Quiz

Perhaps the right answers will filter through.

Questions

1. The Plastic Wrap filter is_____

   a. one of Photoshop's best.

   b. essentially useless.

   c. only used to separate layers.

2. Sumi-e is Japanese for_____

   a. a kind of drawing.

   b. raw fish and rice.

   c. Photoshop.

3. Photoshop "artistic" filters, in general, tend to _____an image.

    a. lighten

    b. darken

    c. sharpen

Answers

1. b

2. a. If you knew sushi….

3. b. If an image is dark to start with, it might turn black.

Activity

Use a picture you already have, or download one of the three used in this chapter, and try out the Artistic, Brush, and Sketch filters. Experiment with different settings and then try applying the same filter a second time. Also, see how fading a filter can make its effect more useful. Try applying a second filter over the first. Some combinations work better than others. See if you can find a combination that turns your photo into a work of art.

HOUR 16

Filters to Distort and Other Funky Effects

So far, the Photoshop filters described have been more or less useful. They corrected a fuzzy image or blurred a distracting background. Or they did something to turn your photo into an imitation drawing, painting, or mixed media construction. In this Hour, you play with some filters that are mostly just for fun. These filters distort, stylize, and pixelate your picture. Most of these are meant for special effects. They're not for every day, but you might find one of two that are actually helpful.

The key to success with these filters is to try as many different combinations of settings as you can with each filter and each new image that you bring into Photoshop. When you encounter a filter that relies on background and foreground colors, try several different color combinations. Try a dark background and light foreground, and then reverse them. It's simple enough to do, if you just click on the double-headed arrow next to the color swatches in the toolbox.

Distort

Distort filters run the gamut from gentle glassiness to image-destroying twirls and even more. Want to make your picture look like it's going down the drain or being blown off the page? These are the filters for you. In this section, you try out filters on this picture of an old millstone used for grinding corn. I chose this picture because it's very simple and has a good range of contrast (see Figure 16.1).

FIGURE 16.1.

Millstone.

The Diffuse Glow Filter

Not all the Distort filters actually distort, such as the Diffuse Glow filter. The Diffuse Glow filter adds a gentle haze of your background color over the lighter areas of the picture. This creates a glow that blends into the image. Hard to say why it is in the Distort family of filters, but it is cool nevertheless.

The controls are Graininess, Glow Amount, and Clear Amount. Try to balance the Glow Amount and Clear Amount. I suggest, for soft glows, that you keep the Graininess setting low. Higher numbers increase the graininess. This might be useful if you want a somewhat speckled look. In Figure 16.2, I used a dark green background and maximum graininess to place a layer of moss on the stone.

FIGURE 16.2.

The Diffuse Glow filter.

Displace

The Displace filter is one of several Photoshop filters that require the use of a displacement map, which works like a texture map. You can find a collection of these in the Photoshop Plug-ins folder. After you set the amount of displacement in the dialog box, you're asked to choose a filter. Figure 16.3 shows a partial list of filters, and Figure 16.4 shows the results of applying the Honeycomb map. The effect you get from this filter depends on which map you choose. You need to try them out to see their effects because the names aren't very helpful.

FIGURE 16.3.

Choosing a displacement map.

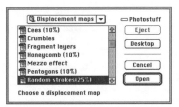

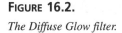 *Displacement maps* are images or patterns that are saved in the Photoshop format and applied as part of a mathematical formula that moves each pixel in the original image according to the values in the displacement map.

FIGURE 16.4.

The Displace filter.

The Glass and Ocean Ripple Filters

I decided to lump the discussion of these two filters together because of the similar effects they can have on an image. They both create displacements that make the image seem as if you are looking through glass or water.

The Glass filter offers you a greater amount of control (see Figure 16.5). You can select a type of texture, such as Frosty, Tiny Lens, or Canvas, and you also can load a texture of your own. Just select Load Texture from the drop-down menu at the bottom of the dialog box.

Use the Smoothness slider to increase the fluidity of the image. Keeping the Distortion low and the Smoothness high will create a subtle effect. Try the opposite for a much more distorted image.

The Invert button at the bottom of the dialog box replaces the light areas of the texture with dark areas and vice versa (see Figure 16.6).

FIGURE 16.5.

The Glass filter.

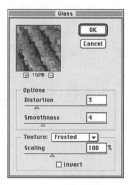

FIGURE 16.6.

The application of the Glass filter.

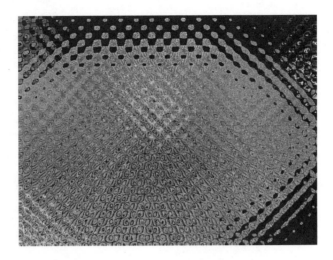

16

The Ocean Ripple filter is quite similar. It creates an effect that makes your image appear as though it is under water. It is an effective filter and easier to use than the Glass filter because it has only two options on its dialog box.

Pinch, Spherize, and ZigZag

The Pinch, Spherize, and ZigZag filters are lumped together, not so much because they do the same thing but because their interfaces are so similar. Figure 16.7 shows the dialog box for the Spherize filter.

FIGURE 16.7.

The Spherize filter dialog box.

Keep an eye on the grid provided at the bottom of the box as you drag the Amount slider higher or lower. It can give you a good indication (as can the Preview box) of what is going on in the image. See the final version in Figure 16.8.

Figure 16.8.

The Spherize filter.

This is a tough filter to master, but a good one to have in your bag of tricks. The Spherize filter can be very useful on occasion, but don't try to force it. If it doesn't look right, try something else.

Also, you can use a negative amount in the Amount slider to generate a hollow instead of a bump. And if this doesn't satisfy your needs, try the Pinch filter or the ZigZag filter, which create very neat pond ripples, too.

The Shear Filter

You can tell a great deal about most filters just by their names, but this isn't one of them. The Shear filter warps images horizontally. (It moves them in relation to the vertical line.) Drag the line in the dialog box, as shown in Figure 16.9. Watch the preview to see the effect of shearing the picture. You also can add more control points on the curve by clicking it at different areas. These control points are like joints; they enable you to redirect the motion of the curve.

Figure 16.10 shows the result of the Shear filter. I've set the image to Wrap Around, so it now looks as if there are two warped millstones.

FIGURE 16.9.

The Shear filter dialog box.

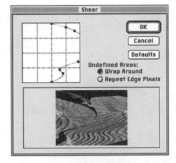

FIGURE 16.10.

The Shear filter applied.

The Shear filter works in only one direction. If you want something to shear vertically instead of horizontally, simply rotate the image before you apply the filter. Then rotate it back again.

The Twirl Filter

The Twirl filter does precisely what its name suggests—it spins an image. You can control the amount of spin with the slider within the dialog box. This is a great filter for creating special effects. So far, I haven't found very many subtle uses for the Twirl filter, but if you can, go to it. It creates wonderful kaleidoscopic effects and can also simulate a swirling drain. It looks great with our millstone, as shown in Figure 16.11.

FIGURE 16.11.

The Twirl filter applied.

Pixelate

When one is "pixilated," according to my dictionary, he's inebriated, but in a charming, bemused, whimsical, pixieish way. Pixelation can be equally whimsical and bemusing, if applied to the right subjects. Misused, it just turns everything into a bunch of dots. Pixelation happens when similarly colored pixels are clumped together to form larger units, which might be square (pixel-shaped) or round, or rounded off by anti-aliasing to whatever form they take. It happens, unasked for, if you're printing a picture at too low a resolution. You end up with large pixels forming jagged shapes that look like they were built out of a child's plastic block set.

When controlled, the effect can be quite interesting. Photoshop includes a set of Pixelation filters that produce different effects based on the notion of clumping together similar pixels. It's best to apply these effects to simple subjects and to those with strong contrasts, such as the example in Figure 16.12.

Crystallize

Most of the Pixelate filter set looks best if the effect is applied as small as possible. Otherwise, the crystals, facets, and so on get so big the image becomes unrecognizable. In Figure 16.13, I applied the Crystallize filter at a Cell Size of 10. It adds reasonable distortion without destroying the lemon shape. In Figure 16.14, I pushed the Cell Size up to 50, destroying the picture. You can even set the Cell Size as high as 300, but it turns the entire picture into one or two cells.

FIGURE 16.12.

Lemon, unfiltered.

16

FIGURE 16.13.

The Crystallize filter applied.

Figure 16.14.

Same filter, over applied.

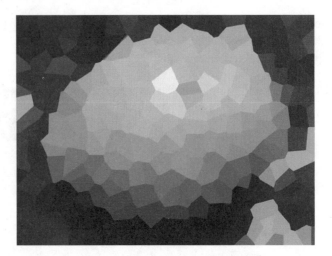

Pointillism and Mosaics

As a former art student, it's fun to go back and recall the first time I was introduced to the work of Georges Seurat. It was a revelation (especially after studying some of the "sloppier" French impressionists) to see these dabs of paint all neatly clustered, forming elegant scenes from a distance, and up close forming equally elegant abstract patterns. It would be nice if the Pointillism filters did the job as neatly and scientifically as M. Seurat. They don't.

This is, however, one case where the smallest setting doesn't work as well as some of the larger ones. I first tried the picture using 3 pixels as the Cell Size. I got a spotty picture, as I expected, but it looked more like video noise than pointillism. Using a slightly larger dot size produced an image a little closer to what I was looking for. But when I tried a much larger size, approximately 25, I ended up with baseballs. Figure 16.15 shows all three effects.

FIGURE 16.15.

*Cell sizes: 3, 8, and
25.*

16

There's a Mosaic setting in the Pixelate effects, but all it does is make larger pixels out of
the smaller ones. The result is the sort of thing used to hide the faces of the people being
arrested on all those late night police shows (see Figure 16.16).

FIGURE 16.16.

Alleged perpetrator.

Stylize

The Stylize filter family offers some wonderful effects. They are creative and you can use them to add final effects or touches to an image. This section touches on the most interesting of the filters: the Find Edges filter, the Glowing Edges filter, and the Wind filter.

Find Edges, Glowing Edges, and Trace Contour

These three effects sound as if they should look alike. They actually do look somewhat alike, with Glowing Edges and Find Edges being much more dramatic than Trace Contour. The Find Edges filter removes most of the colors from the object and replaces them with lines around every edge contour. The color of the lines depends on the value at that point on the original object, with lightest points in yellow, scaling through to the darkest points, which appear in purple. The picture looks like a rather delicate-colored pencil drawing of itself. Find Edges becomes more interesting if you apply it more than once to the same object. Figure 16.17 shows a picture of a flower with the edges traced twice.

FIGURE 16.17.

The first tracing lacked character, but using the filter again made the lines heavier.

Unfortunately, you cannot set the sensitivity of the Find Edges filter. In practical terms, this means that you have to prepare the picture before you trace it. Begin by despeckling, so Photoshop won't attempt to circle every piece of dust in the background. If you don't want the background to show, select and delete it, or select your object and copy it to a separate layer first.

Glowing Edges is more fun because it's prettier, and because you can adjust it to have maximum impact on your picture. Glowing Edges turns the edges into brightly colored lines against a black background. The effect is vaguely reminiscent of neon signs. You can vary the intensity of the color and the thickness of the lines.

In Figure 16.18, I've applied Glowing Edges to the same flower. It works especially well with "busy" pictures with lots of edges. The more it has to work with, the more effective the filter is.

FIGURE 16.18.

Some of the color remains but the background goes black.

Trace Contours, like several of the previous filters, works better on some pictures if you apply it several times (see Figure 16.19). The Trace Contour dialog box has a slider setting for the level at which value differences are translated into contour lines. When you move the slider, you are setting the threshold at which the values (from 0–255) are traced. Experiment to see which values bring out the best detail in your image. Upper and Lower don't refer to the direction of the outline. Lower Outlines specifies where the color values of pixels fall below a specified level; Upper Outlines tells you where the value of the pixels are above the specified level.

FIGURE 16.19.

The flower has been traced several times, with different settings.

I like to use this filter to place different tracings on different layers, and then to merge them for a more complete picture.

The Wind Filter

The Wind filter creates a neat directional blur that looks, strangely enough, like wind. You can control the direction and the amount of wind in the dialog box (see Figure 16.20). This is a great filter for creating the illusion of movement and for applying to type. It works best when applied to a selected area rather than to the entire picture.

FIGURE 16.20.

The Wind filter and its dialog box.

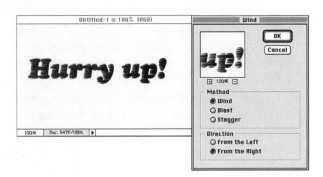

Emboss

Honestly, the Emboss filter doesn't do much for most photos. It turns an image into a bas-relief, though not as well as the Bas Relief filter does. In the process, the Emboss filter converts the image to medium gray. And like the Wind filter, it works very well on type. You can adjust the Shadow Angle and Amount in the dialog box. Figure 16.21 shows a piece of embossed type.

16

FIGURE **16.21.**

Embossing.

Occasionally, you come across a photo, like this portrait of a lion, that almost begs to be turned into a corporate logo or advertising image (see Figure 16.22). In such cases, the Emboss filter can do wonders toward making the picture just abstract enough to be useful. In working with this photo, I found that the angle at which the filter is applied can make a major difference. The following figure shows two different angle settings applied to the same picture. The Height and Amount settings were the same for both.

FIGURE **16.22.**

Embossed lions.

Combining Filters

Some people like things plain. I'm not one of them. I want the whipped cream, marshmallow, nuts, and cherry on my ice cream, and I'm seldom satisfied with using just one Photoshop filter. And with an arsenal of 99 different Photoshop filters (plus dozens of third-party add-ons), why shouldn't we take advantage of as many as possible? In the remaining few minutes of this Hour, look at some interesting combinations.

Texturizer

You can add texture to any photo, no matter what you have already done to it. The
Texturizer filter (Filter→ Texture→ Texturizer) places a pattern resembling canvas,
burlap, brick, or sandstone over your image, making it look as if it's on paper with that
texture. The Canvas texture is particularly nice if reduced in scale. Figure 16.23 shows a
photo of an autumn landscape, first treated with the Colored Pencil filter and then
texturized.

FIGURE 16.23.

*Colored Pencil on
sandstone.*

Dry Brush and Smudge Stick

The Dry Brush filter adds a nice "painterly" quality to this photo of two cats in a chair.
Figure 16.24 shows the single filter applied to it. In Figure 16.25, I added the Smudge
Stick over the Dry Brush, and came up with what I think is an even more interesting
result.

Figure 16.24.

Dry-brushed cats.

16

Figure 16.25.

Cats, drybrushed and smudge sticked. (They hate when that happens.)

The possibilities are endless. If you can imagine a style or treatment for a picture, chances are excellent that Photoshop can do it. As a final picture and final filter combination, here's how you can turn a photo into instant stained glass. Start with any picture that has reasonably large areas of light color. Figure 16.26 shows my original picture, a somewhat fuzzy close-up of a dogwood blossom.

FIGURE 16.26.

Unfiltered dogwood.

To turn this picture into stained glass:

1. Apply the Crystallize filter (Filter→ Pixelate→ Crystallize) with a moderately large Cell Size. I used 30 as the Cell Size in Figure 16.27.

FIGURE 16.27.

Crystallized dogwood.

2. Next, apply the Ink Outlines filter (Filter→ Brush Strokes→ Ink Outline) with the Stroke Length set to approximately 4, and the Light and Dark intensities balanced at approximately 15. Figure 16.28 shows the result—a reasonable rendering of a stained glass window. You can, of course, draw in any lines that Photoshop didn't trace completely, and you can go over the "glass panels" and change their colors if you want.

FIGURE 16.28.

Stained glass dogwood.

At the risk of sounding like a broken record, let me leave you with a final reminder to keep on experimenting. You never know what a filter or combination can do to a particular picture until you try it. The way that Photoshop calculates the filter effects means that some filters can look very different, according to the kind of picture to which they are applied. You can't always predict what will happen, but the unexpected effects are frequently wonderful.

Summary

This hour has been devoted to some of Photoshop's stranger filters: the Distort, Pixelate, and Stylize filters. They're not for everyone—and certainly not for every image—but they're fun to play with and can occasionally create some interesting, unusual, and beautiful effects. Filters can add interesting dimensions to type, also.

Don't hesitate to add a second filter over the first. Many times, the second filter or second application of the original filter can turn a ho-hum picture into something marvelous. At worst, you can always Undo.

Q&A

Q Why do some filters have ellipses after their names, when others don't?

A There are two kinds of native Photoshop filters. The ones with an ellipsis (…) open a dialog box to enable you to select specific settings for the filter being applied. The filters without ellipses are one-step filters; you have no settings to make. The filter is simply applied as it was written. You can apply it a second time to double the effect or fade it by a percentage to lessen the effect.

Q Does the Glass filter include more than one kind of glass?

A This is Photoshop; your choices are virtually unlimited. In addition to the textures provided, you can choose Load Texture from the pop-up menu and open any Photoshop document to apply as a texture.

Quiz

Can you filter out the wrong answers?

Questions

1. A displacement map is_____.

   a. another name for a texture map

   b. a pattern applied as a mathematical formula to move individual pixels in an image

   c. a chart showing how colors shift between your monitor and printer

2. The Spherize filter can make your picture appear to bump ____.

   a. out only (convex)

   b. in only (concave)

   c. either way

3. Pointillism was originally a painting style introduced by _____.

   a. Jean Luc Pontille

   b. Georges Seurat

   c. Leonardo da Vinci

   d. Jean Luc Picard

Answers

1. b
2. c
3. b

Activity

Start with a simple picture and add filters one by one until you can't recognize the image. See how many different filters you can apply on top of each other before the picture disappears.

Go back to your original picture, and use the Colored Pencil filter. This should give you an interesting image. Save it. Try the other filters over it until you find at least three that work well with the Colored Pencil filter. Whenever you have time, repeat this exercise, starting with a different first filter.

HOUR 17

Adding Type to Pictures

If a picture's worth a thousand words, how many more is it worth if we add words to the picture? Well, never mind…. The fact is, though, that sometimes you have to add type to a picture for one reason or another. Photoshop's Type tool has been vastly improved in this revision, but it still isn't the simplest or the most versatile you'll ever encounter. It does, however, allow you to put words over your pictures. From there, you can convert them to paths and fill them with images, apply filters, or use any of a variety of other tricks. We will start with the basics.

The Type Tool

NEW TO VERSION 5 In Photoshop 5, unlike previous editions, you have a choice of setting type horizontally or vertically. The Type tool's popout menu, shown in Figure 17.1, offers four choices. The arrows indicate vertical type, and the dotted lines indicate that type set with that tool will be created as paths, rather than as actual letters. The ability to set paths enables you to do one of Photoshop's neatest tricks—cutting type out of pictures.

FIGURE 17.1.

The Type tools.

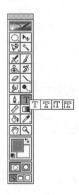

When you click the Type tool and move your cursor over the canvas, you see the familiar I-beam cursor that means you can insert text. Position the cursor where you want the text to start on the page, and then click once. Surprise! Photoshop doesn't place the cursor there for you to start typing. Instead it opens a dialog box, as shown in Figure 17.2.

FIGURE 17.2.

The Type Tool dialog box.

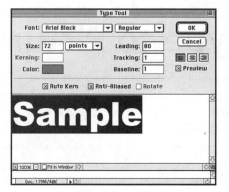

Pop-up menus within the dialog box let you choose a font from those you have installed and set the size, leading, alignment, tracking, and other attributes. By default, text appears in whatever the foreground color is. If you want a specific color, click on the Color box within the Type Tool dialog box to open Photoshop's Color Picker.

The window at the bottom of the box is where you can see what you type. You won't see the text in your chosen color in the window. Type in the window appears in black, but it transfers onto the page in the color you choose. The blinking cursor line indicates that you're ready to type. When you start, your words appear in the window. If you type more text than the box can display, you see scrollbars at the side and bottom of the window.

If you check the Preview box, (which I definitely recommend), you can see the type in its assigned color and size on your page. You might have to drag the Type Tool dialog box out of the way to see it.

After you enter the words and set the type attributes, you must click OK or press Return to position the type. Type always appears on a new layer. Type layers are indicated by a large letter T, as you can see in Figure 17.3. Type layers are named according to the first word(s) you type. If you want to edit your type, click on the T to reopen the Type Tool dialog box.

FIGURE 17.3.

The Layers palette, showing layers of type.

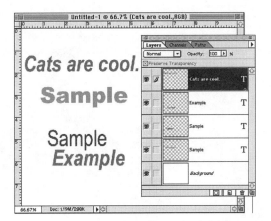

There's one more step to go through before your type is part of the page. Among **NEW TO VERSION 5** the changes in Photoshop 5, the ability to edit type you've already set is one of the most helpful. Of course, you pay a small price for it. The type must be rendered before you can apply the full range of effects to it. You can apply distortion to the layer before it's rendered. Once it's rendered, you can't go back and edit it again. To render the type, use Layer→ Type→ Render Layer, as shown in Figure 17.4.

FIGURE 17.4.

Rendering converts the type to an image.

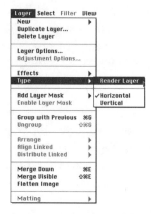

After you place the type on the screen, you can have some fun with it. Apply filters to your heart's content. Pour paint into selected letters. Select the type and distort it. Figure 17.5 shows a few of the things you can do.

FIGURE 17.5.

Filtered, stretched, and distorted type.

Filters are most successful on bold type. Thin, delicate letters tend to get lost. Photoshop can convert most fonts to bold and italic versions, using the pop-up menu next to the Font pop-up menu. Fortunately for type purists, the Shadow and Outline options no longer exist. Besides, there's a much better way....

Drop Shadows

As soon as you start looking for drop shadows, you'll find them everywhere: in magazines, television ads, Web sites, and in every other form of media you can imagine.

Everyone is discovering that as soon as you put a shadow behind some text or an image, it takes on an added dimension that can really make it pop forward into view. It's a nice and easy special effect for giving something more visual weight and making people pay attention.

Here are some tips for effectively using drop shadows:

- Don't use them all over the place! If you use too many shadows, everything pops forward equally and you lose the benefit of using shadows to give attention to one particular object.

- Make sure all your shadows look alike! If you use shadows on multiple objects in the same area, make sure the shadows all go the same way, and make sure the "depth" of the shadow is appropriate. If the shadows are all different and haphazard, people will notice.

- Don't make the shadows too dark. It's easy to go overboard and create deep, saturated shadows that overwhelm what's supposed to be getting all the attention: the foreground image. Keep shadows light and subtle. Figure 17.6 shows what can go wrong.

17

FIGURE 17.6.

Which word looks better? If you can't tell, read the second tip again.

NEW TO VERSION 5 | Photoshop 5 offers its users a powerful and easy Drop Shadow tool, along with Glow, Bevel, and Emboss tools that will do wonders for type and graphics alike. You will find these tools on the Layer→Effects submenu. Follow along to create a cool drop shadow.

1. Create a new Photoshop document with a white background.

2. Select the Type tool and enter some words. For now, don't worry about color, kerning, or setting a baseline. Figure 17.7 shows the basic type.

FIGURE 17.7.

The original art in need of a drop shadow.

The Shadow knows...

3. Open the Layer→ Effects→ Drop Shadow dialog box, as shown in Figure 17.8. (Or use the keyboard shortcut (Command - 1) [Control - 1].) Check the Preview box so you can see your work as you create it.

FIGURE 17.8.

The Drop Shadow dialog box.

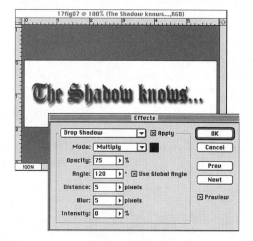

4. Set Mode to either Normal, Multiply, or Darken. Otherwise, you won't see the shadow. Click in the color swatch next to the Mode menu to change the color of the shadow. The Color Picker opens.

5. Adjust the Opacity and shadow Angle as desired, by clicking on the arrows to reach the sliders.

6. Set the distance according to the amount of shadow you want to see. Set the Blur according to how distinct you want the edges of the shadow to be. Click OK to see your drop shadow, as shown in Figure 17.9.

7. You can still change it, of course. Until you merge the layers or render the type, you can make any changes you want.

FIGURE 17.9.

Drop shadow type, with a plain background.

 I find that shadows work better if they're *below* the original image, that is, moved down instead of up when they're offset. When the shadow falls downward, the object looks more like it's popping up.

17

Drop shadows can be tricky. When it looks right, you know it. Trust your eyes to tell you what looks realistic and what looks fake. And be willing to experiment with settings. Try making your shadow twice as blurred as your original setting, or twice as far offset. You might be surprised!

Variation: Shadows on Backgrounds

Of course, drop shadows don't have to occur just over white or solid-color backgrounds. You can have a drop shadow fall over a texture, an image, or anything else that strikes your fancy. Here's an example:

1. First, create the Photoshop image. I started with a photo of flowering dogwood, added type, and copied and pasted one flower to improve the composition. The important thing to remember is to create a *new layer* for each element you want to have a drop shadow (see Figure 17.10). For a refresher on layers, refer back to Hour 11, "Layers."

2. Add a shadow to the text first, by following the steps as in the previous section (see Figure 17.11).

   Notice how you can actually see the texture of the background right "through" the new shadow. The result is a pleasant, realistic effect. You can make even more of the background show through by adjusting the Opacity slider in the Layers palette. Give it a try.

FIGURE 17.10.

The original image before drop shadows.

FIGURE 17.11.

A drop shadow applied to the text.

3. Now create some depth in the background itself. I'll start by adding a drop shadow to the single flower. It's subtle, but it's there. Because that worked well, how about adding shadows to all of the flowers. Using the Magic Wand tool, it's easy to select them from the background and paste a copy into a new layer. I applied the Drop Shadow again to the layer of flowers, and they immediately jumped out from the background. Figure 17.12 shows the final version.

FIGURE 17.12.

Drop shadows at work.

17

Tasteful Typography

There are thousands of typefaces available. Buy them in CD-ROM collections, download them online, use the ones that come with other applications, and so on. Trying out wild typefaces can be so much fun that you might lose sight of the goal—to communicate. Before committing to a design, print out a sample page and hold it up at arm's length. If you can't read it easily, maybe even with your reading glasses removed, try figure out why and consider tweaking the design. It might be a simple matter of making the type larger or giving the lines of type more space (leading). You might need to rethink your background or add an outline. A drop shadow might help— or might make matters even worse. Try combinations of different type and image treatment.

The pros don't use underlining very often, either. The underline habit comes from the old manual typewriter days, when no other typographical tool was available to give emphasis to words. Use bold or italic type styles instead.

Filled Type

The words you paste onto a picture might be filled with meaning. They can also be filled with pictures. Here's how to do my favorite Photoshop trick.

Half the battle is finding a picture to work with. The other half is finding a nice fat type-face that leaves plenty of room for your pictures to show through. I'm working on a logo for a company called Cloud Nine. The first thing I do is flip through my photo files in search of some good-looking clouds. I'll open the picture in Photoshop, crop it, and punch up the contrast a little more.

Then I select the Type Outline tool by pressing the key combination Shift+T to cycle to it from the regular Type tool and vertical Type tool. Now the cursor looks like the familiar I-beam type insertion cursor. Clicking it on the clouds opens the Type Tool dialog box. (Before clicking, I make sure that the horizontal line on the cursor—the type baseline— is where it should be, low enough to catch the clouds.)

I choose Comic Sans from my font list, making it bold as well for a few extra pixels worth of width. And I type the word "Cloud" as large as possible to fit in the area. Figure 17.13 shows this step.

FIGURE 17.13.

Enter the words in the Type Tool box.

When I close the dialog box and return to the picture, I have selection paths in the shape of the letters. Figure 17.14 shows how this looks onscreen.

FIGURE 17.14.

The letters are active paths.

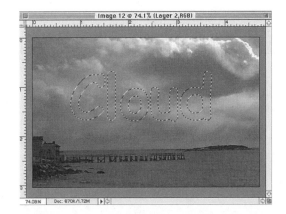

After making sure the letters are centered over the clouds I want to capture, I copy the selection and paste it to a new layer. It's important to copy and not cut. If I use the Cut command, I'll leave holes in my original picture, and that's no good because I have another word to grab from it. First, though, I adjust the color in the picture. The first clouds were pink, as at sunset. These are more blue. Repeating the Type tool process, I enter the word "Nine" and take a different section of clouds.

The next step is to get rid of the original picture because I don't need it any more. But the lettering does need a background. Clouds would probably be appropriate. I start by adding another layer and pouring it full of light blue paint. I also have to pour paint into the interior of the closed letters O and D. After making sure that my foreground color is white and my background color is an appropriate blue, I choose Render Clouds from the Filter menu. Figure 17.15 shows the result.

FIGURE 17.15.

More clouds.

17

The rendered clouds just don't look very impressive, and there's not enough contrast against the lettering. I can make the clouds stand out a little more by adjusting the contrast and color balance. I can also put a drop shadow behind the lettering. And, if that's not enough, I can draw in some little cartoon-like clouds and a bird or two and give them their own shadows. Figure 17.16 shows the final logo, after all of these tricks.

FIGURE 17.16.

Photoshop puts my client on Cloud Nine.

Glows

NEW TO
VERSION 5

Photoshop 5 has another new feature. You can use the Layer→ Effects menu to put a glow around your type, or make it appear as if the letters themselves are glowing. This is a great effect to add emphasis around a piece of text or to make it stand out from a busy background. Figure 17.17 shows a fairly ordinary text and photo combination. (It's a title for a slide show.)

In Figure 17.18, I've applied an Outer Glow around the letters. It's simply another way of defining them from the background and is useful when a drop shadow isn't appropriate. Other objects can glow, too, and we'll discuss these in more detail in the next Hour.

Bevel and Emboss

These two new tools share a dialog box. Both produce raised type: Bevel affects the edges of the type, producing a raised but flat letter surface; Emboss gives the appearance of curved or rounded letters. Figure 17.19 shows examples of both.

FIGURE 17.17.

The letters don't quite stand out enough.

FIGURE 17.18.

The Glow helps separate the text from the background.

You can vary the effect of these tools by changing the Blending modes, by varying the Opacity, and by changing highlight and shadow colors. As always, the best way to see what they do is to experiment with different settings.

FIGURE **17.19.**

The difference is obvious.

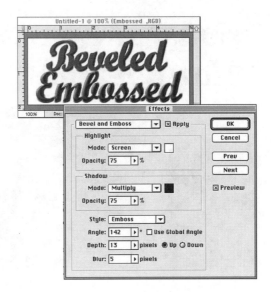

Adjusting Type

Even with the new Type tools in Photoshop 5, it's not the best application for typographic excellence. You have the option to place your type flush left, centered, or flush right. You can adjust the leading between lines and the tracking space between letters, but you don't have the versatility of a program such as PageMaker or even a good word processor that creates Drop Caps, Small Caps, and other fancy tricks.

To make the adjustments, open the Type Tool window and select the type within it that you want to adjust. You needn't change everything if you don't want to. You can, for instance, close up the gap in two letters by selecting them and adjusting the tracking. To adjust the space between two lines of type, increase or decrease the leading.

Summary

Photoshop doesn't have all of the type capabilities of a more traditional graphics or desktop publishing program, but you'll probably never need them. Its Type tool, much improved in Photoshop 5, can handle setting a short headline or title; it's not designed to do more than basic formatting, though. Of course, getting the letters into the picture is only the beginning. After you have the type on the page, you can apply all of Photoshop's filters, Blending modes, and tools to it. If you want to set type, use a program such as PageMaker. If you want to do strange and wonderful things to type, Photoshop has all the tools you need.

Q&A

Q I have a lot of fonts installed, and it takes forever to scroll down the list to find the one I want. Any suggestions?

A Use a font management program such as Suitcase or Master Juggler to sort your fonts into suitcases. Keep a suitcase for serif type and a separate one for sans serif faces, one for display faces, one for special-purpose fonts such as Handbill, StarTrek, or Wild West. Open only the suitcases with fonts you're likely to need.

Q I've typed in the text I want and have rendered it. The problem is I found a typo and when I try to go back and edit the text I can't. What can I do?

A After you render text, it's converted from an editable text layer to a graphic that can't be edited by any of the Type tools. Make sure you have the type you want and it's all spelled correctly before you render it.

17

Quiz

How well do you know your type?

Questions

1. Photoshop 5 can set type horizontally or vertically.

   a. True

   b. False

2. Every piece of type needs a drop shadow.

   a. True

   b. False

3. Photoshop places type on _____.

   a. the background

   b. special type layers

   c. regular layers

   d. adjustment layers

4. If there's a T in the box on the Layers palette, it means

   a. you can double-click it to open the Type tool.

   b. that the layer is a type layer.

   c. effects have been applied to the type.

   d. both a. and b.

Answers

1. a
2. b. Use them sparingly.
3. b
4. d

Activity

1. Download the photo of a plate of pasta from our Web site at `www.mcp.com/info`. Set the word "Pasta" in tomato sauce red over it. Add a drop shadow.

2. Create a textured background. Using the same photo and the Type Outline tool, cut the letters "Pasta" out of the photo and place them over the background. Bevel the edges of the letters and apply an Outer Glow in an appropriate color. Sprinkle with grated cheese and bake for an hour.

HOUR 18

Special Effects

This Hour is going to be a little different: We're going to kick back and explore some of the cool things you can do with the wondrous tool known as Photoshop. Think of this chapter as a collection of recipes—special effects that you can add to your mental list of Photoshop tricks and use again and again. Just follow the steps and you'll be a Photoshop wizard in no time.

Here are the special effects covered in this chapter:

- Glows
- Lighting effects
- Reflections

Very detailed instructions will be given today and I'll use very specific settings along the way. It's important to realize that as you create these special effects with your own images, my settings might not be the best settings for you. Different resolutions, sizes, and colors call for different settings. So when you see specifics, feel free to play with them a bit and see if you can get even better results with your artwork.

Truly, that's the real secret of getting better and better at Photoshop: *Never stop experimenting!*

Glows

The Glow is an easy special effect. It's essentially a drop shadow that isn't offset at all from the original object and is often in a color other than black. In the previous Hour, you learned how to use Photoshop's new Glow tool to apply a glow. Here's a different way to do it.

Let's create a basic glow around an object:

1. I shot this keychain for a jewelry catalog. As is, it's a pretty ordinary picture (see Figure 18.1), but putting a glow behind the object will help emphasize it and make the picture more colorful.

FIGURE 18.1.

The original keychain, sans glow.

2. First, you need to select the object. The Magic Wand tool does a fine job of this. (With this image I "cheated" by selecting the background and inverting.) If there are cutouts, like the open part of the keyring, be sure they're selected, too.

3. Create a new layer and copy the selected object onto it.

4. Return to the background layer and reselect the object (Shift-Command-D) [Shift-Control-D].

5. Expand the selection (Select→Modify→Expand...) by 5 pixels and copy it onto a new layer. Then select the object again and delete it.

6. Make a workpath around the deleted object. Fill the workpath with an appropriate Glow color. Turn off Path to lose the line around it and the color remains on the layer. Figure 18.2 shows this step.

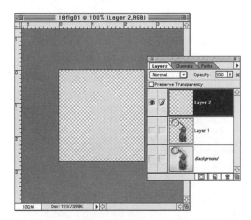

FIGURE 18.2.

Just the Glow layer.

7. Use the Gaussian Blur filter to diffuse the glow. Try a setting between 5 and 10.

8. Assemble the layers, so the glow is beneath the object. If the shadows interfere with the glow, remove them. Figure 18.3 shows the final product.

We've just scratched the surface of Glow effects, so I encourage you to try all sorts of settings and colors. Experiment with the brightness and size of the Glow effect. Also try other Blur filters for glows that imply movement or dimension. Have fun!

FIGURE 18.3.

Catalog photo, glowing.

18

Lighting Effects

Lighting effects refers to a whole range of special effects that are all related to how objects are lit. By illuminating objects in a unique way, you can change the entire feel of an image, drawing attention exactly where you want it.

Our primary tool, as you might expect, is Photoshop's Lighting Effects filter.

1. Start with an original image. Perhaps this is an image that is fairly "flat" as far as brightness is concerned. Perhaps it's an image that simply needs to be more three-dimensional to match its content. (See Figure 18.4.)

   In our example image, the "book" is on a separate layer from the background, so I can light them both separately.

FIGURE 18.4.

Our original image, in need of some special lighting.

2. Make sure the Book layer is active and then select just the book. The Lighting Effects filter works only if you have something selected for it to work on.

3. Choose Filter→Render→Lighting Effects to bring up the Lighting Effects dialog box. Under the Style pulldown menu near the top, select Soft Spotlight (see Figure 18.5). You'll see the preview of your image on the left with the new Spotlight effect.

FIGURE 18.5.

The Lighting Effects dialog box.

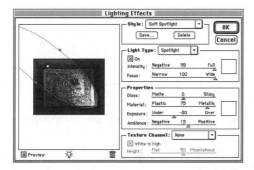

4. Although Photoshop ships with a number of neat default settings, it's fun to play around with the various sliders and values. Don't be intimidated by the number of choices here. For one thing, I don't like how the spotlight is currently falling to the lower right of the image. I want it to shine onto the middle.

   To change the direction and/or shape of the spotlight, simply grab the handles around the oval you see in the left side of the dialog box. You can move them around as you wish. You can even move the center point. Move everything around so it looks something like what you see in Figure 18.6.

18

FIGURE 18.6.

Moving the Spotlight manually.

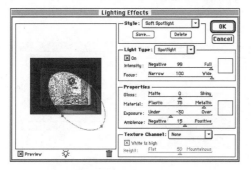

5. Okay, not bad, but the spotlight is too intense and too bright. I played around with the Intensity slider a bit and settled on a value of 50.

6. Now it looks like the unlit parts of the image are too dark. I need to bring the over-all lighting up a bit, so I adjust the Ambience slider up to 35.

7. One more thing: Light doesn't always have to be white. For this image, a softer, more yellow light is more appropriate because of the yellows and reds already in the image. So I click the white square to the right of the Intensity slider, and up comes the Color Picker (see Figure 18.7). As you can see, I find a subtle yellow by setting the RGB values to 240, 255, and 200, respectively.

FIGURE 18.7.

Changing the color of the light itself.

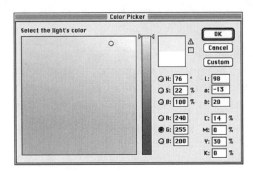

8. I click OK to approve the color and I look over the Lighting Effects dialog box to make sure I like the Preview image. Yup, looks good (see Figure 18.8).

FIGURE 18.8.

All the settings are finally as I want them.

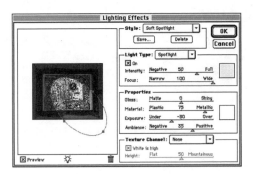

9. I click OK and, after a little processing time, the final image emerges (see Figure 18.9).

If you like, you can also add Lighting effects to the black background as well, to add a further sense of depth to the image.

FIGURE **18.9.**

*The book with a warm
spotlight highlighting
the area I want to
focus on.*

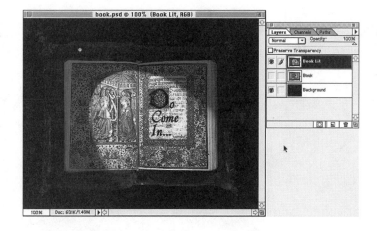

Reflections

If you often find yourself bringing various images together in Photoshop (and I predict
you will), you can't simply toss the images together and have it look realistic. As we've
seen, effects like Shadows are essential to creating a realistic-looking environment.
Creating reflections is another technique for doing this.

Let's look at an example to see how you can add reflections to your toolkit of special
effects:

1. Let's say I have a yellow flower (which I do) that I want to insert into an image
   I've created. First, I use the various Selection tools to extricate the flower from its
   original photographic background. Then I place the tulip (on its own layer, of
   course) into my new image (see Figure 18.10). By the way, the tile is simply the
   Filter→Texturize→Mosaic filter.

   I think you'll agree that the effect isn't very realistic. It looks like the flower and
   background came from two different sources (which they did, but I don't want it to
   be so obvious!).

2. To start working on a reflection of the tulip in the floor tile, duplicate the tulip
   layer (refer back to the "Drop Shadows" section for details). In the Layers palette,
   move this new layer (I named it Reflection) below the original tulip layer, because
   we want the reflection to appear underneath the tulip.

3. With the tulip's Reflection layer active, select Layer→Transform→Flip Vertical.
   This flips the reflected tulip onto its head. If you hear muttering in Dutch at this
   point, ignore it.

18

FIGURE **18.10.**

The flower in its new environment.

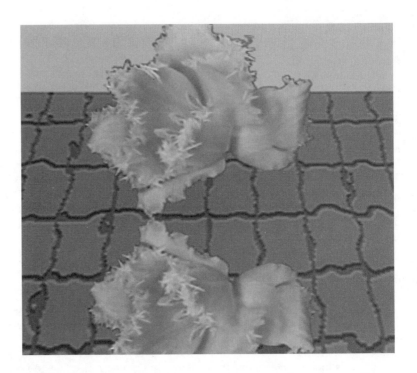

4. Select the tulip's Reflection and use the Move tool to move it down. (Hold down the Shift key as you move the selection, so that it moves straight down and not at all horizontally.) Move it down so that the "two tulips" precisely meet without any tile visible between them (see Figure 18.11).

FIGURE **18.11.**

The tulip flipped and moved down into place.

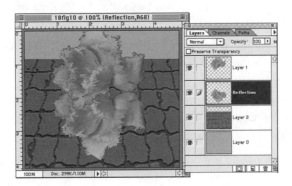

It looks like a reflection, right? Well, sort of. It looks like a reflection only if the tile floor is *perfectly* reflective, like a mirror, which obviously no floor is.

5. To make the reflection realistic, some of the tiles have to show through, just as we saw with drop shadows. Deselect the tulip reflection so the image is easier to see as a whole. Then adjust the Opacity slider in the Layers palette until the reflection looks more realistic and blends in with the floor (see Figure 18.12). My floors are freshly waxed, so I took Opacity down to 40%.

FIGURE 18.12.

With Opacity reduced, the reflection looks much more realistic.

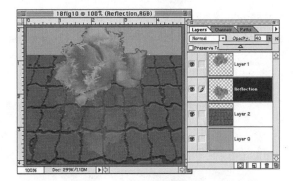

If you're satisfied with the reflection as it is now, then you're done. Unfortunately, I'm picky and seldom satisfied. The reflection still looks too perfect to me. No floor is that smooth.

6. To introduce a little "dirtiness" into the reflection by blurring it slightly, it's time for another trip to the Gaussian Blur filter. I use a setting of just 1 pixel to get the effect I like (see Figure 18.13).

FIGURE 18.13.

The reflection is now slightly blurred, which is what a realistic floor does to reflections.

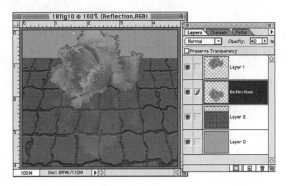

18

Okay, now it's looking good. The tulip image is now interacting with the floor image, creating a realistic effect. There's just one more thing bugging me: the wall behind the tulip. Shouldn't the tulip and wall interact? Shouldn't the tulip be casting just a bit of a shadow on the wall? I think so.

7. I create a drop shadow as I normally would. Duplicate the original tulip layer, select the new tulip, and fill it with black. Don't forget to send it behind the tulip.

   Instead of offsetting the whole shadow, however, I need a kind of Perspective shadow. The bottom of the shadow should match the bottom of the original tulip, and the top of it should be cast above the tulip onto the wall.

8. To stretch the shadow, select Layer→Transform→Distort. Grab the top middle handle that appears and drag it upward to about what you see in Figure 18.14. Double-click within the box to approve the change.

FIGURE 18.14.

Stretching the tulip's shadow onto the wall.

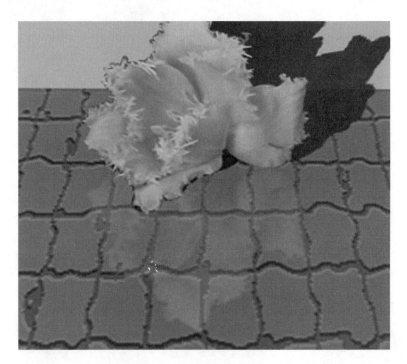

9. Deselect the shadow. Obviously it's too dark and too sharp.

10. Time for another Gaussian Blur. I want a really fuzzy shadow, so it looks like the tulip is being illuminated by ambient light, not a specific light source. A value of 12 pixels looks good.

11. Finally, I grab the Opacity slider and move it down to 60%, so the shadow looks lighter and the wall texture shows through a bit (see Figure 18.15).

FIGURE 18.15.

The finished image, with reflection and shadow.

18

Well, I'm satisfied. The image now looks like one piece instead of three disparate images thrown together. That's what special effects like Reflection can do for you.

Summary

A "special effect" isn't about specific instructions and narrowly defined settings—it's about experimenting with all that Photoshop has to offer and being pleasantly surprised by new discoveries. As you use Photoshop's features (especially its filters) more and more, you'll uncover an endless stream of special effects. This chapter is just a small taste of what's possible. Have fun creating your own special effects!

Q&A

Q How would you place a reflection in water?

A Much the same as what we did on the tile floor, except that I'd apply an appropriate Ripple filter to the reflection, as well as blurring it. Depending on the kind of water, you may want to apply Blur first, and then Ripple, or vice versa. Try both and see which looks more correct.

Q **Just how did you learn how to do all this! It all seems so complicated—filters, effects, selecting things, changing colors, modifying options. Argh!**

A I learned the way you're learning—one step at a time. I studied my pictures and decided what effect I wanted to achieve and then kept trying things until I got the picture to look the way I wanted it to. When I have some free time, I like to turn on Photoshop and use it like a video game. I open a picture and see how long it takes me to completely lose the original image. It sounds silly, but I learn a lot from these sessions.

Quiz

How do special effects affect your photos?

Questions

1. How many kinds of lighting effects are there?

    a. Three: Spot, Omni, and Directional

    b. 17, including colored spots and multi-light patterns

    c. Two, On and Off

2. A Glow is a drop shadow that's not offset.

    a. True

    b. False

3. Reflections face in the _____ direction as the object reflected.

    a. same horizontal, opposite vertical

    b. same vertical, opposite horizontal

    c. Either...it depends on where the Mirror surface is.

Answers

1. b.

2. a., (and in a color, instead of black)

3. c. Think about it.

Activity

Take some time and study reflections. Look at yourself in your coffee table (you may have to shine it first!). Go outside and see the reflection of trees in water—even in a puddle or pothole in the road. Find a book (or look on the Internet) of M.C. Escher and look in particular for "Three Worlds," "Puddle," and "Rippled Surface."

Download the photo of the lemon from our Web site, and place it on a reflective surface. Position the reflection beneath it and a shadow behind it. Experiment until both look natural.

18

HOUR 19

Photoshop Plug-ins and Add-ons

By now, you have seen, if not used, most of the 99 filters that came with your copy of Photoshop. There couldn't possibly be any more, could there? Well, Photoshop is kind of like those fashion dolls or action figures that kids of a certain age demand. You can't just buy Batman and Robin or Barbie. You need the Batmobile, Stately Wayne Manor, Barbie's Dream House, yacht, and RV.... After you see how much fun you can have with the basic filters, you'll want Eye Candy, KPT and Convolver, Photo Tools...and at least several dozen of the latest shareware filters, too. And the list goes on.

You've probably also considered buying a graphics tablet and more RAM. (You can never have too much.) Maybe you also need a faster computer to make all these tools work a little more efficiently. You don't have to have any of these things, but for the next hour, let's pretend we're kids in a candy store. We'll sample everything possible.

Where to Get Them

Commercial plug-in sets, such as the KPT, Chromatica, and Eye Candy packages described below, can be found in mail order catalogs or at your friendly local computer dealer (who'll be even friendlier once you start buying all these goodies).

On the other hand, you needn't spend a lot of money. It often amazes me how very many talented and generous people there are who not only write useful software, but then turn around and give it away, or sell it for such a pittance that they might as well be giving it away. I am speaking, of course, of shareware and the authors who spend many long nights polishing a program, and then upload it to CompuServe or AOL, or to the Web. If you go searching in appropriate areas for Mac or Windows software, you should find plenty of new and useful Photoshop plug-ins.

I did a Lycos search on Photoshop filter and got back a list of hundreds of sites that were triggered by that combination of keywords. Here are some good ones to get you started.

`http://pluginhead.i-us.com/plugin.htm`

`http://the-tech.mit.edu/KPT/`

`http://www.mediaco.com/nvr` (Windows only)

How to Install Them

Few things could be simpler than installing an individual filter. Simply drag it into the Photoshop filter folder, if you're using a Mac. Windows users, place it in the folder Photoshop\Plug-Ins\Filters. Then, restart your computer, and the new filter will appear in the list under the Filter menu. If you purchase a set of filters, such as Alien Skin's Eye Candy, there's an installer included, which automatically places the filters where they belong. Installed third-party filters appear in the filter list after Photoshop's native filters. Figure 19.1 shows my current collection.

FIGURE 19.1.

The Filter menu.

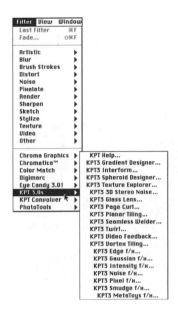

Kai's Power Tools

Kai Krause is a legend in the field of computer graphics. He's the guiding genius behind Kai's Power Tools, Bryce, Convolver, Vector Effects, Final Effects, Goo, Soap, and probably many goodies yet to be announced. Power Tools (also known as KPT) 3, the current edition, comes with an "Explorer Guide" rather than a manual. There's much to explore, but as Kai says in a foreword, you really don't need to read the guide book. The interfaces are designed to be as intuitive and as interesting as possible. There are excellent help screens available within each filter (look for a question mark and click it). The goal of these filters, along with doing interesting things to your photos, is to do interesting things to your mind and to your way of working with the computer. By the way, you can find Power Tools in mail order catalogs or on the shelves of your local software store, for about $49.

MetaToys

One of the coolest, if not the most useful, of Kai's tools is the MetaToys Lens. If you think of a Swiss Army Knife and turn it into a magnifying glass that does tricks, you'll have the beginning of an understanding of the Lens f/x (see Figure 19.2). Each of the

19

lines and bumps and buttons on it does something. Clicking the words *Lens f/x*, for instance, opens the menu of effects available with this tool, allowing you to switch without going back to the Photoshop screen. Effects that the Lens applies are Pixel, Gaussian, Noise, Edge, Intensity, Smudge, Glass Lens, and Twirl.

FIGURE 19.2.

Kai's MetaToys Lens f/x tool.

The gray marks along the left side, along with the two red balls on either end, control the intensity and opacity of the effect you're applying. The left side handles intensity and the right opacity. Clicking either ball and dragging up increases the percentage, and dragging down decreases it. The third ball, when present, controls the directionality of the effect. Clicking and dragging this third one applies that direction to the effect, if it's an effect that can be directional. In the figure, we're using the Kaleida effect, which treats the image as if it were viewed through a kaleidoscope.

The top button is the Preview button. It toggles your view through the lens between the center of the image and whatever the lens happens to be on top of. You can drag it all over the image to preview the effect on different areas. You can also drag it across the rest of the screen to see what your menu bars, trash can, or recycle bin looks like with the effect applied.

The lower button is the Reset button. It returns all the settings to their defaults. The gauge directly below the Reset button is the Options gauge. Pressing it opens the menu listing options for applying the effect. You have, generally speaking, the same options you have when applying any other Photoshop effects: Normal, Darken, Lighten, Multiply, and so on. Remember that after you apply a KPT effect, you can still go back and fade it using Photoshop's Fade settings.

When you have adjusted the effect the way you want it, click the small green dot at the bottom right of the lens to apply it. If you decide you don't want it, click the red dot instead to cancel and return to the regular Photoshop screen.

The Kaleida effect makes nifty stained glass windows but isn't especially useful otherwise. Some of the Lens f/x that *are* useful include the Pixel effect and the Smudge effect, which can make interesting textures and backgrounds.

Texture Explorer

Speaking of textures, let's check out Kai's Texture Explorer. It comes with a library of default textures, all of which are generated mathematically; hence, they demand little in the way of memory or hard drive space.

The Texture Designer interface is somewhat intimidating at first glance. The large square on the right is the source texture and the squares surrounding it hold derivative textures, all recompiled each time you make a change. As you can see in Figure 19.3, you can use your own image as the source for texture generation. Clicking any of the initial 16 derivative textures makes that texture the source, and 16 new variations are generated, which can repeat until you get tired of clicking. If you find one you like, you can protect it by clicking it while pressing (Option) [Alt]. This puts a red line around it, protecting it and keeping it from changing when you next change the source texture.

FIGURE 19.3.

The Texture Explorer.

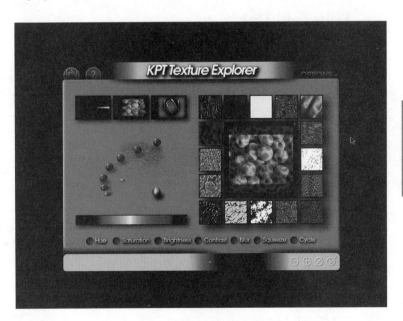

19

The collection of red or aqua balls on the left is the Mutation Tree. (Note the shadow of a tree beneath.) These balls represent the degree of mutation that the filter adds each time you create a new texture set. The bottommost ball applies minimal mutation, and so on up the tree to the top ball, which is maximum mutation. This gives you results that don't even remotely resemble the source. Clicking the balls on the mutation tree results in new mutations, based on the same source.

The multicolored globe changes the gradients used to generate colors for the derivative textures. Each time you click the color ball, Explorer applies a different gradient. The strip below it shows the current gradient. Clicking the strip brings up a pop-up menu that lets you select a preset from hundreds that are included.

The words at the bottom of the screen each represent a control that affects the gradient on which your texture is based. You can change any of these by clicking and dragging right or left.

The three small windows near the top of the screen represent Rotation, Opacity, and Glue. The Rotation window lets you rotate your source texture by clicking and dragging. The Opacity window lets you adjust the opacity of the gradient, making it more or less transparent, by clicking and dragging left or right. The same window also, when you double-click it, cycles through the sample backgrounds so you can see the results of applying your texture to different kinds of images.

Spheroid Designer

The interface is a little weird. According to the book, it "may seem like a bunch of balls dropped into a pile of mud" but is "actually a bunch of spheres dropped onto an old, stale brownie." Hey, those are Kai's words, not mine. Weird, yes. Powerful, you betcha. The Spheroid Designer gives you pseudo-3D modeling power in what's really only a two-dimensional program. You can take an image, convert it to a relief, and turn it into one, several, or hundreds of spheres, balls, little roundish things...whatever. Figure 19.4 shows the Spheroid Designer in operation.

The sample sphere at the center shows the work in progress. It's the equivalent of a Preview window. The four smaller clusters of spheres around it are the light sources you can apply to your sphere. Click once on the larger ones to turn them on and use the small, marble-sized ones to control the color, position, intensity, and highlight intensity of each light source. As with any of Kai's tools, clicking the logo lets you see the effect in full screen form. Figure 19.5 shows the sphere applied over the original image.

The three balls at the lower left of the screen in Figure 19.4 control the curvature of the sphere, the glossiness and amount of ambient light around it, and the opacity. Clicking and dragging on these balls changes their settings.

FIGURE 19.4.

Kai's Spheroid Designer.

FIGURE 19.5.

Adding spheres to the picture.

19

There are many more dots and balls and other goodies to click on in this interface. The clustered balls determine how many spheres you'll generate. The Mutation Tree in the upper left corner of the screen, as in the Texture Generator, gives you random variations on your sphere. You can set bump polarity, height, rotation, and zoom with the four small dots below and to the right of the Bump map panel. The best way to figure out what the various buttons and dots actually do is to experiment. You won't get bored with this tool, and even if you do nothing else for a week, you won't discover all its possibilities.

 Some of these operations can take a great deal of memory. If you can't place your sphere over the background you want to, close that file and save it to a new, blank screen. Then you can merge the two images later.

More Tools

You want more? There are other KPT tools that do interesting and occasionally useful things. Glass Lens adds distortion to an image. Gradient Designer does what its name implies, but being one of Kai's tools, it does it with an interesting and unique interface. Page Curl makes your picture look as if it came from an old, dry book. Seamless Welder creates images that wrap around a 3D object with no visible seam. Twirl sends your picture through a tornado, with variables as to its intensity and direction. It also contains the Kaleidoscope filter that makes your pictures look as if you're seeing them through an actual kaleidoscope.

KPT Interform is another kind of texture designer. It merges two "parent" textures to make a "child" texture and animates the process as a QuickTime movie. Figure 19.6 shows the interface.

KPT Convolver

If those initials seem familiar, they should. Convolver is another Kai creation. You could think of it as Power Tools' more practical-minded brother. Convolver has two functions: corrective and creative. If you only use it for one of these, you'll be happy with your investment, but you'll be missing half the fun. The good thing about Convolver is not so much what it does, although it's extremely powerful and definitely useful, but its biggest feature is that it brings all the tools together. When you're tweaking an image, you don't have to keep going back to the menu to get new tools. Everything's right there. If changing the saturation affects something else, you don't have to go very far to fix it.

FIGURE 19.6.

Interform combines textures and motions.

Figure 19.7 shows Convolver in Tweak mode (your other two choices are Explore and Design). The large central diamond is the Preview window; the smaller one above is called the Current Kernel Tile and is used to select a portion of the image to mutate in Explore mode.

FIGURE 19.7.

Making multiple adjustments with Convolver.

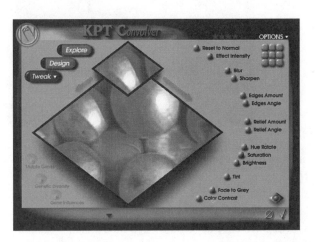

19

Along the right side of the screen are the Image controls. To apply one, click its button and drag right or left. Numbers appear in the bar below the Preview window to tell you what settings you're using. Most of these tools can be applied as a negative as well as a positive. Saturation, for instance, starts at 100% when you first click the button. Dragging left lowers the saturation to amounts less than 100%, while dragging right raises it. How high? I stopped after 3200%.

> Exploration is its own reward with Convolver, but there are more tangible ones as well. To encourage you to poke around, the program includes some hidden tools. They're called stars and the idea is that you'll get one after you've shown you really use the program. Each one adds a new tool when you're ready to apply it. It takes a while to work up to all five stars.

Design mode uses the Image controls in pairs, taking the central diamond and breaking it into 15 windows, each representing a combination of two Image control effects in a different degree of variation. That sounds confusing, but it should become clear when you look at Figure 19.8.

FIGURE 19.8.

Convolver in Design mode.

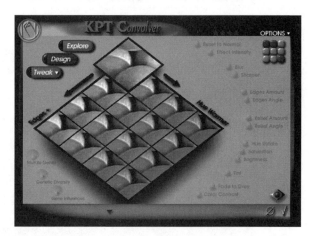

You'll notice an arrow along each axis of the diamond and a label denoting one of the effects. There are nine different options for each axis, and considering that they can go positive or negative, that makes 18 possible settings for each axis. Multiply that by 15 tiles of variations, and 10 degrees of intensity for each setting, and you end up with a lot of options. The difference between Design mode and Tweak mode, other than the difference in the interface, is that Design mode has the Image effects divided into logical pairs, while in Tweak mode, you can adjust them individually.

One of Convolver's best features is the multiple undos. You can undo—and of course, redo (Command/Ctrl-R)—up to 200 levels of change.

Explore mode is the creative side of Convolver. It applies new mutations based on some combination of colors and textures every time you click the mouse. Although it's not especially useful for cleaning up a poor quality photo, it could turn something you don't know why you shot into a work of art.

Alien Skin Eye Candy

Kai's not the only one who invents interesting plug-ins for Photoshop. The guys over at Alien Skin have come up with a set of goodies, formerly called Black Box but in this version renamed Eye Candy. It comes in both Mac and Windows flavors and can be found at your local software store or mail order source for about $125. Some of the Eye Candy effects are probably not for everyday use, unless your day job is designing covers for a science fiction magazine. Others, however, like drop shadow and perspective shadow, could be very useful.

The Alien Skin interface changes according to the effect you're applying, but the basic screen (shown in Figure 19.9) remains the same.

FIGURE 19.9.

Alien Skin Eye Candy.

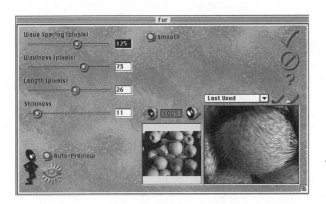

19

In this example, I've created a box of fur-covered apples. Fur is one of the 21 Eye Candy effects, along with smoke, fire, jiggle, squint, swirl, and a lot more. You can adjust all possible parameters of each of these effects, making the fur wavy, long, or shiny, the smoke dense or wispy, or whatever you can think of.

Applying many of these effects requires first selecting an area to which the effect will be applied, or adding a layer for it. A few, like Antimatter, simply do their thing. Antimatter inverts the brightness without affecting the colors or saturation value. Darks become light and lights go dark.

How to Create Glass Distortion

Possibly the most useful of the Eye Candy effects is Glass. In Figure 19.10, we're looking at one of my favorite scenes through a sheet of bumpy glass. The Glass effect is achieved by simulating three different effects: reflection, refraction, and light filtering. To use the Glass distortion effect, follow these steps.

FIGURE 19.10.

Using Glass distortion.

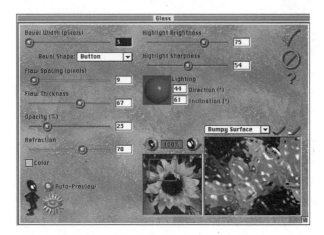

1. Start with an image that is basically simple. Glass works best on uncomplicated photos. Select the Glass filter from the Eye Candy list.

2. Set the Bevel Width. This controls both the width of the smooth outer edge of the glass and the apparent thickness of the glass. Larger values, used with high refraction, make your glass seem thicker. Smaller values, with low refraction, make the glass appear thinner.

3. Flaw Spacing and Flaw Thickness create the ripples in your glass. Smaller Spacing increases the frequency of flaws, while larger Thickness makes them more obvious.

4. Use the Color box to select a color or shade of "dirt" for the glass. A very light gray suggests a dusty window without affecting the colors of the original picture. Use the Opacity slider to determine how much of a color tint is applied to the glass. Higher values add more color. Lower values allow the picture to show more clearly.

5. Set the smoothness. Higher values remove small ridges in the bevel.

6. Refraction is the most important control for "glassiness." It controls the amount your picture is warped by the glass. The scale runs from 0 to 100%, but only the low end of it lets your image remain intelligible. Setting refraction past 50% reduces the underlying photo to vague shapes.

7. Highlight Brightness and Highlight Sharpness affect only the white highlights that appear on the "bumps." Higher values here give a glossier effect. Direction and Inclination can be set by typing numbers into their boxes or by dragging the ball around until the lighting looks right.

8. Watch the effect of each change in the Preview window as you make it. When you like what you see, click the check mark to confirm it and return to Photoshop, or just press Return or Enter. If the overall effect is too much, undo it and lower the settings or use Photoshop's Fade command to moderate it.

As is true of any of these tools, the more you explore, the more you'll learn about working with it.

Extensis PhotoTools

PhotoTools is a comprehensive set of plug-ins that makes working with Photoshop easier and more pleasant. (Find it at the usual software sources for about $125.) It includes a version of Intellihance (a "smart" filter for exposure correction), and it has lots of other goodies as well, including a toolbar that you can set up for faster access to your favorite Photoshop tools. The first thing PhotoTools does is to add another menu to your screen, with its own options and filters. Figure 19.11 shows the PhotoTools submenu. As you can see, there are tools to bevel and build buttons, to cast shadows and glows, and even to work with type.

FIGURE 19.11.

Extensis PhotoTools.

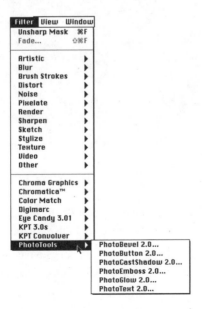

19

You can download limited-time, full-working versions of all the Extensis plug-ins on the World Wide Web. Go to www.extensis.com and check out the Photoshop plug-ins for Mac or Windows. They're good for 30 days in demo mode, and then you can register by phone with a credit card.

PhotoText

If there's only one reason to buy PhotoTools, it's the type tool, PhotoText. As you probably noticed, Photoshop still doesn't have a whole lot of flexibility with regard to type setting. PhotoText makes up for this lack by letting you place type over a picture and adjust the position of individual characters while you're typing it. The PhotoText window is shown in Figure 19.12.

FIGURE 19.12.

PhotoText is terrific!

You can set width and tracking for your type, adjust leading, and set anti-aliased, justified, flush-left, flush-right, or centered type at the click of a mouse, just as in any other good graphics program. Text handling was formerly Photoshop's only deficiency, and this tool definitely fills in the gap. Even better, it's easy to use. Here's how:

1. Prepare your background first. Remember that a too-busy picture makes type harder to read, so fade it down or reduce it to two colors as we've done here.

2. Open the PhotoText window. Choose a font and size and click the T icon to place a text block. Position the cursor where you want to start typing and set your type.

Drag the handles on the text block to make it larger if necessary. Type is set in a new layer, so you needn't worry about covering background elements.

3. Use the arrow icon or just press and hold the Option key to bring back the Pointer tool, so you can move your text around on the screen if you decide to reposition it. Adjust the leading and tracking in the windows above the Preview screen. Change the color with the Eyedropper and Color Picker windows.

4. If you're using larger fonts (over 14 point) and want to apply anti-aliasing to prevent jaggies, click the anti-alias button, under the Color Picker.

5. When your page is as you want it, click the arrow icon (top button) to save it, or the X button to cancel. Closing the window also cancels the type.

You can change type attributes on individual characters by selecting them with the Type tool, or on the entire text block by selecting it. Because the type is set on a new layer, you can easily apply Photoshop's Type Paths tool to turn it into a selection and use it for special effects. Headlines set in this way, because they can be properly kerned and letter-spaced, look better than those done directly in Photoshop.

PhotoGlow

Want to put a glow around those letters? It's a cinch if you have PhotoTools installed. Select the object, open the PhotoGlow box, as shown in Figure 19.13, and set up exactly as much glow as you'd like. PhotoGlow works on any selection, making it even more versatile than Photoshop's own Glow tool.

FIGURE 19.13.

All that glows isn't necessarily gold.

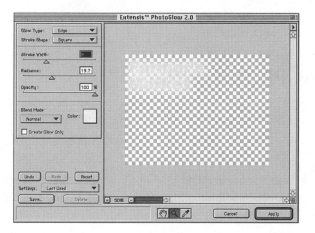

19

PhotoBevel

Sometimes it's fun to put a frame around your work, even when it's only going to be seen on a screen. Web page photos and art for audio/video presentations take on added emphasis if you treat the edges. PhotoBevel is a very neat and easy way to do just that. Figure 19.14 shows a beveled frame around a picture.

FIGURE 19.14.

Beveled edges add importance.

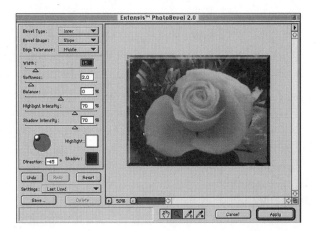

There are more PhotoTools, too. The Button tool is great for Web page buttons. You can turn any picture or textured surface into any of a dozen or so different button shapes. CastShadow automates the process of copying a shape, filling it with black and feathering it to look like a real shadow. Emboss is similar to Photoshop's own embossing filter but has a few more variables.

Extensis PhotoFrame

A new plug-in from the PhotoTools people gives you the ability to add a premade frame around your art. PhotoFrame comes with several different kinds of frames, and you can adjust them as you place them around a picture. Figure 19.15 shows the PhotoFrame window.

Each frame can be scaled, rotated, colored, blurred, or made opaque as needed. Additional CD-ROM volumes of frames are available, and you can download others from the Web or make your own.

Figure 19.15.

Frames include water color, canvas, and photographic plate effects.

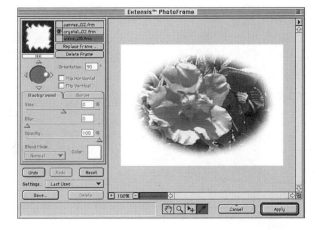

Intellihance

Personally, I think the color and exposure adjustments that you can do in Photoshop are one of the most enjoyable parts of using it. However, a lot of people don't enjoy messing with curves and levels, and brightness and saturation. If you're among them, Intellihance was written for you.

Open a picture, select Intellihance from the Filter menu, and click the button or press (Command-F) [Control-F]. That's all there is to it. A few seconds later, your screen blinks and there's the corrected image. Intellihance makes its corrections based on preferences you've previously set.

If you have a bunch of similar photos, you can fine-tune one of them using the Preferences window, shown in Figure 19.16, and then simply click the Enhance button on each of the subsequent pictures. You like snappy contrast and despeckling darks only? No problem. Intellihance remembers and corrects the picture the way you would. Only it probably does the job a little better, and a lot faster.

19

FIGURE 19.16.

Intelligent color correction with Intellihance.

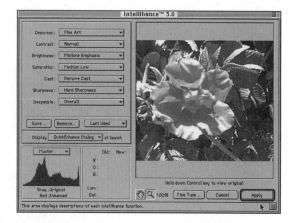

Chroma Graphics

Chroma Graphics creates some very user-friendly plug-ins for Photoshop, including Chroma Color and Chroma Palette—the two components of Chromatica. They've recently developed Magic Mask and Edge Wizard as well, and another plug-in, ChromaZone, is due out shortly. What do they do? Chromatica simplifies the business of selecting and changing colors in an image. Magic Mask and Edge Wizard handle masking and edge selection functions more gracefully than Photoshop itself.

Chromatica

Suppose you have a picture of a yellow flower. Now, suppose you really *need* a picture of a blue flower. Can you select the yellow flower and turn it blue? Sure you can, in any of several different ways. Will it look right? Yes, if you use Chromatica. Instead of just pouring one color over another or fiddling around with the Hue slider, you can make changes that match the full dynamic range of the original. You don't lose any of the detail or the subtle shading that vanishes when you try to make color changes by brute force.

Figure 19.17 shows a rose that I have selected and turned blue using Chromatica. Well, you're seeing it in gray, but trust me, it's a very natural-appearing pale blue on my screen.

Figure 19.17.

Blue roses? Why not?

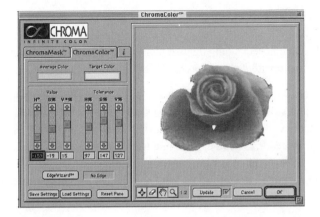

Chromatica is actually a combination of tools that first masks an object and then lets you recolor it. Chromatica's masking tool, Chroma Mask, works by letting you select a small sample of the object to create a precise mask. You can then use the color wheel and Hue, Saturation, and Value sliders to further refine your mask. After you make the selection, switch to ChromaPalette, as shown in figure 19.18, to make the color change.

Figure 19.18.

Blue, red, green, or any other color—it's your choice.

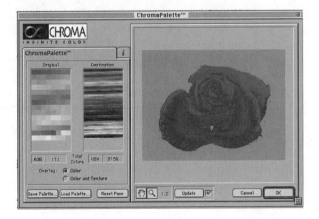

19

The masking aspects of Chromatica can also be found in MagicMask, another Chroma plug-in. MagicMask, like Chromatica's masking tool, uses color sampling, and also has a Magic Lasso that seeks out edges of a selected object for you, making selection a snap. You can even create density masks to work with difficult gradients such as skin tones.

EdgeWizard is a Chroma plug-in that blends edges. This may not seem like a big deal, but if you've struggled with Photoshop's edge feathering tool and gotten a halo around your feathered edge, or an otherwise unsatisfying result, you'll love EdgeWizard. It's shown in figure 19.19. You can blend edges in a particular direction, or apply Gaussian blur. You can even choose a Variable Color Edge and EdgeWizard will analyze the image under your mask to determine the best possible edge. Threshold and Transition sliders provide tools for fine-tuning the effect.

FIGURE 19.19.

The Edge Wizard at work.

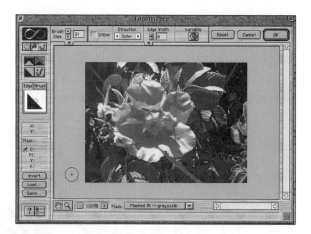

Summary

In this hour, we checked out some of the cool third-party filters you can use with Photoshop. The most versatile and complete package is MetaTools' Kai's Power Tools (KPT 3.0), although it's probably not the easiest to use. Alien Skin's Eye Candy filter set includes a great many really odd filters, such as Fur and Fire, as well as very simple-to-apply drop shadow and glow filters. Extensis PhotoTools is another wickedly neat set of plug-ins. They're a little less weird than the others, and the set includes an excellent TextTool that's far easier to use than Photoshop's own; it's also much more versatile.

I strongly recommend PhotoTools. Intellihance will save you time compensating for bad scans or lousy photography. Finally, Chromatica gives you the mask, color change, and edge blending tools you need to do professional quality work.

Q&A

Q Is there a way to design your own Photoshop filters?

A The CD-ROM includes a plug-in called Filter Factory, which supposedly lets you do so. It's a fairly complicated procedure and the documentation is lacking. Probably the best (easiest) way to get custom effects is to use KPT Convolver, either alone or in combination with other filters.

Q How do I make stars appear on the KPT Convolver palette?

A Like the joke that asks "How do you get to Carnegie Hall?"...Practice! The more new things you try with Convolver, the closer you get to adding more stars and more tools.

Quiz

Can you plug in the correct answers to these questions?

Questions

1. Where do plug-ins appear?

    a. On the Plug-ins palette.

    b. At the bottom of the Filter menu.

    c. At the top of the Window menu.

2. Which of the following is NOT an Eye Candy effect?

    a. Fur

    b. Fire

    c. Squint

    d. Slime

3. Convolver rewards your use of it with

    a. stars

    b. additional tools

    c. refund of the purchase price

    d. a & b only

19

Answers

1. b.

2. d. (But if you start with green glass, you can create a reasonably slimy effect.)

3. d. Hey, stars are nice, but more toys are better.

Activity

Turn on your modem and cruise to Extensis (`www.Extensis.com`). Download the PhotoTools and Intellihance plug-ins, and try them out for yourself.

Do the same for Eye Candy. (`http://www.alienskin.com/eyecandy/ec_demo.htm`)

Hour 20

Compositing

Compositing can be known by other names. It can be "combining" or making a collage or photo-montage. Whatever it's called, the goal is the same: to make one picture from pieces of other ones. Photoshop is the ideal program for this kind of work for several reasons. First, because it has the tools to assemble pieces of different pictures. Second, because it gives you the ability to work in layers. Third, because its filters enable you to blend pictures and add shadows and reflections more easily and effectively than any other graphics program.

You can use the techniques described here, along with the ones you've already learned, to produce all sorts of surrealistic images, and (for many people) this is what Photoshop is all about. For others, myself included, compositing is more a way of making up for deficiencies in the original picture.

Sources for Images

Pictures are everywhere. You can download thousands of images from the Web. You can buy CDs full of photographs and line art. And, of course, you can either scan conventional photos or import from a digital camera into Photoshop.

When you start thinking about combining images, you'll probably realize that some pictures are more suitable than others for this kind of use. You can even classify some as backgrounds, others as objects, and some as the raw materials from which to create special effects. As you browse through your own pictures and look at collections of stock photos, some images will jump out at you and you'll begin to see possible combinations.

Stock photos? If you're not familiar with the term, you should be. Stock photos are pictures that are made available to you, either royalty-free or for payment (usually the latter), to do with as you see fit. You can use them in your reports, in ads, or practically any way you want, as long as you're not reselling them as is, or using them in any way that's libelous, defamatory, pornographic, or otherwise illegal. Be sure you read and understand the licensing policies before you use them.

Point your Web browser toward www.adobestudios.com to see some really good stock photography. Alas, you can't use any of the pictures in the Adobe Image Library without paying for them. The screen versions all have a large Adobe logo imprinted on them, but you can get a feel for what's available and how much it costs.

Extensis PhotoDisc is typical of stock photo collections. The PhotoDisc collection includes over 50,000 pictures of everything you can imagine. A few samples are included on the PhotoTools and Fetch CDs. Figure 20.1 shows a page from their catalog. There's no reason you can't use these kinds of images in combination with your own. If you need something basic, like a slab of concrete to use as a background, it will be faster, cheaper, and just as effective to use one from stock. Let's start compositing with a couple of images from the stock catalog.

Of course, as you wander around town with your digital camera in your pocket, you can start your own stock collection, too. In fact, it's one of the ways you can make money with your pictures, allowing you to invest the profits in more software and higher resolution cameras.

FIGURE 20.1.

Stock photos.

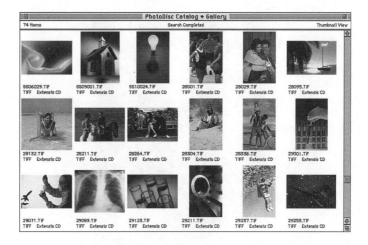

 If you are interested in learning more about digital photography, look for *Teach Yourself Digital Photography in 14 Days*, from Hayden Books, ISBN 1-56830-405-6. It's a good one—I wrote it.

Making One Picture from Two

Looking through the catalog of stock photos, I noticed a picture of a light bulb and one of a rose. Combining them could give us an interesting image. First, open the light bulb in Photoshop, because it will be the main image (see Figure 20.2).

Then open the rose picture. Because it's horizontal and the other one is vertical, the first steps will be to rotate (Edit→Transform→Rotate) it and crop it. Figure 20.3 shows the rose after this step.

20

FIGURE 20.2.

And there was light.

FIGURE 20.3.

Cropped and rotated.

This is still not what's wanted here. I need it to stand up straight. I'll select it with the Rectangle Marquee and free rotate it until the flower is vertical. Check out the action in Figure 20.4. Now it's oriented correctly.

FIGURE 20.4.

Standing tall.

There are several ways to get rid of the background, but the easiest is to select the rose and copy it, leaving everything else behind. After doing that, jump back to the light bulb picture and make a new layer. When you paste the rose into it, the screen looks like Figure 20.5.

FIGURE 20.5.

I moved it over the bulb.

20

Now we're about halfway there. The rose is just a little small, so we'll scale it up until it fits inside the bulb. Layer→Transform→Scale puts a scaling box over the flower, so I can resize it to fit properly inside the bulb. While I'm at it, I'll take the Eraser and trim the stem to fit. Figure 20.6 shows the results of this step. Because the rose is on a separate layer, I don't have to worry about damaging the background.

FIGURE 20.6.

Trimmed to fit.

It looks almost right, but the rose appears to be on top of the light bulb instead of in it. Reducing the opacity of the layer to 70% gives the flower the same sort of milkiness as the light bulb.

As a final touch, deselect the rose layer for a moment, and select the light bulb. Applying the Eye Candy Glow filter to the bulb, as shown in Figure 20.7, turns on the light. At the same time, we can add a little pink to the glow to suggest that the rose, rather than just the bulb, is glowing. Figure 20.8 shows the final picture.

FIGURE 20.7.

The Glow filter adds some light.

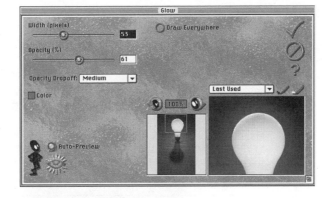

FIGURE 20.8.

A rosy glow, perhaps?

Controlling Transparency in Overlaid Images

It's extremely simple to paste one opaque image over another one—you just do it. Transparent images are harder to work with, though Photoshop makes it a little easier by giving you Transparency control.

When you're creating a multi-layered picture, as in Figure 20.7, you have two ways to control the way the layers blend. One is the Opacity slider. You can set any degree of opacity, from 100% all the way down to zero, at which point whatever's on the layer has completely disappeared. You can also control the effect by using the Blending Modes menu. By applying different modes to different layers, you can control the way each layer overlies the others.

Realistic Composites

Creating an image that's not meant to be completely realistic is relatively easy. Faking realism is a lot harder. The main things to consider in making composites are:

1. Keep your backgrounds simple.

2. Isolate the elements on different layers for easier editing.

3. Make sure the pieces you combine are in the proper scale for each other.

4. When you're done, merge the layers for a smaller file.

Remember also that adding shadows, reflections, or other special effects can make a big difference in the end result. Watch out for perspective, too. If it's wrong, you'll know it, although you may not know exactly why.

The series of pictures that follows shows a problem that I encountered with perspective and how I solved it.

Figure 20.9 is a photo I shot of an old windmill on Cape Cod. It was an overcast day in the middle of a hot summer. The sky is gray and the grass is more brown than green. As for the flowers along the fence...they're best forgotten, but the windmill itself is interesting. What can I do to improve this picture?

FIGURE 20.9.

Not very exciting.

On that same trip, I found a pretty cottage with a rose covered fence (see Figure 20.10). Perhaps the fence from that picture could replace the boring one? It looks as if it might work, but first we'll have to get rid of everything that's not fence.

FIGURE 20.10.

Can we make this fence fit?

20

Selecting with the Polygon Lasso and deleting removes the sidewalk and everything below it. Cropping and then using a combination of the Magic Wand and the Eraser gets rid of the rest, leaving nothing but fence and flowers. Figure 20.11 shows just the fence.

FIGURE 20.11.

Fence minus every-thing else.

I'll make a new layer on the windmill picture and copy the fence into it. Then I need to select and remove the white background that imported along with it, but that's a matter of two clicks with the Magic Wand and one click of the Delete key. With the fence moved into position, I see one minor problem. I stood to the left of the fence and to the right of the windmill (see Figure 20.12).

FIGURE 20.12.

Oops. The perspective is wrong.

Flipping the fence is easy. I just select Layer→Transform→Flip horizontal and the fence reverses itself. Now it looks better. Applying some extra roses with the Rubber Stamp helps fill in some gaps, and adding clouds to the (selected) sky completes the effect. To place the clouds, I used an Airbrush with a blue slightly darker than the sky color. After some experimenting, I decided to use Darken Only as the Blend mode when I brought in the sky, so it didn't overpower the very delicate lines on the windmill blades. As a final step, I'll merge the layers. Figure 20.13 shows the final photo, much improved from the original.

FIGURE 20.13.

All it needed was a new fence and some enhanced color.

Replacing a Background

Remember that tiger with the chain link fence in the background? We hid the fence, but it would be nice to put him somewhere a little bit wilder. My friend Linda took a picture of a waterfall, somewhere near Easley, South Carolina. It's a nice shot, but it could be more exciting. Maybe we can put the tiger into it. Figure 20.14 shows the waterfall and Figure 20.15 is the original tiger.

20

FIGURE 20.14.

A nice ordinary picture.

FIGURE 20.15.

And a nice friendly tiger.

The first thing to do is to isolate the tiger, but because the background is so complicated, the Magic Wand won't be much help. I can select and delete it a piece at a time with the Rectangle Marquee and Lasso, but that would take quite a while. Instead I'll start with the Polygon Lasso and work around the big cat. I then circle it around the top of the screen so that I've selected more or less everything behind him (see Figure 20.16.) What I can't select and delete, I can erase.

FIGURE 20.16.

Deleting the background.

To make it easier to blend him into a background, select the white space behind him, and choose Select→Inverse to select just the tiger. Then I apply Select→Feather to feather the edges by four pixels. In Figure 20.17, I have copied the feathered tiger and pasted him onto a new layer in the waterfall picture.

FIGURE 20.17.

Uh oh... too much tiger.

20

Trouble is, he's too big for the rock. While he's still selected, I can use Edit→Transform→Scale and shrink him down to a more comfortable fit. A little air-brushing around the edges, and a little dodging and burning to make his head stand out from the water, and we're done. He looks like he belongs there. Figure 20.18 shows the tiger in his new home.

FIGURE 20.18.

Notice how nicely his stripes relate to the waterfall.

So you see, combining pictures isn't at all difficult. You simply need to prepare them by removing unwanted backgrounds or other bits, and then assemble them in layers. Don't forget to merge the layers when you're sure that you're done working on the picture. Otherwise, your files, if they have several layers, can be quite large.

"Composites" from Nowhere

You've seen in some of the earlier hours that Photoshop can create art "from scratch," as well as editing and altering existing photos. As a final attempt at compositing, let's see what we can make out of nothing. I'll start with a new page and apply a gradient as a background.

Photoshop 5 has more Gradient options than ever before. Gradients can be linear, radial, angled, reflected, or diamond-shaped, and can have as many transparent or opaque colors as you wish. To create a gradient, follow these steps:

1. Choose the kind of gradient you want to apply from the pop-out menu, and double-click to open its Options window, an example of which is shown in Figure 20.19.

FIGURE 20.19.

Gradients and the Gradient Options window.

2. Use the Type: menu to choose Radial or Linear blend. I want to use Linear blend, which applies the colors in a straight line from one point to another. Click Dither to create a smoother blend.

3. Choose a color combination from the pop-up menu. The Preview bar at the bottom of the window shows the currently selected gradient. If it's not precisely what you want, that's okay.

4. Click the Edit button to open the Gradient editor, shown in Figure 20.20.

FIGURE 20.20.

The Gradient editor.

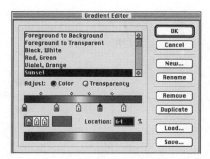

5. Select the Color button to adjust the colors in the gradient.

6. Click the left square beneath the Gradient bar to change the starting color. The triangle above it turns black, showing that you're editing that part of the gradient. To change the color, click the Color swatch and choose a color from the Color Picker, or click either the foreground or background selection box (marked F and B, respectively) to pick either of those colors. You could also hold the cursor over a color on the gradient to sample, and when it becomes an Eyedropper, click it.

20

7. Click the right square and follow the procedures above to change the ending color of the gradient.

8. Drag the diamond(s) above the gradient left or right to adjust the midpoint, or blend points if there are more than two colors.

9. Click and drag an additional color selection box to the gradient to add another color. Choose F or B or the empty box to add another color. Clicking it opens the Color Picker so you can choose the color.

10. Click OK when you are satisfied with the colors on your gradient.

11. Use the crosshair cursor that automatically appears to draw a line on the screen where the gradient should be applied.

In Figure 20.21, I have drawn a line from top to bottom to fill the screen with my gradient. It's starting to look like a sunset, which is what I had in mind, but it needs a sun. I'll use Eye Candy's Star filter to create one. Figure 20.22 shows the Star designer box and Figure 20.23 shows the star applied.

If you want to start from scratch, don't bother to select an existing gradient. Just click the Edit button to open the editor. Then click the New button and give your new gradient a name. Proceed as above to define its colors.

FIGURE 20.21.

The Gradient applied.

FIGURE 20.22.

Eye Candy Star filter.

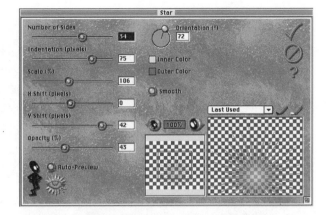

FIGURE 20.23.

Adding a sun. (Well, okay, it's a star, but so is the sun.).

20

That's good but not perfect. Applying the Ocean Ripple filter to the lower part of the star gives it a little more of a watery quality. As a final touch, I drew in a sailboat, copied it on a separate layer, and flipped it vertically. After again applying the Ripple filter to it, I faded the reflection. Figure 20.24 shows the final picture.

FIGURE 20.24.

Sunset sail.

Summary

Composites, montages—whatever you call them, they're simply combinations of two or more images, carefully merged. Use your own pictures, stock photos from collections, or create images by combining techniques and filters. It's fun and it's effective. It's one of the things Photoshop does exceptionally well. Be sure to spend some time playing with compositing.

Q&A

Q. Can I apply a filter to a gradient?

A. Certainly. It's easiest if the gradient is on a separate layer. Just make the gradient the active layer and apply any filter or combination you like. The results often make an interesting background for other pictures, too. Start by trying the Texture filters and some of the brushstroke ones. These are generally successful.

Q. I tried importing a building to another photo, but it just doesn't look right. Why not?

A. There could be a dozen different reasons, but the three most obvious are: scale, perspective, and lighting. The import may be too big or too small for where you put it. It may need to be skewed into a different perspective. You may also be trying to put a shadowless, noon-time picture into a late afternoon background. When you select pictures to combine, try to match sizes, orientation, and time of day. If that's not possible, you can still make it work, but you will have to do more correcting.

Quiz

Now that you know how to put pictures together, see if you can put these questions and answers together.

Questions

1. Any picture you download from the Web can be considered a stock photo.

   a. True

   b. False

2. Photoshop has _____ different kinds of gradients.

   a. two

   b. three

   c. five

3. Name one thing you'll have to master to make good composite images.

   a. Zen

   b. Filters

   c. Layers

Answers

1. b. Be careful, as many images are copyrighted and you could get into legal trouble if you use them commercially. If you're just messing around with Photoshop at home, you're probably safe.

2. c. Can you name them? If not, start Photoshop and explore the toolbar where the Gradient tools reside.

3. c. You'll have to know several Photoshop techniques to create composite images, but being a pro at using layers is indispensible.

20

Activity

To experiment with compositing, find two of your own pictures or two stock photos, one landscape and one portrait. Remove the background from the portrait subject, and place him or her into the landscape. Add shadows or reflections if necessary to make the person look as if he or she was photographed "on location." To see how I placed my kids in front of the Golden Gate Bridge, go to `home.earthlink.net/~momcat`.

HOUR 21

Photo Repair—Black and White

Fixing damaged or "just plain lousy" pictures is the number one reason why most people buy Photoshop. It can really work miracles on old, torn, faded photographs and it can also make up for most, if not all, of the flaws in your snapshots. Photoshop can be used to recompose a picture that's off-center, tilted, or has too much empty space. You can edit out the power lines and trash cans that spoil the landscape. You can even remove unwanted former spouses, or that awful boyfriend your daughter finally dumped from family portraits. It's nowhere near as difficult to get rid of them onscreen.

Easy Fixes

Let's start by looking at some of the things you can do to fix up an old picture that may have faded, yellowed, or been damaged. First we'll consider a couple of old family photos that need a little bit of adjusting and touching up. We'll run (literally) through the steps involved in fixing them and the tools you'll need to know how to use. (Remember, you can always flip to the front of the book to refresh your memory about these tools, too.) Finally we'll take an extremely damaged picture and work through it step by step, until it looks like new again.

Some pictures don't need very much work. The photo in Figure 21.1 was taken in 1905 but has been kept in an album away from sunlight for most of the past 93 years. It's turned a little yellow, but all in all it's remarkably well preserved.

FIGURE 21.1.

This needs only minor touch-ups.

To fix this picture, we first crop the borders to remove any unnecessary edges and rotate the image so the porch isn't tilted. Then we set the mode to Grayscale, which removes any color information that the scan picked up and immediately eliminates the yellow and brown tones. Next we use Curves (Image→Adjust→Curves) to tweak the contrast a little. By using Curves, we can lighten the light tones without affecting the darks. In Figure 21.2, the very slight curve in the window lets you see just how subtle this adjustment is. Figure 21.3 shows the results of the steps we've taken.

A couple of spots in the picture could use some minor enhancement. We'll apply the Burn tool to darken some areas where the contrast could be a little better. By applying the Burn tool only to the shadows and with a low Percentage setting, we can darken the lady's hair without darkening the sky behind it. Similarly, applying Burn to midtones separates the lady's jawline from her high whalebone collar. Figure 21.4 shows the final result.

FIGURE 21.2.

The curve adjustment is very slight.

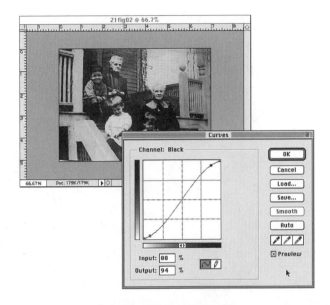

FIGURE 21.3.

Much improved.

21

FIGURE 21.4.

Well-preserved photos, regardless of age, can be digitally enhanced.

Many Photoshop users make a habit of applying the Dust and Scratches filter (Filters→Noise→Dust and Scratches) to every scanned photo. This is often a mistake because, although it does make dust particles less obvious, it also softens the focus of the picture. If you decide to try it, evaluate the results carefully, using the Preview check box to toggle back and forth, turning the filter preview on and off until you're certain that it's an improvement.

A second family picture, this one an early Polaroid only 50 years old, is in much worse shape. It is both yellowed and faded, and it has a couple of thumbprints and a crease right through the middle. Even when it was shot, the contrast wasn't very good. The untouched photo is shown in Figure 21.5. Can we rescue it?

Again we'll start by cropping and then go to Grayscale to get rid of the yellow tones. There's a good deal that can be cropped out of this photo, improving the composition as well as avoiding the fold line. The contrast ratio in this picture isn't as good as in the previous one, so our next step will be to attempt to improve it. The Levels window shows the histogram for this picture, which tells us that the whites are too dark and the darks not dark enough (see Figure 21.6).

This one needs more serious work.

FIGURE 21.6.

Changing the Levels adjusts the contrast.

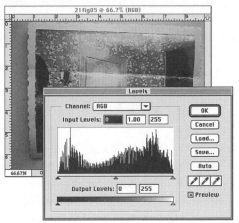

Resetting the black and white points helps a great deal. Resetting the midpoint to the center of the peak in the histogram helps even more. The best way to learn to make these adjustments is to work on a copy of a "bad" picture and simply experiment with the settings until you see the picture looking the way you want it to. Notice what happens when you move the sliders to the right or left. Figure 21.7 shows the corrections so far.

21

FIGURE 21.7.

Better, but not as good as it could be.

Using the Eyedropper

Sometimes you need to paint over part of an image, either to fill in scratches or to remove unwanted lines, spots, or in-laws. Use the Eyedropper tool to select a color to paint with. Simply click the Eyedropper on any color (or in this case, shade of gray) in the image that you want to replicate, and that color becomes the foreground color, ready to apply with the Paintbrush, Airbrush, or whatever painting tool you choose. Double-clicking the Eyedropper opens its Options window. A pop-up menu gives you the choice of a single pixel color sample or of taking an average color from either a 3×3 or 5×5 pixel sample.

Someone picked up this print before it dried and left a thumbprint right in the middle. Right now it looks like glare on the painted door. With the Eyedropper, Brush, and Smudge tools, we'll repair the damage. All we need to do is to pick up the appropriate background gray from elsewhere in the picture, paint it in, and smudge it a little bit so it blends. At the same time, we'll lighten the face of the man on the right.

Using the Eyedropper tool in a situation like this is much easier than trying to match an existing color or shade of gray on the color wheel. All you need to do to paint in the background is to find another spot in the picture where the color or gray shade is the same one that you'd like to use. Select the Eyedropper and click it to make that color the foreground color. Then use your brush to paint in the selected shade. Smudge the edges very slightly if necessary to make the new paint blend in (see Figure 21.8).

FIGURE 21.8.

You can see the changes from "Before" in Figure 21.5 to "After."

Taking a closer look at the family's faces, we can see white spots, which are apparently an artifact from the scan, because they aren't on the original. Figure 21.9 shows a close-up view, before and after retouching. Because the area to work on is so small, we use a single-pixel brush as a Smudge tool and set it for only 20% Pressure to not overdo the smudges. When you are working on corrections this small, it's much easier to apply them gradually and let the effect build up than try to do it all in one pass.

FIGURE 21.9.

A little spotting and smudging does wonders.

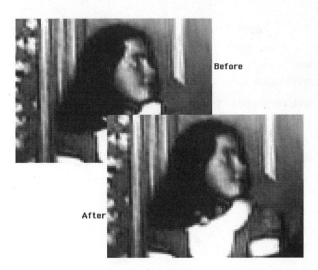

Before

After

21

Rubber Stamp

The Rubber Stamp tool is perfect when you need to copy small pieces of the picture and paste them elsewhere. Technically it's a cloning brush. It samples from a chosen point in the image and duplicates it, exactly as if you'd made a rubber stamp of the selection. Figure 21.10 shows the Rubber Stamp tool and its Options window.

FIGURE 21.10.

The Rubber Stamp tool's icon looks just like a rubber stamp.

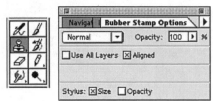

To select a point to clone from, press Option (Mac) or Alt (Windows) while you click the mouse on the spot you want to copy. Then release the key and start stamping by moving the mouse to the new spot and clicking. You can stamp as many times as you need to.

Because the Rubber Stamp tool functions like a brush, you can apply all the Brush modes, such as Dissolve, Multiply, and so on. The size and shape of the Rubber Stamp area will be the same as the Brush size and shape you have selected. You can also apply the same Opacity settings that you would to any brush. Feel free to flip back to review these tools and settings in greater detail.

The Rubber Stamp Options window lets you select among several ways for the Stamp to operate:

- **Clone (aligned):** When you select a reference point, the Stamp creates a duplicate of the image anywhere you start painting, expanding the duplicated portion of the image as you go. Conceivably you could reproduce the entire image, if you have enough blank canvas.

- **Clone (non-aligned):** After you select your reference point and start painting, the duplicate portion of the image expands only while you continue to hold down the mouse button. When you release it and press it again, you start painting another duplicate image from the same reference point.

- **Pattern (aligned):** You can define a pattern and stamp it with the Rubber Stamp tool. Use the Rectangle Marquee to select a piece of image to use as a pattern, and select Define Pattern from the Edit menu. Now when you use the Rubber Stamp, the pattern is tiled over the area as you stamp.

- **Pattern (non-aligned):** Select a pattern as above, but each time you release the mouse button and then press it again, the pattern starts over instead of tiling.

- **From Snapshot:** Use the Rubber Stamp to apply changes to your image selectively. Make the change, take a snapshot of it, then undo the change and apply it selectively with the Rubber Stamp. You can take a snapshot of your image by choosing Take Snapshot from the Edit menu.

- **From Saved:** This works like a magic eraser. Where you stamp, the image reverts to the way it was the last time you saved. It's essentially the opposite of the process above. Instead of selectively applying the changes, you're selectively undoing them.

- **Impressionist:** This is more or less useless. This stamp applies the last saved version of the image in a smudged, spotty, uneven pattern.

When you use the Rubber Stamp tool to retouch, always choose a soft-edged brush in a size only slightly larger than the scratch or blemish you're hiding. Retouching is generally easier if you enlarge the image first.

For this next photo, we'll need the Rubber Stamp tool and probably all the tricks in the book. As you can see in Figure 21.11, this picture has been folded, ripped, faded, and generally beaten up. We'll go through this one step by step, so you can see exactly what happens at each stage.

Cleaning Up a Picture, Step by Step

To make this picture, or any other, look like new:

1. Crop the image to remove the border and any unnecessary parts of the image. (Anything you remove doesn't have to be retouched.) Select the Cropping tool from the toolbox. (It pops out from the Selection Marquee when you hold the mouse button.) Drag it across the picture, holding the mouse button down. Use the handles on the Cropping window to fine-tune the selection, and then double-click inside the window to crop the image.

21

FIGURE 21.11.

*This will take some
work.*

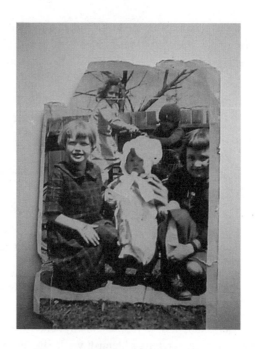

2. Set the mode to Grayscale (Image→Mode→Grayscale) to remove the colored stains.

3. Open the Histogram window (Image→Histogram). Look at the histogram to see what needs to be done to equalize the contrast (see Figure 21.12). In this case, both the white and the dark points need to be reset. To make these changes, we'll need to adjust the levels.

4. Open the Levels window (Image→Adjust→Levels) and adjust the levels by dragging the dark point to the right until it's under the beginning of the dark peak of the histogram. Drag the white point to the left until it's under the beginning of the white peak. Figure 21.13 shows our adjustments.

FIGURE 21.12.

The histogram shows a lot of lights.

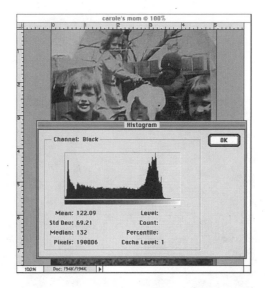

FIGURE 21.13.

Adjusting the levels improves the contrast.

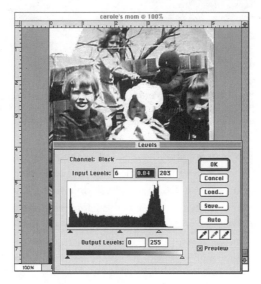

5. Now we'll try out the Dust and Scratches filter (Filters→Noise→Dust and Scratches). In this case, it seems that the good it does outweighs the slight fuzziness it adds (see Figure 21.14 to see the filter applied). Click OK to apply the filter.

21

FIGURE 21.14.

*Removing dust can
also remove detail.*

6. The filter took care of some of the dust but left most of the scratches. Use the
   Rubber Stamp tool to cover them. Select the tool and open the Brushes and Options
   windows (Window→Show Brushes and Window→Show Options). Choose a small
   brush and set the Opacity to 90%. Choose Clone non-aligned, pick the dark tone

adjacent to the scratch, and start stamping it out. Remember to set a spot to use as a stamp, and press Option (Mac) or Alt (Windows) while you click the mouse on the spot you want to copy. Figure 21.15 shows the partially treated photo. Remember to change your stamp selection as the areas the scratch runs through change value.

FIGURE 21.15.

Help stamp out scratched photos!

21

7. The best way to remove the scratch across the girl's face is to use a Paintbrush and repaint the face, rather than trying to stamp it. To make the task easier, enlarge the picture. Click the Magnifying Glass tool at the bottom of the toolbox to enlarge the picture.

8. Select the Eyedropper tool and click the medium dark gray on the right side of her bangs. Choose a small Paintbrush and paint over the scratches, changing shades of gray with the Eyedropper as you need to. Figure 21.16 shows before and after views of this step.

9. At the same time, you can use the Smudge tool to remove any light spots and to fill in the background between Rubber Stamp impressions.

FIGURE 21.16.

Be careful not to apply paint too evenly.

10. Next apply the Dodge and Burn tools as needed to bring out details. Dodging lightens the image and burning darkens it. Sponging increases or decreases the saturation of colors. Figure 21.17 shows these useful tools. (Flip back to Hour 9, "Moving Paint," for more details on using them.) Select the Dodge tool and set its Exposure to 25%, so the effect will be gradual.

FIGURE 21.17.

The Dodge tool looks like a lollipop, the Burn tool like a hand, and the Sponge tool like a sponge.

11. We can dodge the boy's face and the other dark areas and burn a little where there are light spots. The effect will build if you release the mouse button, then click it and go over the same area again. Be careful not to overdo it. Figure 21.18 shows the final version.

FIGURE 21.18.

Compare this to the picture we started with.

21

Applying Tints

It was common in the early days of photography for pictures to be brown, blue, or silver instead of plain black and white. Sepia toning, which gave a warm reddish-brown color, was the most common and one we tend to associate with most "old time" photos.

If you want to restore the sepia tone to a picture you've been working on, Photoshop gives you several ways to accomplish this. Perhaps the easiest is to reset the mode to CMYK or RGB, depending on whether the finished photo will be viewed onscreen or printed, and then use the Hue/Saturation window (Image→Adjust→Hue) to add color. After you open the window, as shown in Figure 21.19, check the Colorize box, as well as the Preview box. Then move the sliders until the image looks the way you want it to. Click OK when you're satisfied with the color.

FIGURE 21.19.

The statue of Myles Standish was digitally photographed in February, 1998. It only looks like 1898.

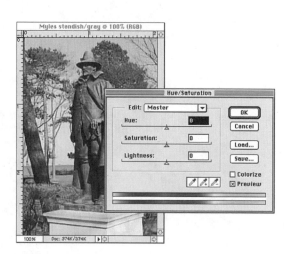

Duotones

A somewhat richer tone can be achieved by using Duotone mode, which combines the grayscale image with a colored ink. Duotones are often used to extend the gray range of a photograph, because a typical printing press is capable of reproducing only about 50 shades of gray, while Photoshop can generate 256.

To create a duotone, start with a grayscale image. Within Duotone mode, you also have the option of adding colors to make a tritone or quadtone. Although duotones are usually composed of black plus a single color, as in Figure 21.20, there's no good reason why you can't use two colors instead, especially if the end result is to be displayed on a Web page or as part of a desktop presentation, rather than in printed form.

Figure 21.20.

To create a tritone, add another color.

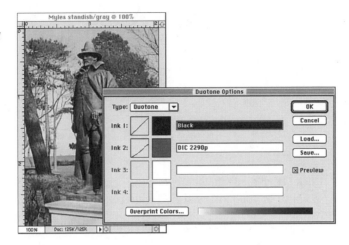

Figure 21.20.

To create a tritone, add another color.

Because it has a nice range of grays, the photo of Myles Standish is a good candidate for conversion to a duotone. To make a duotone from a grayscale image, follow these steps:

1. Open the Duotone Options window (Image→Mode→Duotone).

2. Select Duotone from the Type pop-up menu, if it's not already selected (refer to Figure 21.20). This menu is in the upper-left corner of the dialog box.

3. Choose colors for your duotone by clicking the color swatches. Choose black or a dark color for Ink 1 and a lighter color for Ink 2. You must select the Photoshop Color Picker, rather than the system Color Picker, in order to access the Custom colors (PANTONE process colors). If you need to switch to the Photoshop Color Picker, close this window temporarily by clicking Cancel, and open the General Preferences window (File→Preferences→General or Command/Control-K). Set the Color Picker to Photoshop and click OK. Reopen the Duotone Options window and proceed as above.

4. Use the curve windows within the Duotone Options window to adjust the curves for your two colors. (They're the small windows with diagonal lines, just to the right of the words "Ink 1" and "Ink 2.") If you click the small window, it expands to a full-size curve grid, which works just like the regular one (see Figure 21.21). Click to set points and drag to adjust the curve. You can't see the effect on the image, but you can see it on the strip of tone in the Duotone window.

21

FIGURE 21.21.

Here we're adjusting
the curve for Ink 2.

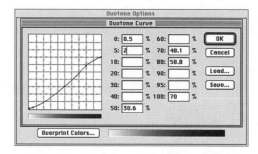

5. Click OK to apply the duotone to the image. Unfortunately there's no preview available. If you're not satisfied with the result, undo it and try again.

Using blue as the color with black gives you an image that replicates an old, black-and-white TV set. Using a light to medium brown with black gives a pretty good imitation sepia, as does a combination of red and green.

"Hand-Colored" Photos

Years ago, before color film was readily available, it was common to see hand-tinted photos. These had been painstakingly overpainted with thinned out watercolors to add a pale suggestion of color to the picture. The Photoshop Paintbrush and Airbrush are well suited for re-creating the look of a hand-colored photograph. You can even do the whole Ted Turner routine and colorize stills from your favorite Marx Brothers movie or Bogart classic. (You can find lots of movie stills and movie star pictures on the Web to practice on.)

After you have cleaned up the image that you want to hand-tint, change the mode back to Color, either RGB or CMYK, as you did above for the duotone. Double-click the Paintbrush tool to show the Paintbrush options, if this window isn't already open. Set the Blending mode to Color and the Opacity to somewhere between 15 and 20%. Remember to keep the mouse button down as you paint, because letting up on it and clicking it again adds a second 20% of color over the image.

If you have large, uncomplicated areas to tint, use one of the Selection tools, such as the Lasso or the Magic Wand, to select the area. Select a foreground color and choose Fill from the Edit menu, as shown in Figure 21.22.

FIGURE 21.22.

Use Fill for large areas. It's faster and smoother than painting.

When the Fill window opens, set the Opacity to about 25% and choose Color from the Blending mode options. Set Foreground Color on the Use pop-up menu. Click OK to fill all the selected areas with your chosen color at that opacity. If it's not enough, either reopen the Fill window and apply it again, or undo it and set a higher percentage. If it's too much, undo and set a lower percentage.

Summary

We have been looking at ways to repair photographs that need help. When you have old, cracked, torn, or faded pictures, you can use a variety of Photoshop tools to cover up the imperfections and restore the image. The Eyedropper tool enables you to select a color or gray tone and apply it with any of your painting tools. The Rubber Stamp clones a selected piece of the picture and places it wherever you want it, as much or as little as needed to cover a crack, fill in an empty space, or cover objects you want to hide.

Tinting old photos can be managed in any of several ways. Toning may be applied by colorizing or by turning the picture into a duotone, tritone, or quadtone. Hand-coloring can give you a different "old" picture look.

Q&A

Q How can I remove my ex-husband from a group shot of the family?

A It depends on where he is in the group and what's behind him. If you can drag the background to cover him, that might work. Otherwise, perhaps you can find some other face the right size and colors to replace him. (Leonardo di Caprio, perhaps?)

21

Adjust the size and position of the new face on a separate layer. Blur the face you want to hide and use the Opacity slider to bring in the replacement. If you leave it at about 80%, it should merge right in.

Q OK, I've retouched all the old family photos, what do I do now?

A The next logical step is to buy a package of photo-quality glossy paper and print them out as photos. Kodak, HP, and Epson all sell glossy paper for inkjet and bubblejet printers. It's about the same weight as photo paper and it makes your pictures look really good.

Be sure to save the files for future use, too. CD-ROMs and Zip disks can hold several generations of family photos and can be stored in very little space. If you keep a backup copy in a safe place, like a bank safe deposit box, your precious family history is fire and flood proof.

Quiz

If you don't know the answers, retouch your score.

Questions

1. Burning is the opposite of _____.

    a. covering

    b. filling

    c. dodging

2. The Rubber Stamp tool prints _____.

    a. text

    b. a clone of whatever you have selected

    c. random shapes and designs

3. How many colors of ink are in a duotone?

    a. one

    a. one plus black

    c. any two, not necessarily including black

Answers

1. c. Dodging lightens the image. Burning darkens it.

2. b. Though c might be fun...

3. c. Though black is usually one of the two, it needn't be.

Activity

Find a picture in need of retouching, or download one from our Web site. Clean it up as much as you think necessary and save a copy. Convert the copy to a duotone. Hand-color the original using transparent tints. Notice how the duotone looks like rotogravure pages from the 1930s, while the hand-colored version looks like photos from the '40s or '50s. Think about how you might use these techniques with your own work.

21

HOUR 22

Photo Repair—Color

Last Hour, we worked on some black-and-white pictures that needed help. This Hour we'll do the same with color. You can adjust the colors to fix a picture that's faded with age or has too much red, green, or some other color in it. You can compensate for slight to moderate under- or overexposure, but you can't put back an image that's just not there, unless you paint it in.

You can take the red out of your daughter's eyes or the unearthly green out of the cat's eyes. Does your teenager wonder how she'd look with orange or green hair or a half-shaved head? Try it on the screen first. Maybe she'll settle for a second set of earrings.

Color Retouching

So far, all the pictures we've worked on are old, black-and-white photos. You can use most of the same tools and tricks in color. You may find that color retouching is even easier than working in black and white. The color tends to disguise some of the manipulation.

Figure 22.1 is a photo of my parents and some friends, shot sometime in the 1950s. The color might not have been good to start with, and as the picture has aged, it's gotten worse. Now it's mostly pinks and reds. (I know, it's hard to see this in black and white. Use your imagination.)

Using the Curves window, as shown in Figure 22.2, I can adjust the Red channel to remove most of the unwanted color. Rather than trying to remove all of it, which would turn the image too blue, it's better to compromise and leave a faint warmth. To adjust a single color with the Curves window:

1. With the image open, open the Curves window (Image→Adjust→Curves).

2. Choose the color closest to, or the complement to, the color that needs adjusting from the pop-up Channels menu. Choose Red, Green, or Blue if those colors need lessening. If there's too much yellow, add blue. If there's too much magenta, add green. If there's too much cyan, add red.

3. Drag the curve up to increase the amount of the color. Drag it down to decrease the amount by adding the complement. Watch the Preview as you drag. Click OK when the colors look right.

FIGURE 22.1.

This picture turned red with age.

FIGURE 22.2.

*Adjusting the red chan-
nel separately lets us
get the red out.*

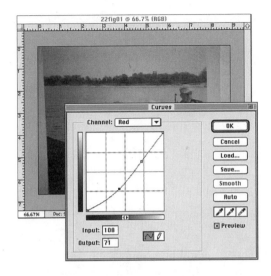

22

This photo needs some additional tweaking to increase the Saturation now that we've taken out the excess red. It also needs some Brightness and Contrast adjustment and some cropping to improve the composition.

The smudge at the top of the picture can easily be removed either with the Rubber Stamp tool or by lassoing a piece of sky and placing it over the spot. This is a simple way to fix large, plain areas. You can also use it to hide something like a trash can by dragging shrubbery over it.

To use the Lasso tool for this purpose:

1. Select the Lasso tool from the toolbar. Open the Feather dialog box (Select→Feather) and set the Feather Radius to somewhere between 3 and 6 pixels. This will help the copied sky blend in.

2. Select a piece of sky the same color as the sky behind the smudge by circling it with the Lasso.

3. With the dotted line Marquee flashing, choose the Move tool and press (Option) [Alt] as you drag the selection. (See a close view of this in Figure 22.3.)

4. Repeat as needed, selecting different pieces of sky if the color changes behind what you need to cover. You can also use this trick to hide any other parts of the picture that you don't want.

5. Press (Command-D) [Control-D] when you're finished dragging and copying to deselect the selection. Figure 22.4 shows the cleaned-up picture.

FIGURE 22.3.

Be sure to cover all of the smudge.

FIGURE 22.4.

The finished picture minus smudges and clutter.

Fixing Red Eye

You've seen red eye. It's not a problem in black-and-white photos that you colorize, but it's often a problem in color pictures of people and animals taken with a flash camera.

22

Basically what happens is that the flash reflects off the blood vessels at the back of the eye and puts an eerie red glow into the pupils of anyone looking straight at the flash. Cats, by the way, can also display a similar phenomenon called "green eye," caused by the flash reflecting off taurine crystals in the back of the eye. You can avoid this if you make sure your portrait subject, human or otherwise, isn't looking directly at the flash, and by making sure there's plenty of light in the room so the subject's pupils have contracted as small as possible.

Figure 22.5 shows a portrait of a cat suffering from a combination of red and green eye. This one was shot in a dark room and the flash caught the cat staring wide-eyed. If we correct the off-color eyes, it will be a nice picture.

FIGURE 22.5.

Even printed in black and white, the eyes look wrong.

The correction is actually quite easy. Here's how to do it:

1. Open the image and zoom in on the eyes by clicking the Magnifying Glass.
2. Use the Magic Wand to select the parts that need to be corrected (see Figure 22.6).

FIGURE 22.6.

Cat's eye selected at 200% magnification.

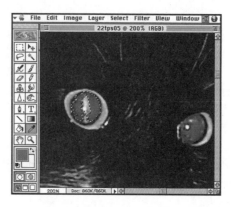

3. Choose the Paint Bucket tool. Set the Foreground color to black. Double-click the Tool icon to open the Tool Options window and set the Paint mode to Darken with an Opacity of about 80%. This setting darkens the eye while maintaining the detail.

4. Pour the paint carefully into the pupils of the eyes, making sure not to pour it into any white or colored highlights in the pupil (see Figure 22.7). You may need to click different selected parts of the pupil in order to cover all of it. If you accidentally fill one of the highlights, Undo. If you want to accent the highlights more, use a single pixel Pencil (select the smallest possible Brush size) and touch up as needed.

FIGURE 22.7.

The highlights in the pupils are called catchlights.

5. Press (Command-D) [Ctrl-D] to deselect the eyes so that you can evaluate the effect of the change. Figure 22.7 shows the finished cat.

The semi-opaque black that we poured in effectively darkened the pupils without losing detail. You can use this technique any time you have a small area in a picture that needs to have the color changed drastically. Be careful not to select any part of the image that you *don't* want to change.

How Much Change Is Okay?

Editing a picture to improve the composition is entirely reasonable, if it's a picture for your own use, but this is precisely what got the esteemed *National Geographic* magazine in trouble some years ago. They were doing a piece on Egypt and sent a photographer to get pictures of the pyramids. The art director studied the pictures and decided the composition would be better if he moved one of the pyramids closer to the next. As soon as the issue was published, astute readers began calling and writing to the magazine to complain. An apology appeared in the following issue, but simply knowing that the manipulation was possible waved a red flag for many people both inside and outside the publishing industry. The question has been debated ever since. How much change is okay? How much is too much?

It's clear that you can't always believe what you see. The supermarket tabloids frequently feature pictures that stretch the bounds of believability. Remember the one of the President shaking hands with the "space alien"? Or the "big foot" carrying off the scantily clad woman? (Why was she dressed like that in the snow anyway?) On the other hand, if a model is having a bad hair day or her face breaks out, retouching is required and expected. Where do you draw the line?

The answer depends on how the picture is to be used. Reputable newspapers and magazines tend to have strict guidelines about what they'll allow for photo manipulation. The general rule seems to be that if a change affects the *content* of the photo rather than its appearance, you can't do it. You can lighten a too-dark picture of the politician, but you can't change the soda can in his hand into a beer can (or vice versa).

"Editing" a Picture

There are times when you have to remove more than a scratch or a small imperfection from a photo. Sometimes you have to take out larger objects in order to save a potentially good picture. Figure 22.8 shows just such a photo, a nice collection of lobster pot markers, hanging from a pier down on Cape Cod. I'm going to want to turn this photo into a Photoshop "watercolor," but there's a lot of stuff that will distract from the markers, including an electrical box, the diagonal props for the railing, the pier, and other railings behind them.

FIGURE 22.8.

Many things in here need to come out.

1. First let's crop the picture to improve the composition. Select the Cropping tool from the toolbox and drag a rectangle that includes most or all of the buoys but cuts off the top and sides of the photo (see Figure 22.9). Double-click inside the rectangle or choose Image→Crop to remove the non-selected part.

FIGURE 22.9.

That takes care of the railings and the dock.

2. The next step is to get rid of those supports. The easiest way to do this is to copy and drag pieces of adjacent space to cover them. First use the Lasso tool to select a small piece. Then click the Move tool (it's the pointer with crosshairs at the top-right corner of the toolbox). Hold down (Option) [Alt] and drag the selection. This copies it as you go. If you use the Smudge tool with heavy pressure, you can drag the colored buoys down so they overlap and disguise some of the diagonals (see Figure 22.10).

22

3. We still have a couple of rusty pipes and an electrical box to disguise. Starting with the box, I'll copy a piece of the picture directly above it and, using the Move tool and the (Option) [Alt] key, I can drag it straight down to cover. Keep the Option key pressed to copy the selection instead of just moving it. A couple of quick swipes with the Smudge tool finishes the job and turns a while blob into another buoy.

4. The pipes are best covered up with a bit of ocean. When you're working in small areas like this, use the Zoom tool to enlarge the picture (see Figure 22.11).

FIGURE 22.11.

After we copy enough water, we can smudge it to make it more even.

5. Figure 22.12 shows the picture at this stage. The box and pipes are gone, replaced by water and miscellaneous shapes.

6. Now is a good time to do any last-minute color adjustments. I checked the levels on this picture and decided that they didn't really need any tweaking, but it seemed a little over-saturated, so I lowered the saturation by about 5 points. Now, as a final treatment, we can apply a filter. Even though my original concept was to use the Watercolor filter, I tried and preferred the Cut Out filter. Figure 22.13 shows the final piece of art.

FIGURE 22.12.

Nothing but buoys.

FIGURE 22.13.

Please come and see this in color on the Web page.

Putting Back What Was Never There

I don't know which of my kids decided to crop my picture of a tiger washing up after lunch. He obviously didn't know Photoshop, because he trimmed the picture down to size by ripping off the edges. I still like the photo and I think there's enough background left that I can restore it. Figure 22.14 shows the raw scan.

Step one is to crop the picture down enough to lose the extra space (see Figure 22.15). Step two will be to copy pieces of ground to fill in the holes.

FIGURE 22.14.

Poor tiger.

22

FIGURE 22.15.

Cropping removes many of the gaps but leaves some.

Instead of just dragging and copying the background, I'll cut and paste to as many new layers as needed and vary the opacity so the background doesn't all look the same.

After filling the gaps, I'll apply the Unsharp mask filter to improve the focus a little. (Some of the detail was lost in the scan.) See the results in Figure 22.16.

FIGURE 22.16.

That looks much better.

But he looks kind of crowded there. Suppose, instead, we use Edit→ Transform→ Scale to shrink him down and put him in the courtyard of a mock medieval castle. Slide him around until he looks comfortable. Figure 22.17 shows the tiger in his newer, larger home.

FIGURE 22.17.

That's even more interesting.

22

The point of this exercise is that there's no picture too damaged to rescue. The only limit to what you can do with your pictures is your own imagination. If you have a digital camera, shoot lots of backgrounds and keep them in a special file on your computer or on a Zip drive. Then when you have a problem photo, like the ripped tiger, you have ready-made scenery to drop the subject into.

Summary

Color repair isn't much different from black-and-white photo repair, except that you need to be a little more aware of the colors and color Blending modes. Off-color photos are fixed with Photoshop's regular color adjustment tools. Retouching to get rid of obvious flaws and red eye is best accomplished with the Brush and the Eyedropper, and with the image enlarged so you can see what you're doing. Use layers to protect your original while you're working, and merge the changes when you are satisfied with the results.

Q&A

Q If the picture I need to repair doesn't have enough background to copy or doesn't have a good background, what should I do?

A Remember that Photoshop allows you to have more than one file open at a time. You can "borrow" from another picture and copy the selection onto a new layer of the picture that needs fixing. Shrink it or enlarge it so the texture is in scale with the rest of the scene, and then copy and paste it as much as you need to.

Q What color mode should I be working in? CMYK, RGB, Indexed, Lab, or Grayscale?

A How are you going to use the picture? If it's going on a Web page or as part of a desktop presentation, stick with RGB. If it's going to be printed and is a color image, use CMYK. If it's a black-and-white photo and you don't intend to colorize it in any way, Grayscale is your best bet.

Quiz

By now, you should know these.

Questions

1. "Red eye" is caused by _____.

    a. excessive consumption of caffeine

    b. impossible deadlines

    c. light reflecting off the back of the eye

2. If a picture is too yellow, add more _____.

    a. cyan

    b. blue

    c. white

3. Old color photos most often look too _____.

    a. blue

    b. red

    c. washed out

Answers

1. All of the above.

2. a. Cyan is the color wheel opposite of yellow.

3. b. Color dyes often shift toward red as the print ages.

Activity

Find some of your own photo portraits that have bad "red eye." Scan them into the computer and use the tricks you have learned to restore normal eye colors.

HOUR 23

Printing

We're almost done....You've created some wonderful Photoshop art and you'd like to hang it on the walls and send copies to your friends. (You'd probably also like to add these masterpieces to your Web page, but you'll learn that next Hour.) Even in this brave new world of the Internet, CD-ROM, and other electronic media, printing isn't going away and it never will. Getting your image to output correctly is as important as any other step in the process of image creation, and that's why it deserves its own chapter.

Printing should be easy, right? Hit the Print command and watch your image emerge on paper. Unfortunately, getting Photoshop images to print well can involve quite a few variables and decisions. In this chapter, we'll look at what those are, from choosing a printer through setting up inks, separations, halftones, and other issues.

Be warned. Some of this stuff gets into deep detail and gets very technical, and some of it is irrelevant if you only print to one kind of printer. Feel free to ignore the sections that don't relate to the kind(s) of printing you do. If *none* of it makes sense, stick with the default settings. Your pages will be, at the very least, adequately printed.

Choosing a Printer

You know this already: Lots of printers are out there, as well as lots of printing technologies. How you print obviously depends a lot on what printer you're using. In fact, the printer you use can and should influence how you work in Photoshop and how you prepare your image, because you'll want to create a final image that will best print from your particular printer.

An entire book could be written about all the varieties of printers. In this section, we'll make do with a snapshot of what's available: inkjet printers, laser printers, dye-sublimation printers, thermal wax printers, and imagesetters.

Inkjet Printers

At the most inexpensive end of the spectrum are inkjet printers, almost all of which can deliver acceptable quality color printing (depending on your definition of "acceptable," of course). Examples of inkjets (sometimes also called "bubble jets") include Apple's StyleWriter printers, HP's Deskjet, and Epson's Stylus printers.

Inkjet printers are not necessarily PostScript-compatible, which means some of them can't print PostScript information that might be in your documents. For most Photoshop images, however, this isn't a problem.

 PostScript is a page-description language that lets any two devices (computer and compatible printer) describe and reproduce exactly the same page.

The quality of output varies tremendously on an inkjet printer, from fair to excellent, depending on how much you want to spend. High-end inkjets, like the Iris, can cost tens of thousands of dollars but can be perfect for graphics professionals.

Laser Printers

The laser printer is the professional standard and a good balance of price, quality, and speed. Laser printers abound from well-known companies like Apple and Hewlett-Packard.

Most laser printers output 300 to 600 dpi (some up to 1200 dpi) and are particularly good with halftone and grayscale images. Some can subtly alter the size of the printed dots, thus improving quality. Speed is generally better than that of inkjet printers, although they tend to be more expensive.

Dye-Sublimation Printers

Dye-sublimation printers are expensive photographic-quality printers, but you get what you pay for. Image quality is superb, but these printers use special ribbons and paper. You can't use ordinary paper with them and the specially coated paper is expensive. You probably can't afford one of these, but many service bureaus have one, so you can always output there if you want to.

Thermal Wax Printers

Thermal wax printers also provide excellent quality color output, but at prices comparable to laser printers. What's more, wax printers are now supporting common paper stocks, and not just special paper. So as you can imagine, these printers are becoming increasingly popular. Because of the materials they use, thermal wax printers are especially useful for producing transparencies.

Imagesetters

Imagesetters are printers used for medium- or large-scale commercial printing jobs. These large, expensive machines burn the image onto photographic film or paper. That film is then developed and used to make printing plates that are used for the actual printing. We're talking high resolution here: 1,200 to 2,400 dpi, or even better.

Imagesetters don't print in color per se. Instead, you have to create a separate image for each color you want printed. These are called separations and we'll talk more about them later.

Preparing the Image

Here's the best strategy if you know you'll want to print your final Photoshop image: Keep the printer in mind throughout the entire process! Different printers output differently, so knowing your printer enables you to adjust your image for its particular behavior and, thus, guarantees the best possible image on the final printed page. This is particularly true for full-color images.

With that in mind, always configure Photoshop to the monitor and printer you'll be using, and do this before even considering printing anything important! This configuration involves several different areas: setting up monitors, printing inks, separations, and separation tables.

23

RGB Setup

NEW TO VERSION 5 Photoshop 5 has changed the way color is managed, both onscreen and for printing. It's added the capability of using some very sophisticated high-end color printing equipment and associated files. It's also given users the option of choosing how color information is sent to the monitor. This directly affects the colors that you see onscreen, so it's important that you do not change your monitor setup once it's correct.

There are a couple of ways to decide what's correct. Adobe's experts suggest that you leave the default settings in place. This means that you'll be using RGB, which is a standard setup that gives you accurate color on most kinds of monitors. Mac users have ColorSync, which calibrates the monitor and specifies the correct profile. Figure 23.1 shows the default settings. Refer to the Photoshop manual for more information.

FIGURE 23.1.

The default settings for RGB Setup.

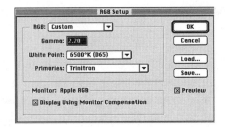

 Note that you can also save and load various settings you create via the Save and Load buttons.

CMYK Setup

Choose File→Color Settings→CMYK Setup to bring up the dialog box used to control the conversion tables Photoshop uses to define color settings (see Figure 23.2). The primary use of this dialog box is to configure Photoshop's color settings so they match a printout from a new printer or press. This way you're sure that future print jobs will be what you expect, based on what you see on your monitor.

FIGURE 23.2.

*The CMYK Setup
dialog box.*

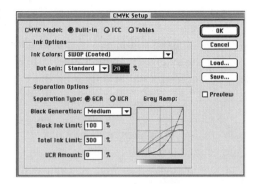

You won't have to mess with these settings much, if at all. Photoshop's default settings work well for most mid- to high-end printers, so feel free to skip this section if you don't need it. For the ever-curious, however, here are the options in the dialog box:

- The Ink Colors pull-down menu is for choosing your printer or paper type. You should select the option that most closely matches what you're using, so that the colors also closely match what appears onscreen. There are a lot of choices, and you even have the opportunity to create a custom choice. If these don't look familiar to you, then chances are you don't have to worry about them.

  The default is SWOP (Coated), which is the U.S. industry standard for color separation printing.

  By the way, Coated refers to glossy paper (as in most magazines), and Uncoated refers to regular paper, like the page these words are printed on. Newsprint refers to, you guessed it, newspaper.

- The Dot Gain option relates to the fact that, for different kinds of paper, the ink used soaks into the paper and spreads outward differently. Some papers have a higher dot gain because the ink is absorbed more readily and tends to spread out into thicker dots when printing.

  You can easily adjust how Photoshop compensates for dot gain. Lower values for this setting mean the printed dots are smaller, thus creating a lighter image. Higher values mean larger dots and darker images.

- The Separation option is used (only by experts) to adjust how Photoshop combines CMYK inks to print colors. Again, in the vast majority of situations, you'll never need to touch these settings. Photoshop's default values are excellent. Only mess around with these settings if your print shop or service bureau tells you to and shows you how.

Grayscale Setup

Here you have only two choices: RGB or Black. I tried both settings in printing a grayscale picture on an HP Deskjet printer. There was no visible difference. Check the Photoshop manual for advice or ignore this setting.

Profile Setup

NEW TO VERSION 5 Photoshop 5 can embed information in its files that tells the computer opening the file what sort of monitor it was created on and what printer settings are intended to be used. This is important if you work in a situation where Photoshop files are opened on different platforms, using different kinds of monitors, or printed to several different kinds of printers. Photoshop can make the necessary conversions so that you'll see the same colors on your Apple monitor that your client sees on his or her NT workstation. Printed pages should also look the same, color-wise, whether they emerge from a NewGen Chromax dye sublimation printer, an HP color laser, or the generic Japan Standard Proofing System. Figure 23.3 shows the Profile Setup box.

FIGURE 23.3.

The Profile Setup box.

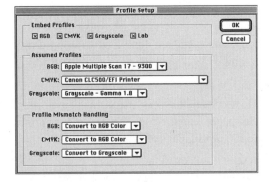

Setting Up the Page

Okay, our image is ready. Now we have to take care of the page setup. Select File→Page Setup to get to this very important dialog box (see Figure 23.4).

Important: This dialog box can look different depending on what print driver you have selected! For example, although many Macintosh laser printers use the standard LaserWriter print driver that results in the dialog box you saw in Figure 23.4, other printers ship with their own print drivers. HP Deskjet, for example, ships with a print driver that makes the Page Setup dialog box look like what you see in Figure 23.5. Most of the options are the same; they just appear a bit different. You'll also see additional features offered by individual printers.

FIGURE 23.4.

The standard Mac Page Setup dialog box.

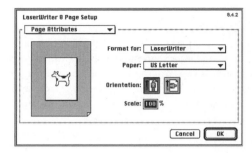

FIGURE 23.5.

The Page Setup dialog box for my Mac HP Deskjet 855C printer.

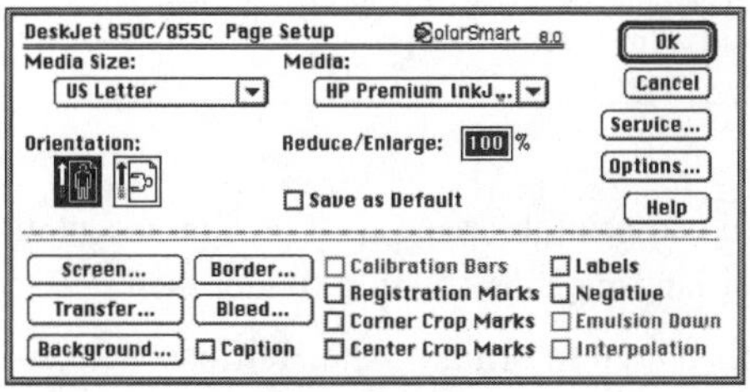

Okay, let's go through all the standard options one by one. I'll only cover the basic and intermediate settings; if you want to play with the other settings, talk with your print shop. (Note that not all options will be available in every situation.)

- The name of the printer always appears at the top. Make sure it's correct!
- **Properties:** On Windows machines, you can click this button to access a dialog box that enables you to change things such as paper size, layout, printer resolution, halftone settings, and so on.
- **Paper:** Choose the size of the paper you're printing on. On the Mac, if you change the paper, you can see the preview in the upper-left of the screen change accordingly.
- **Source:** On Windows machines, you might be able to choose the paper tray for the printer to use.
- **Layout:** Choose how you want the printed files to be laid out on the printed page.
- **Reduce or Enlarge:** Want the image to print smaller or larger? Adjust this percentage appropriately.

Later, when you actually hit the Print button (see the next section), you might run into a problem with files that are large in dimension. If the image dimensions are larger than the dimensions of the page you're printing on, Photoshop tells you. You can then choose to either print anyway, resulting in only part of the image printing, or you can cancel and adjust the Reduce or Enlarge value so the whole image fits on the page.

Also, Photoshop always prints images at the center of the page. You can't change this, I'm afraid.

- **Orientation:** You can print the page with portrait orientation (so the page is taller than it is wide) or landscape orientation (wider than tall).
- **Screen:** Press this button to bring up the Halftone Screens dialog box (see Figure 23.6). By default, Use Printer's Default Screens is checked and you won't be able to change anything else. Uncheck this option if you want to customize the other halftone options. Most of the time, Photoshop's default settings work fine.

FIGURE 23.6.

The Halftone Screens dialog box.

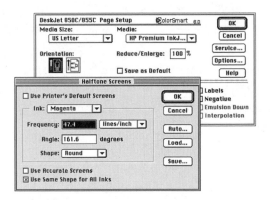

If you need to adjust these settings, here is where you can change for each ink (C, M, Y, and K) the frequency (lines per inch) of the dot grid, the angle of the grid, and the shape of the dot used. If you're printing to a PostScript Level 2 printer, you probably want to check the Use Accurate Screens box.

- **Transfer:** Click this button to bring up the Transfer Functions dialog box (see Figure 23.7). Here you can adjust the transfer curve—in other words, change the gray values so they print lighter or darker, depending on your needs. Most printers ship with the capability to calibrate themselves, so it's unlikely you'll need this feature.

FIGURE 23.7.

The Transfer Functions dialog box.

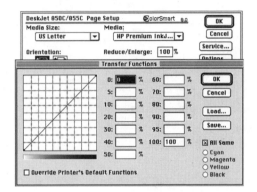

23

- **Background:** Want to print a background color on the page around your image? Hit the Background button and you'll be greeted with the standard Color Picker (see Figure 23.8). Whatever color you pick is used for printing only and does not alter your actual image file.

FIGURE 23.8.

The Photoshop Color Picker on the Mac.

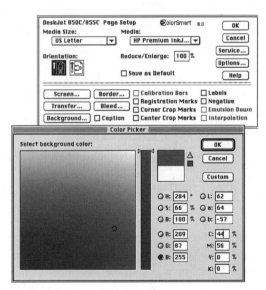

- **Border:** Similarly, if you'd like a border around your printed image, press the Border button. In the resulting dialog box, you can set the width of the printed border (see Figure 23.9). The border is always black; you can't change the color. (Like Background, using this feature doesn't affect the actual image file.)

FIGURE 23.9.

The Border dialog box.

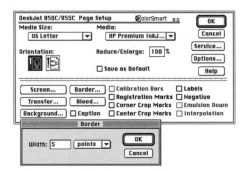

- **Bleed:** Bleeding means that part of the image goes right off the edge of the paper and is not printed at all. There isn't supposed to be any border or empty space between the image and the edge of the page. (Note that this feature won't work in every printer. Some printers are incapable of printing to the very edge of a page.)

  Clicking the Bleed button results in the appropriate dialog box, where you can define the bleed area of an image (see Figure 23.10). Higher values move the crop marks within the boundaries of the image, so that less of the image gets printed. You can't bleed an image more than an eighth of an inch.

FIGURE 23.10.

The Bleed dialog box.

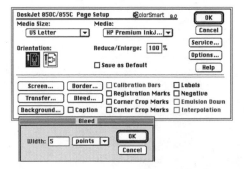

- **Caption:** Check this box and on the printed page you'll see whatever text appears in the Caption area of the File Info dialog box for that file. (To get to this dialog box, choose File→File Info and make sure Caption is selected on the top pull-down menu.) This can be helpful for providing contact info or copyright details next to your image.

- **Calibration Bars:** Check this box and Calibration and Color bars will be printed next to your image. A Calibration bar is a row of 11 gray squares of different values, and a Color bar is a row of 11 colors. These bars can help when trying to calibrate to a specific printer, or to see how a specific printer prints. (This option is available only if you're using a PostScript printer.)

- **Registration Marks:** Activate this feature and a variety of registration marks prints out around the image. You'll get bull's-eyes (which look like what you'd expect), star targets (two crossed lines within a circle), or precise pinpoint marks (two simple crossed lines), depending on your printer. (We'll actually see some of these marks in a bit.) These marks can be helpful for aligning color separations.

- **Corner Crop Marks:** Corner crop marks appear around each corner of your image, defining where the image should be trimmed. They are simply horizontal and vertical lines.

- **Center Crop Marks:** These crop marks are centered along each side of the image, defining the exact center of the image. They look like two crossed lines.

- **Labels:** You can have the filename print next to the image with this check box. If you are printing color separations, the name of the appropriate color channel is also printed on each color plate.

- **Negative:** With this checked, the printer reverses the values of the image. That is, the whites become black and the blacks become white, and everything in between shifts accordingly. You end up with a negative version. This option is useful if you're printing to film for commercial offset printing, because these images usually need to be negative.

- **Emulsion Down:** Check this setting and your image will print out as the horizontal mirror image of the original. Everything gets flipped left to right. Your print shop will tell you if you need to print this way for some reason.

- **Interpolation:** Interpolation refers to some printers' ability to resample an image as they print it. That is, any PostScript Level 2 printer can take a low-resolution image and resample it on-the-fly, so that the resolution is improved and the printout is of better quality. This is valuable only if you're dealing with low-resolution images.

Figure 23.11 shows what a sample printed page looks like with some of the options checked.

FIGURE 23.11.

A printout showing various crop marks.

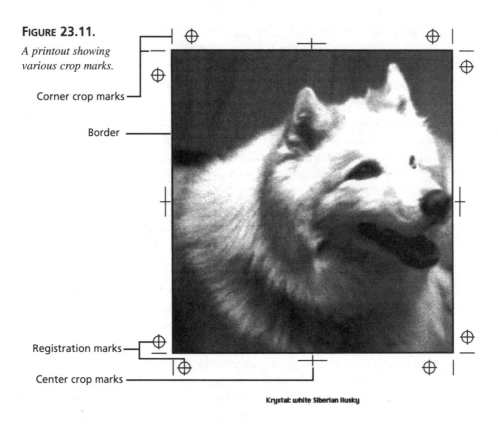

Corner crop marks

Border

Registration marks

Center crop marks

Krystal: white Siberian Husky

Before you continue, make sure that whatever you want to print is currently visible onscreen. By default, Photoshop prints all visible layers and channels. If you want to print just certain layers or channels, make them the only ones that are visible, and then print.

Printing the Page

Okay, now we're getting around to finally printing the image. I told you there were a lot of printing variables, didn't I?

Let's pull up the Print dialog box using File→Print (see Figure 23.12). The first thing to be aware of is that this dialog box looks different, depending on what printer you have, what platform you're running on, and what mode the image is in. Let's look at all the fields and options.

FIGURE **23.12.**

The ultimate dialog box: Print.

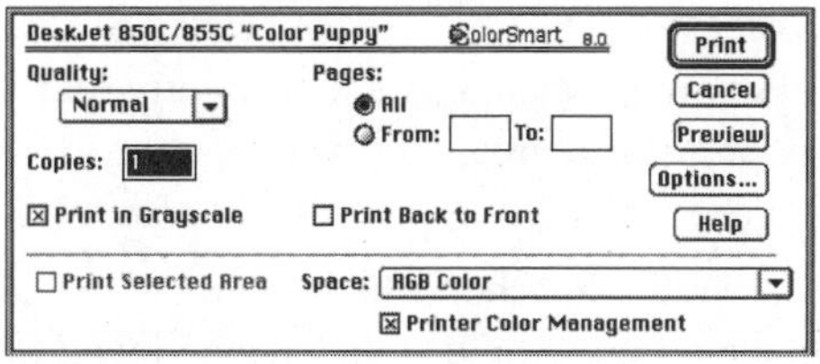

- **Copies:** How many copies of the document do you want printed? Enter a number here.

- **Pages:** This area (called Print Range in the Windows version) specifies the range of pages to be printed. This setting is irrelevant in Photoshop, because each document consists of only one "page."

- **Paper Source:** Here Mac users can define which paper tray to use.

- **Print Quality:** Windows users can often specify a printer resolution here, such as 300 or 600 dpi. Mac users can often specify Best, Normal, Econofast, or some variation on this theme.

- **Destination:** You can print to the printer, obviously, but you can also print to a file. Printing to a file means saving the printed output as a PostScript or EPS file. (This option only works if you have selected a PostScript-compatible printer.)

  Select File and the Print button now says Save. Click it and you'll see the Save dialog box, where you can name the file and select what format of file you want (see Figure 23.13). You can also choose an encoding scheme (ASCII is best for PostScript files and Binary can speed up printing for printers that accept binary data). Level 1 Compatible means that the file prints on all PostScript printers, whereas Level 2 Only files work only on PostScript Level 2 printers. Finally, you can specify if you want font information embedded in the file, and for which fonts.

FIGURE **23.13.**

Printing to a file.

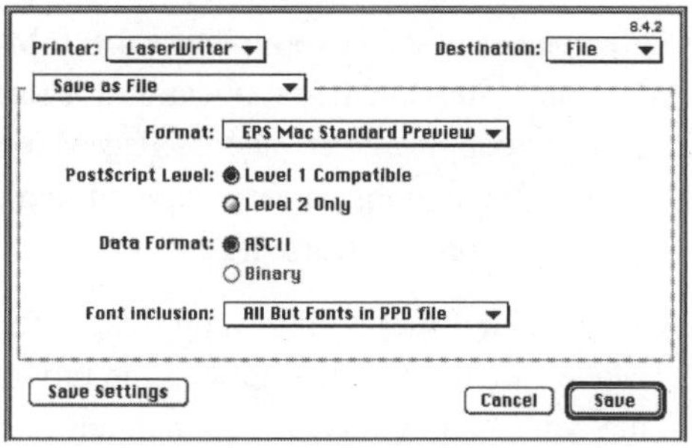

- **Print Selected Area:** When this box (simply called Selection for Windows users) is checked and you have a rectangular area currently selected in your Photoshop image, you can print just that area. This works only with rectangular selections created with the Marquee tool. Also, it doesn't work for feathered selections.

- **Encoding:** Here you tell Photoshop which encoding method to use when it sends the image data to the printer. ASCII is understood by all PostScript printers, so it's a safe bet. Binary encoding is more compressed and can thus be faster, but it doesn't work on all printers. Finally, JPEG encoding is faster yet, but it results in some loss of data, because JPEG is a lossy compression scheme. JPEG encoding works only with PostScript Level 2 printers.

- **Print In:** You can decide here how to print the image: in grayscale, in RGB colors, or in CMYK colors. For some desktop printers, RGB gives better results. (Try both, if you're unsure, and see which looks better to you.)

- **Print Separations:** This option appears in place of the Print In option *only* if the image is currently in CMYK or Duotone mode and the composite color channel is active. Check this option and Photoshop prints each channel as a separate color plate. For example, a CMYK document would print as four separate pages, one for all the cyan data in the image, one for magenta, one for yellow, and one for black.

- **Options:** Strangely enough, Options isn't always one of your options. On a non-PostScript printer, such as the HP Deskjet series, you'll see the Options button as one of your choices in the Print dialog box. Options lets you select Intensity, Half-toning, and Color Matching. Leave all three at Auto unless you're printing a photograph. If you are, choose Photographic from the Color Matching menu, which will give you the best possible color reproduction.

- And now, at long last, when everything's set to your satisfaction, click Print to print!

So that's how to print from Photoshop, but as you'll probably discover, printing directly from Photoshop doesn't happen as often as you might expect. Most of the time, images created in Photoshop are brought into another application for final placement and output. Most often these are page layout applications, such as PageMaker and QuarkXPress. Photoshop images can even be brought into other image-editing applications, such as Painter and Illustrator, and can be printed from there.

The main thing to watch for when printing Photoshop images from other applications is the format of your file. Make sure it's compatible with the program you're bringing it into; if it's not, believe me, you'll know! Other than that, any settings related to the image, such as custom colors or halftone screens, are automatically brought with the image.

Papers

What you print on makes almost as much difference as how you do the printing. You can get various types and weights of paper for all kinds of printers. There are special papers for inkjet and for laser. If you want your picture to resemble a photograph, consider investing in a pack of "photo weight" glossy paper. It's a much thicker paper with a glossy surface that really does help make your inkjet- or laser-printed picture look like something that came out of a real darkroom, rather than a digital one.

You can get coated papers for printing color on inkjet printers. These give you photo quality prints with a matte surface, rather than the glossy one. Transparency paper is clear acetate film, specially treated to accept the inks. Use it to make overhead projection slides and overlays.

Label stocks come in all kinds of sizes and shapes and literally hundreds, if not thousands, of different kinds and weights of paper for both inkjet and laser printers.

Finally, you can buy packs of iron-on transfer paper (for color laser or inkjet printers), which lets you put your images on T-shirts, aprons, tote bags, or anything else that you can iron onto. Follow the instructions with the paper and don't forget to flip your image before you print it, so it reads correctly.

I generally use inexpensive photocopying paper for most of my work. It's fine for printing a quick proof to see how a picture comes out. For work that a client will see, I use a coated paper, however, because the colors are brighter and don't bleed into each other. If I want the picture to look more like a darkroom photo, I'll pay the dollar per sheet to print it on special glossy paper.

Summary

Printing Photoshop images isn't difficult; there are just a lot of decisions to make along the way. This chapter discussed those choices, from initially preparing an image for printing, to setting up the page, and finally setting the Print options. The wonderful thing about printing is that if you don't get a gorgeous printout the first time, you can simply change settings and try again! Provided you have enough paper and ink, of course....

23

Q&A

Q I love the idea of putting pictures on T-shirts and so on. What should I know before I start?

A Iron-on transfer paper works best with white or light-colored cotton or cotton/poly-ester blends. Transfer with a household iron on its highest setting or in a professional heat press. Iron the fabric first and be sure it's cooled before you place the transfer on it. Also, back up the single layer of fabric you're ironing onto with a sheet of cardboard. This prevents the dye from bleeding through and giving you a second image on the back of the T-shirt. Press firmly and expect to iron a large, full-page image for two to three minutes. Keep the iron moving enough so you don't scorch the fabric. Small images are easier to manage and take less ironing time. To avoid fading the transfer, wash shirts inside out and do not bleach.

Quiz

See if you're a print guru by answering these questions.

Questions

1. Dye sublimation printers need special paper.

   a. True

   b. False

2. Registration marks look like _____.

   a. the letter R in a circle

   b. a cross in a circle

   c. four concentric circles in CMY and K

3. RGB stands for

   a. initials of Roy G. Biv, inventor of Color Sync.

   b. Raster, Gray, Black.

   c. Red, Green, Blue.

Answers

1. a

2. b

3. c

Activity

PaperDirect is a company that sells more different kinds of papers for more purposes than you can possibly imagine. Visit their Web site (`www.paperdirect.com`) to see how to get a sample kit of their papers and envelopes. Take a field trip to your local computer store or a really good office supply store to see what kinds of papers they have for your printer. Treat yourself to a package of high-quality paper and try printing some of your best work.

23

HOUR 24

Photoshop for the Web

Wow! You're almost finished; this is the last chapter. You've learned enough to work effectively with Photoshop, even if you haven't yet mastered all the tricks and time-saving features. The rest will come as you do more work with the program. This final hour is devoted to one of the newest and best uses for Photoshop—putting your work on the World Wide Web.

You've heard about the Web and have probably "surfed" it with your favorite browser, such as Internet Explorer or Netscape Navigator, but let's take a moment to review what is really going on out there in cyberspace. First of all, although the Web is what you might call a *virtual space*, meaning that it creates the illusion of space and distance, it also exists in a physical space. It is comprised of computers called *servers* that serve files across networks that stretch around the world. The computers can be anything from super-charged SPARC stations to minis and mainframes, or a machine not unlike the one sitting on your desktop. These machines run software that can *talk* with your machine via what are known as protocols.

Thus, when you type a *URL* (*Uniform Resource Locator*) into your browser to get access to a Web site, a message made up of electronic pieces of information called packets goes out to these remote machines. These machines then send back the files for which you have asked. The files that make up all the sounds, pictures, and text of the Web then have to travel across phone lines. This creates a problem that you have to keep in mind as you create graphics for your Web site. Phone lines are slow and there is only so much information that can travel at a time. If you are lucky enough to have an ISDN or T1 connection, you are doing okay—speed-wise. A 28.8Kbps (kilobits per second) modem is fairly fast. A 14.4 modem is fairly slow. We used to be satisfied with 2400bps modems, but those were the pre-Web days, when we only used our modems for email and perhaps accessing chats on CompuServe or America Online.

The most popular language used to publish documents on the Web is *HTML* (*Hypertext Markup Language*). HTML isn't really a computer programming language, so relax. It is, as its name suggests, a *markup* language. A series of relatively simple *tags* enable you to specify how text appears in the browser, images, and links to other sites. HTML isn't difficult to learn, but you really don't even need it. There are programs, including desktop publishing programs, Web browsers, and word processors you may already own, that can translate your pages into HTML with just a couple of mouse clicks. All you need to do is to lay out the page the way you'd like it to look, with your Photoshop pictures pasted in. You do have to make sure they're in a compatible format, though. Because Web pages can be viewed on all kinds of computers, the graphics have to be in a format that's common to all.

File Formats and File Size

The first thing that you need to learn is the type of file format to use for the Web. There are two standard choices: GIF (Graphics Interchange Format) and JPEG (Joint Photographic Experts Group). There's also a third, newer format known as PNG (Portable Network Graphics). It promises to be the best choice of all three but is not supported by older browsers. Use it if you like, but be aware that not all software can read it.

The most important thing to remember, regardless of the file format you decide to use, is that the Web has limited bandwidth. This means that if you create an absolutely beautiful image and it weighs in at something like two megabytes, on a 14.4 modem it will take forever to download. This is not to say that you *can't* create images with as large a file size as you want. I am just suggesting that few Web surfers out there will have the patience to sit there and wait while your 2MB image downloads. If you know that your primary audience is surfing from home with slower modems, you might want to keep your Web pages well under 30 Kilobytes apiece.

This is the challenge of Web development. There are ways around it, but you will ultimately have to make sacrifices. It's okay though…everybody does it.

> If you have some big files that you want to publish on the Web, don't fret. There are ways around the big file issue. Most surfers won't mind the wait for a big file if they have a warning. Give them a thumbnail version of the image and tell them how big the file is. That way, they can decide for themselves if they want to spend the time waiting for the download. A little courtesy, as in all aspects of life, goes a long way on the Web.

JPEG (Joint Photographic Experts Group)

Depending on your needs, JPEG could be the best file format for you. It is great for photographs and other continuous tone images, primarily because it allows you to use 16 million different colors. (Of course, some Web browser programs can't handle that color depth. Instead, they display a "reasonable approximation" of your artwork.) JPEG maintains color information but does, however, employ a *lossy* compression scheme, which means that you can adjust and reduce the file size—at the expense of the image quality.

To save as a JPEG, you need to work in RGB mode within Photoshop. This is reasonable because RGB is the "monitor" viewing mode, and Web images are going to be seen on—that's right—an RGB monitor. Figures 24.1 and 24.2 show the JPEG Options box, which opens whenever you elect to save a file as a JPEG. It gives you several choices.

FIGURE 24.1.

The JPEG Options dialog box.

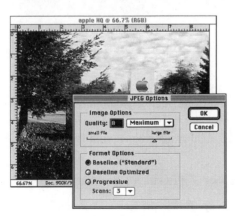

24

FIGURE 24.2.

Saving a smaller file.

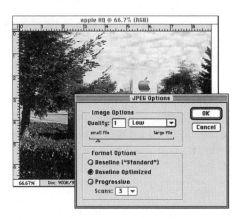

In Figure 24.3, the figure on the right is 64 kilobytes. The figure on the left is 208 kilobytes. This is a staggering difference in file size for a minimal difference in file quality.

FIGURE 24.3.

Two JPEG files with similar quality but very different file sizes.

Give any image that you plan to take to the Web a close look. Use the File→Save a Copy command so that you don't lose your original image and try some different compression. If using a heavy compression ratio (one that reduces the file size a great deal) causes degradation to the image quality, save again with less compression to get a better quality image.

Also notice the section in the JPEG dialog box that prompts you for format options.

- **Baseline (Standard):** This is the standard option.
- **Baseline (Optimized):** This option optimizes the colors in the file. When I tested to see if Optimized created a larger file, I was surprised to see that the Optimized file was actually smaller than the Baseline standard file.

- **Progressive:** For Web work, this is your best bet. Progressive means that your file is visible within a Web browser faster and then refined by subsequent passes or *scans* as more file information is downloaded. Notice the dropdown menu that becomes active when you select this option (see Figure 24.4). It enables you to specify how many scans you will permit before the image is finished downloading to a user's browser. A good choice would be three, but if your file is fairly large, go with four or five.

FIGURE 24.4.

Setting the number of progressive scans.

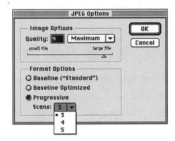

24

Always keep your Web browser open when you are creating Web graphics. This enables you to take a look at them to determine their quality.

Also, don't be fooled by how quickly File→Open File in your browser opens one of your files. These files are on your hard drive, or *local*. When a person has to go out on the Web to get your pages, the process is slowed down incredibly.

GIF (Graphics Interchange Format)

GIFs are your other (current) option for Web file formats. Since they're limited to 216 colors, they're not as good as JPEG for continuous-tone art. GIFs enable you to save files with transparent backgrounds, which are extremely useful when you are creating buttons and other round graphics. Photoshop does not allow you to have anything but a square or rectangular canvas, so if you don't save your button as a transparent GIF, you end up with a white square of canvas around the image.

A good way to select which file format is right for you is to visit Web sites that have graphics similar to what you want to publish. To find out what kind of file format an image is, simply click the image. On a Macintosh, click and hold the image until a dialog box appears. On a Windows machine, click the image with the right mouse button.

In the dialog box, choose to save the image. When you are prompted for where you want to save the image, note the file extension—.jpg for JPEG or .gif for GIF. Click OK to save the file or click Cancel if you are just looking.

Backgrounds, Buttons, and Bouncing GIFs

I admit that I have mixed feelings about backgrounds on Web pages. These can really add personality to a Web site, but they also can make reading the text of your site really difficult and frustrating. To quote Web designer David Siegel, "Gift-wrap makes poor stationery."

That said, however, if you use backgrounds with discretion, they can add to a site's presence and look. Fancy buttons are commonplace on Web pages, and you'll even see GIF animations: dogs wagging their tails endlessly, cats catching mice, balls bouncing...it's enough to make you dizzy. Photoshop can supply the graphic elements for any of these goodies.

Creating backgrounds, buttons, and animated GIFs, however, is really way beyond the scope of this book. If you want to get serious about Web page design and using HTML, run back to your local bookstore or computer store and look for Hayden's *Photoshop Web Magic* and *HTML Web Magic*. They're great sources for tips and tricks to spiff up your Web site.

If you want to stay casual about Web design but still end up with good-looking pages, use one of the graphic Web layout packages that let you paste up the pages as you want to see them. Figure 24.5 shows my own Web site, which I'm working on in Netscape Communicator.

Some Web design programs even come with buttons and other goodies you can apply to your page, as well as instructions on how to put your own graphics onto their buttons. Nothing could be easier. After you're done playing, it makes the conversion to HTML for you in the background and gives you files ready to upload to your Web page provider.

FIGURE 24.5.

Web page layout in Communicator is almost fun.

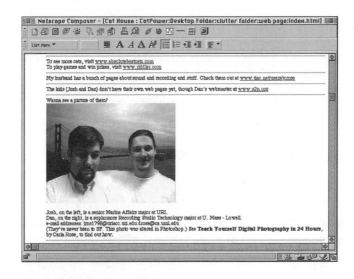

Preparing Text for the Web

HTML Web standards include a handful of different type sizes and fonts, some for headings, some for text, and some for "emphasis." Uh-huh. "Bo-ring," to quote the kids. However, you're not necessarily limited to what HTML has to offer. If you want an elaborate title for your page, create it in Photoshop, using filled letters, filters, drop shadows, glows, or whatever other special effects you like. Crop it tight and save it as either a GIF or JPEG. Figure 24.6 shows one that I created for my page. Compressed, the file is only 39Kb.

FIGURE 24.6.

Saved as a JPEG.

24

You have the option of converting your file to JPEG or to GIF. One good thing about text is that it usually, but of course not always, is applied to a white background. If this is the case with your Web site, there is no need to go through the trouble of exporting a GIF89a file. Just make sure that your background is white and save it as a plain GIF file.

> There's one "rule of thumb" that professional Web page designers apply to choosing formats. With line art or anything with a limited palette (fewer than 255 colors), choose GIF. With photos or full-color art, choose JPEG.

When designing images for the Web and writing the HTML code, save yourself work as often as possible, because new problems and new challenges always appear—usually when you least expect it. When you're absolutely sure that you've got it right, that's when it refuses to work.

Take heart. You are by no means alone. The sign of the Photoshop pro is the one who realizes that there are about 10 ways to accomplish any one given task. Keep experimenting and never give up.

Making Pages Load Faster

The bottom line is, you can't. The page will load as fast as the server can send it and the recipient can receive it. Those are both factors beyond your control.

What you can do, though, is make sure that your page is arranged so there's something to see while the graphic loads. Bring up a Welcome headline first, and then add the background. If there's a graphic that will take some time to load, bring up a block of text before the graphic appears. The load time for the picture will seem much shorter if the person waiting has something else to read or think about.

Keep your images small or put up a thumbnail and link the full-size picture to it, so visitors have the option of waiting to see the big picture. Remember that some people use text-based Web browsers and don't see images at all. If the content of your picture is important, put a text description of it on the page, too. (This also helps make your Web site handicapped accessible, which is a nice thing to do for the estimated two million visually impaired Web users.)

Summary

In this final Hour, we looked at putting your work on the Web. We examined what file formats the Web uses and how you might best choose the right formats for your own work.

So what comes next? You've finished your 24th Hour and you know a lot more about Photoshop than you did when you began. That doesn't mean you know it all, but you now have the tools—your imagination, creativity, and a basic understanding of Photoshop. There is still plenty out there to learn and experiment with.

Above all else, have fun!

Q&A

24

Q Can I mix the kinds of images I use on a Web page...some JPEGs, some GIFs, a PNG...or will that cause everything to crash?

A There's no reason not to mix image types. Choose the type according to the content of the image. Realistic photos look best as JPEG or PNG files. Graphics with limited color are most efficiently stored as GIFs.

Q What's the trick for using a picture as a page background?

A Keep it small and apply the picture as a tiled background. If you keep the edges blurry, they blend smoothly, avoiding that floor tile look. Save your file as either a GIF or JPEG with the name "background." Your Web page creator program should be able to insert it automatically, but if not, use the HTML tag <body background = "background.gif">. (Or .jpg, if appropriate.)

Q If I want to put my pictures up on the Web, but only for my friends to see, can I protect them?

A There are lots of ways to do this. The easiest is to put them on a "hidden" page. This is a second page on your site, but not linked to the first. Instead it has a separate address, like home.myservice.net/mypage/hidden.htm. Give your friends the direct URL to this page. No one who doesn't know it's there will be able to reach it.

Quiz

This is your final exam. No cheating, please.

Questions

1. What do I have to do to a Photoshop .psd file before I can put it on the Web?

    a. Attach a copyright notice.

    b. Flatten the image and save it as a .jpg, .gif, or .png file.

    c. Get a model release on any recognizable people.

2. HTML stands for

    a. Hypertext Markup Language

    b. Hand-coded Type Meta Language

    c. Has Trouble Making Lines

3. What's the most important thing to remember about Photoshop?

    a. Experiment

    b. Experiment

    c. Experiment

Answers

1. b., but a. and c. are a good idea, too.

2. a.

3. The most important thing is that there's no wrong answer. Keep trying new things, new combinations, and new approaches. Photoshop is a wonderful tool, but without *your* creativity and imagination it's just software.

Activity

After you've chosen some of your best Photoshop work and put it up on your own Web page, send me an email (momcat@pinkcat.com) with your page location, and I'll give you a critique of your work. No Web page? Attach no more than three JPEGs to your email. Expect a response within five to seven days (or sooner unless I am swamped with requests).

Appendix A

Photoshop 5 Palette Quick Reference

Navigator Palette

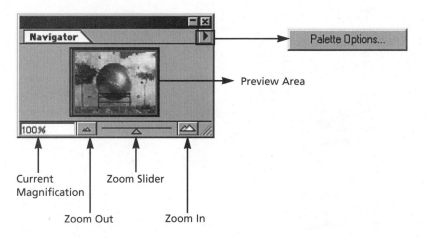

Palette Options...

Preview Area

Current Magnification

Zoom Slider

Zoom Out

Zoom In

Info Palette

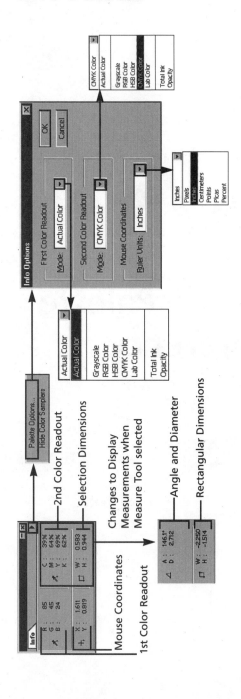

Color Palette

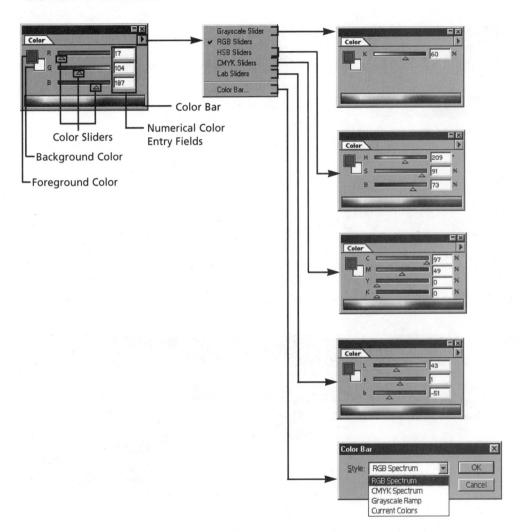

Color Bar

Numerical Color
Entry Fields

Color Sliders

Background Color

Foreground Color

Swatches Palette

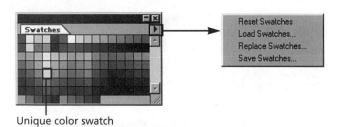

Unique color swatch

Brushes Palette

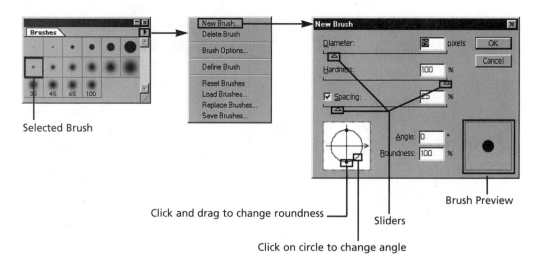

Selected Brush

Brush Preview

Click and drag to change roundness

Sliders

Click on circle to change angle

History Palette

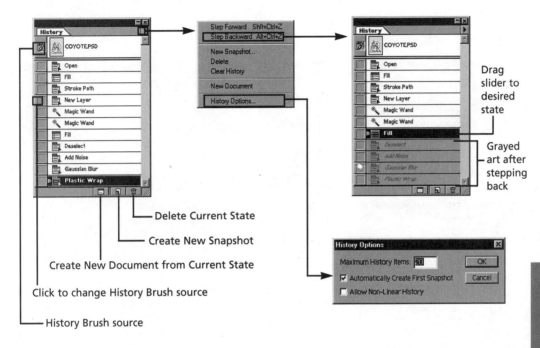

— Delete Current State

— Create New Snapshot

Create New Document from Current State

Click to change History Brush source

— History Brush source

Actions Palette

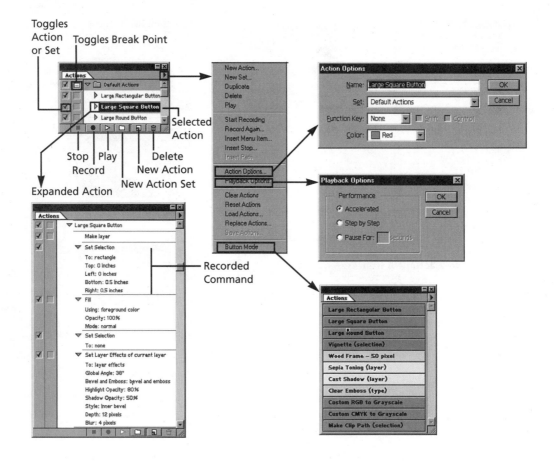

Toggles Action or Set

Toggles Break Point

Stop

Play

Record

Delete

New Action

New Action Set

Expanded Action

Selected Action

Recorded Command

Layers Palette

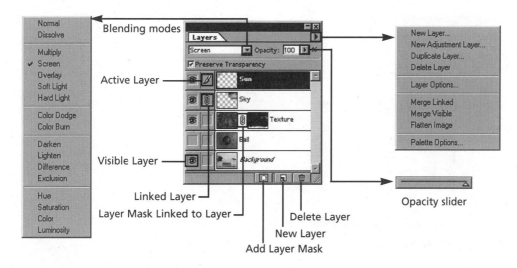

Blending modes

Active Layer

Visible Layer

Linked Layer

Layer Mask Linked to Layer

Delete Layer

New Layer

Add Layer Mask

Opacity slider

A

Channels Palette

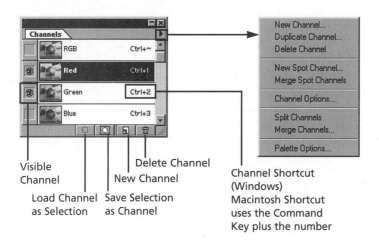

Visible Channel

Load Channel as Selection

Save Selection as Channel

New Channel

Delete Channel

Channel Shortcut (Windows) Macintosh Shortcut uses the Command Key plus the number

Paths Palette

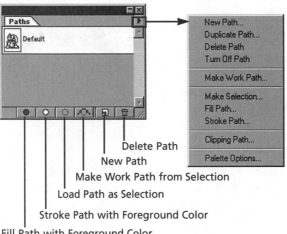

Delete Path
New Path
Make Work Path from Selection
Load Path as Selection
Stroke Path with Foreground Color
Fill Path with Foreground Color

INDEX

M

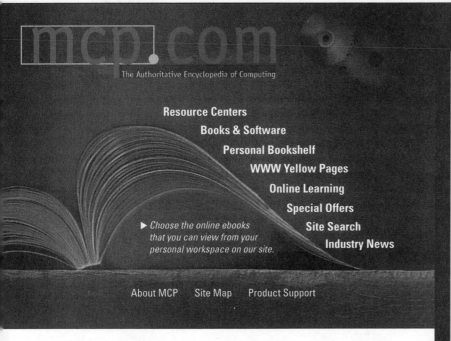